Women at the Center

WOMEN
AT THE
CENTER

Life in a Modern Matriarchy

PEGGY REEVES SANDAY

CORNELL UNIVERSITY PRESS

Ithaca & London

First published 2002 by Cornell University Press

Printed in the United States of America

Library of Congress Cataloging-in-Publication Data

Sanday, Peggy Reeves.
    Women at the center : life in a modern matriarchy / Peggy Reeves
Sanday.
        p. cm.
    Includes bibliographical references and index.
    ISBN 0-8014-4004-1 (cloth : alk. paper)
    1. Minangkabau (Indonesian people)—Social life and customs. 2.
Matriarchy—Indonesia—Sumatera Barat. I. Title.
DS632.M4 S265 2002
305.89'922—dc21   2001006790

Cornell University Press strives to use environmentally responsible suppliers and materials to the fullest extent possible in the publishing of its books. Such materials include vegetable-based, low-VOC inks and acid-free papers that are recycled, totally chlorine-free, or partly composed of nonwood fibers. For further information, visit our website at www.cornellpress.cornell.edu.

Cloth printing   10 9 8 7 6 5 4 3 2 1

For
Eggi and her family,
Endri,
the people of Belubus,
and my many Minangkabau friends
Terima kasih

If there is no winnow for the rice
How can it be cleaned?
If my mother is no more
On whom can I lean?

I have come home to Canduang
To her rumah gadang.
The stairs are broken and the door is closed.
Oh, tell me my people where has she gone?

If my dear mother is at home
My worries are over.
When I am sad, she soothes my heart.
When I need her, she gives advice.

Without her I am nothing.
With whom will I talk?
I feel so lost, I can only cry.
It is late, I must hurry home. . . . Oh, Mother.

— Ratok Koto Gadang

Contents

V Millennial Musings

Preface

It was already dark on the evening of July 6, 1996. From my seat in the back of the Jeep that brought us from the coastal city of Padang, I saw Wik grab a broom and start sweeping as soon as she realized who was pulling into her driveway.

"Ibu! Ibu! Ibu!" Agoes yelled, pointing at me and Serge with delight as we walked in the front door. It was obvious from the bags of newly threshed rice stored in the living room that we were not expected. Agoes danced around us, his little body arching like a streak of lightning. He stared up at me in sheer amazement and then yelled to his mother, Ibu Wik, "Amak, Ibu Peggy, Ibu Peggy."

Eggi, Agoes's older sister, appeared with a broad smile on her face. I embraced her gently in the Minangkabau way, inhaling as I touched my cheek to hers. Because Agoes was still a little afraid of me, I offered him the more formal greeting. Bending down to his level, I held out my palm. At first hesitant, he stopped just long enough to extend his little hand, holding it stiff as a board. We touched palms and then drew our hands back to our hearts.

The look on the faces of Agoes and Eggi expressed what I felt on arriving in Belubus—joy at returning again to my adopted home, anticipation at what would transpire, excitement at the prospect of catching up with the family. I could see how Eggi and Agoes had grown during the nine months of my absence. Eggi was now a girlish nine and Agoes had left the toddler stage behind.

Eggi was named after me in July 1987 after her birth ceremony in the house I had just entered, which was my home during visits to the village. For years, both before and after Eggi's birth, I returned to Belubus annually to learn as much as I could about the customs that the Minangkabau people refer to as "matriarchal." Belubus is a village of some 1100 inhabitants located in the highlands of the province of West Sumatra in Indonesia. This is one of hundreds of villages forming what is known as the Minangkabau "heartland" or "world."

The Minangkabau are the largest and most stable matrilineal society in the world today. Numbering some four million people in West Sumatra, the Minangkabau are the fourth largest ethnic group in the archipelago. They are well known in Indonesia for their literary flair, democratic leanings, business acumen, and "matriarchal" ways. On my first visit I encountered many people who proudly referred to their society as a *matriarchaat*, a term used by Dutch colonial officials in the nineteenth and early twentieth centuries to describe the Minangkabau. Long since incorporated into the local lexicon, *matriarchaat* today operates as an ethnic label marking the Minangkabau as distinct among Indonesia's three hundred ethnic groups.

This book is a memoir of an intellectual and personal journey into the heart of matriarchy as I came to know it. It is a tale about a special relationship, a special people, and a special place. Every year from 1981 to 1999, with the exception of five years between 1990 and 1994, I returned to West Sumatra, usually to Belubus. I was alone until 1988, when my husband, Serge Caffié, joined me for the first time. Thereafter he accompanied me every year, and Eggi's village became our summer home.

The Minangkabau matriarchaat has managed to resist and accommodate the patrilineal influences of immigrant kings, traders, and religious proselytizers who for centuries sought to establish a base in the gold- and pepper-rich regions of central Sumatra. Today the Minangkabau people are aware of the threat to their "matriarchal" customs posed by modernity. Tradition and modernity coexist, sometimes uneasily, in the cities of West Sumatra. Malls, universities, banks, and bookstores share the street with traditional marketplaces in the capital city of Padang. The colorful cities of the highlands attract tourists from all over. Buses link most villages to urban centers. Satellite dishes beam CNN, Asian MTV, Indonesian soap operas, and Japanese and Indian movies to village homes and food stalls. All of these influences filtered into Belubus in the early 1990s, once the village was wired for electricity and acquired year-round road access. How these diverse influences are accommodated in village life is part of my story.

My journey into the heart of the Minangkabau matriarchaat has convinced me that a challenge to the Western definition of matriarchy—rule by women—is long overdue. This vision of matriarchy has produced more than a century of squabbling. It arose in the nineteenth century by analogy with "patriarchy" or "father right," not from ethnographic studies of female-oriented social forms. Matriarchy was defined as the mirror image of patriarchy, its female twin.

Armed with this definition, countless scholars went looking for primitive matriarchies during the twentieth century, but they turned up nothing. It is impossible to find something that has been defined out of existence from the start. Defining a female-oriented social order as the mirror image of a male form is like saying that women's contribution to society and culture deserves a special label only if women act and rule like men.

Despite anthropology's dedication to seeing things "from the native's point of view," a dishearteningly high number of my distinguished colleagues have stepped up to the plate to take a swing at this imaginary, empirically empty social form. Finding no society where females as a class ruled like men, mainstream anthropologists proclaimed the universality of male dominance and struck the word *matriarchy* from their lexicon.

The excision of matriarchy from the anthropological canon on the grounds that women don't rule obscures the dominant role played by maternal meanings in many societies. To neglect or underestimate the social power of this role because women do not flood the domain of male politics has always struck me as excessively androcentric.

A number of feminist writers within and outside anthropology are not so myopic. Many understand the social implications of maternal meanings and refer to a female ethos that emphasizes love, duty, and common commitment to a sacred tradition. Following anthropology's lead, most of these writers have avoided the term *matriarchy*, choosing instead replacement terms like *gylany*, *matrix*, *matristic*, *matricentric*, or *matrifocal* to avoid any connotation of gynecocracy. These scholars speak of the sexes as being on an equal footing, egalitarian, or "linked" rather than "ranked," in a "partnership" rather than a "dominator" relationship. This characterization fits the Minangkabau, as many anthropologists have been at pains to point out.

I prefer to retain the term *matriarchy* out of courtesy and respect for Minangkabau usage. As an anthropologist I see my task as one of understanding what the Minangkabau mean. I hope the reader will agree with my conclusion that rather than abolishing the word, it should be refurbished. Had the original definition been based on what was known of female-oriented societies in the nineteenth century, matriarchy would have had a very different genealogy in anthropological usage. This chronicle of my journey includes the kind of ethnographic analysis that might have led to a different conceptualization.

How the Minangkabau conceive of their world is a central theme in my story. My experience of the centrality of women in the Minangkabau world at the end of the twentieth century is the stage from which I speak. I suggest that the concept of matriarchy is relevant in societies where maternal symbols are linked to social practices influencing the lives of both sexes and where women play a central role in these practices.

The least of my hopes is that this book conveys the respect for women that characterizes Minangkabau culture and permeates social relations in villages like Belubus. My greatest hope is that the reader comes away with an understanding of the stability of the Minangkabau matriarchaat in social life and an appreciation of the world view on which it is based. If this comprehension gives the reader an incentive to rethink female-oriented webs of significance in other contexts, I will have accomplished my goal.

Any public performance in West Sumatra that touches on the story of the Minangkabau people opens with an apology something like this:

> I offer a thousand apologies
> And ask a thousand pardons
> For retelling the story only the people can tell.

Following the Minangkabau way, I open this book with a general apology. Recognizing that only the Minangkabau can tell their story, I apologize for daring to offer my own version. Mine should be viewed not as a retelling of their story but as the chronicle of a personal journey that spanned almost two decades. In honor of the Minangkabau stress on "what is right and proper," I weigh my words carefully so as to be true to my anthropological vision and that of the Minangkabau.

My view must be taken as one of many. The Minangkabau have a saying for describing differences among villages, which applies to the differences between one writer's view and another's:

> In different ponds, different fish;
> In different fields, different grasshoppers.

Different writers will capture different refractions from the prism of Minangkabau culture. Men will inevitably see more of male culture, women more of women's culture, for the simple reason that one spends much time in sex-segregated settings. Those who study religion will highlight the role of Islam, neglecting perhaps the public role of women's ceremonies in village life. Yet, because all Minangkabau see their matrilineal system as unchangeable and in need of safeguarding, I hope to leave the reader with some conception of its fundamental characteristics.

Departures are also an occasion for apologies in Minangkabau life. Whenever I was about to leave Eggi's village to return to the United States, each member of the family would ask forgiveness for whatever slights, wrongs, or breaches of etiquette they may have inadvertently committed during my stay in the village. I reciprocated in like manner, apologizing for my Western insensitivity to Minangkabau ways. These conversations, which were deeply felt on both sides, were always tinged with the sadness of separation. Ibu Idar, Eggi's great aunt and my mentor, and Wik, Eggi's mother, who was like a daughter to me, never cried, for that was not their way, but I always did. So did Eggi and the other family members who were always present to say good-bye: Ibu Wel, Eggi's maternal grandmother, along with Ibu Ida and Ibu Os, Wik's sisters. Pak Edi, Eggi's father, expressed his feelings by looking more serious than usual.

In the Minangkabau spirit, I apologize to these members of my adopted family and to the people of Belubus for anything they might find offensive in these pages. Without them I could not have written this book. They gladly answered my questions, allowed me into their homes, and treated me like family. They helped shaped the vision of this book and made my journey unforgettable.

Endri and Pak Boestami were of great assistance. Over the years, En (Minangkabau names are always shortened) was my close companion, driver, research assistant, adopted son, and friend. During the thousands of miles we traveled together to and from Belubus and Padang, and elsewhere in West Sumatra, En and I talked about what we had learned and what it all meant. Over the years En became a superb research assistant, transcribing tapes, translating from Minangkabau to Indonesian, photographing ceremonies, and in my absence making exploratory trips to interesting historical sites. Pak Boes, En's boss, made this mobility possible by lending me a car and allowing En time off from his position as an employee of Museum Negeri Adityawarman, the state museum in Padang, which Pak Boes founded and directed for many years.

Through Pak Boes and his associates, Pak Herman and Ibu Ita, both of whom became directors of the museum after Pak Boes retired, I met and interviewed some of the most important figures in Minangkabau life and letters. They arranged my first interview with Pak Idrus Hakimy, the author of the defining texts on Minangkabau *adat* (customs) read in villages throughout West Sumatra. Pak Idrus was always available for an interview whenever I tracked him down, usually at his daughter's house in Padang. His son-in-law, Bahrizal, translated these interviews during the early years when I was learning Indonesian.

Suwati Kartiwa introduced me to West Sumatra. She was a graduate student at my university in 1981 when I was contemplating which matrilineal society to visit. As curator of ethnology at the National Museum of Indonesia in Jakarta, Suwati had done fieldwork in West Sumatra through Pak Boes and the museum in Padang. She convinced me to go to West Sumatra and arranged my first trip with Pak Boes, who sent members of his staff to greet me at the airport. Later, Suwati also arrived and we all went off on a tour of West Sumatra.

I owe the greatest debt to my children. Julie, who grew into a pragmatic feminist and positive thinker during the years of my travels, asked many key questions along the way. Eric, a student of philosophy while I was writing this book, inspired me to compare the philosophical bases of the Minangkabau matriarchaat with themes he encountered in ancient Greek literature and philosophy. The comparison yielded some intriguing commonalities.

I thank Julie and Eric for their strength and endurance over the years. When they were very young, I left them for what I thought would be only one summer but turned into many. I missed them dreadfully and was never sure that it wasn't a mistake to leave them. I was often aware of the paradox in leaving my children to study motherhood in a faraway land. I am grateful to their father, S. C. Sanday, who was always dedicated to the well-being of our children. Without him I would not have been able to leave. Yet, even with their father's steady presence, my absences were not always easy for them. To my children I offer a thousand apologies and ask a thousand pardons.

In later years, Serge was my constant companion, sitting beside me on the long airplane trips and holding my hand when I was sick in Belubus. We shared the emotion of the poignant songs sung by women late into the night on the Belubus ceremonial stage, and Serge delighted with me in the comradery of village life. I thank him for the thousand insights he shared during our stays in Belubus. His understanding of matriarchy from the vantage point of his French intellectual heritage, and his close association with Simone de Beauvoir, enriched my comprehension and provided new ways of thinking about what we experienced. His presence also enabled me to check my reactions through male eyes.

All these people were my guides. Somewhat like the guardian angels of my girlhood, they sit on my shoulder as I write, guiding my fingers on the keyboard, ever present in my mind. I thank them for making it possible for me to learn firsthand how Minangkabau men and women together uphold and defend *adat matriarchaat* (matriarchal customs).

I thank them also for the good times, for their smiles, for their steadfast devotion, and, most of all, for enriching my life beyond measure.

Writing this book was another kind of journey. I thank the people who read my drafts at various stages. Sheila Murnaghan, a colleague in classics, and Eric Cheyfitz, of the English Department at the University of Pennsylvania, provided important feedback at crucial moments. Evelyn Blackwood, a fellow Minangkabau scholar who worked in a village near Belubus and published a book on the social webs of female power, not only helped me to work my way through the labyrinth of my mind but confirmed my impression that what I was finding in Belubus was not unique.

My students clarified what was working in the text and what was not. I thank them for their enthusiasm and honest feedback, in particular Frank Cho, Erin Reilly, and Rachel Aronin, who worked with me in crafting the final touches.

Finally, I want to acknowledge the support of colleagues at the University of Pennsylvania. As the directors of the University of Pennsylvania Museum, Robert H. Dyson Jr. and his successor Jeremy A. Sabloff funded my trips through museum research funds. Jeremy Sabloff encouraged me to develop an exhibition of ethnographic photographs, which was displayed at the museum in 1997. This exhibition then traveled to West Sumatra and was shown at the Museum Negeri Adytiawarman in Padang in 1998. Another important financial source was the Research Fund of the University of Pennsylvania. I am also grateful for the feedback and support of colleagues in the Department of Anthropology, particularly Sandra Barnes, Gregory Possehl, Paula Sabloff, and Greg Urban.

Most of all I thank the Minangkabau people to whom I dedicate this book.

Women at the Center

Coming Home, 1996

> In our opinion the structure of a matriarchal society as can be found in Minangkabau is advantageous to individual development, of both males and females, as can generally be seen in the case of Minangkabau women and men. A Minangkabau woman is self-confident because she is not dependent on her husband who has been "collected." . . . In her behavior she is free to act as she pleases. Minangkabau women are people who have confidence in themselves, who are active and full of initiative in economic, political, religious, artistic, and other spheres of life.
>
> Sutan Takdir Alisyabbana, "Sistem matrilineal Minangkabau"

My first landing in Padang in 1981 came just before the holiday that celebrates the end of the Islamic fasting month of Ramadan. The plane was filled with people from all over Indonesia heading home to their villages. Those who could speak English told me they had gone *rantau*—that is, migrated. But now they were coming back to the village of their birth, to their mother's household. The excitement and expectation was palpable. The passengers chatted and strolled up and down the aisle as if everyone were one big family. Their laughter, smiles, and extraordinary friendliness wrapped me, a puzzled foreigner, in a cloak of good will. From the start, I felt welcome in this new land.

Every year as my plane descended toward the Padang airport, nestled between the Indian Ocean and the lush green mountains of central Sumatra, the sight of the buffalo horn–shaped rooftops of the houses gave me a sense of coming home. In Belubus and on the plane, people recited a famous proverb to explain why the village of their birth was the

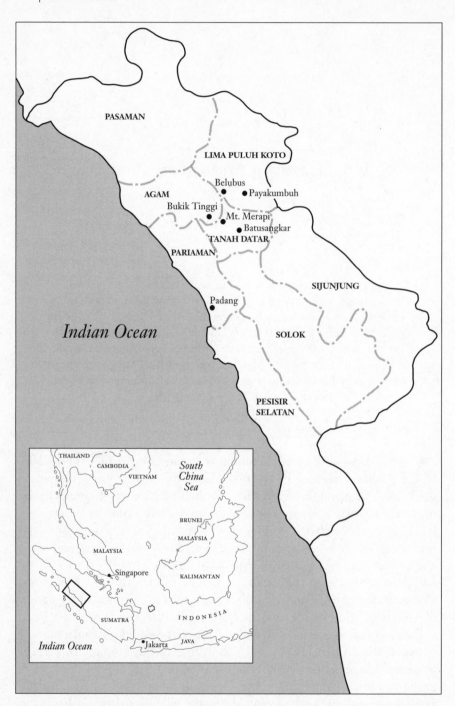

Province of West Sumatra

center of their world, the place they always returned to and where they wanted to be buried.

> Even if it rains gold in other lands
> And it rains stone in mine
> I will always return to my beloved village.

This proverb provided the first key to unlocking the meaning of *adat matriarchaat*, the phrase some villagers used to refer to their female-centered customs.

Few Americans have the opportunity to return to the house of their early memories. We tend to be dispossessed, alienated from our ancestral roots, wanderers searching for fame and fortune. The Minangkabau are also wanderers, but the umbilical cord of their ancestral past is never cut because matrilineal property is held in perpetuity for future generations. Grounding motherhood in the land gives a transgenerational solidity to memories and ensures the cultural importance of all stages in the cycle of life—particularly birth, marriage, and childbearing—from one generation to the next.

Thinking back through mothers and foremothers has a decided social meaning in Minangkabau village society. A daughter's connection to her foremothers is lifelong. Not only is her livelihood tied to the clan land of the common ancestress, but so is her marriage. On her wedding day, flanked by her maternal kin, a bride collects her husband from his mother's house and takes him to her mother's house, where the two live until they establish a household of their own on the bride's clan land. Daughters are the transgenerational links in the maternal chain through which pass ancestral land and matrilineal titles. If there are no daughters, the line ends. The man who holds the matrilineal title, the *penghulu*, helps with the management of the land, but he cannot pass these lands on to his children. Customs like these are at the core of the body of customary law the Minangkabau call *adat Minangkabau*.[1]

The sense of homecoming sharpened when I was greeted at the airport by a group from the Minangkabau state museum. For years, Pak Boestami, the museum's founder, met me with Endri, my driver, who always came with suitcase in tow, ready for the challenge of exploring his culture with me once again. In later years Pak Herman, the new museum director, met me with En.[2]

The reunion always carried over to my favorite Padang restaurant, where I was treated to the ritual meal celebrating a return. As one might expect in a mother-centered culture, commensalism is at the heart of social relations. As I ate this homecoming meal, dormant memories stirred and the mantle of Minangkabauness enveloped me once again.

Through food one imbibes the Minangkabau character. The social and psychological centrality of food is dramatically evident in the ritual feeding of rice and peppers to the newborn infant. The staple dish of red-hot peppers tempered with the soothing blandness of white rice reflects the Minangkabau passion for celebrating and synthesizing oppositions. Colorful displays of symmetrically arranged cakes and sweets alongside plates of hot red and green peppers mixed with onion, garlic, and lemon tangibly express the coexistence of passion and harmony in Minangkabau life. To eat, appreciate, or prepare Minang food is to be Minangkabau.

I usually stayed a week or so in Padang seeing colleagues, renewing ties with friends, arranging for a car with Pak Boestami, and shopping for provisions. On this trip during the summer of 1996, my eleventh and Serge's fourth, our Padang sojourn was marred by Serge's fall into an open five-foot-deep rain gutter when we were walking down an unlit street. The ordeal taught us much about traditional and modern medicine as practiced in West Sumatra. A doctor in a nearby clinic assured Serge that nothing was broken. But later that evening we learned that in West Sumatra anyone who takes a bad fall goes to a specialist in massage, whose job it is to fix broken bones and straighten the spine. Usually these are *dukun*, magical healers known for their ability in massage.

As it turned out, En had studied massage with a family member. After confirming the doctor's diagnosis he gave Serge his first massage of the summer. Later in Belubus, Serge was treated by a dukun widely known for his expertise in setting bones and massage. Along with deep massage the dukun advised hot compresses made from local herbs. To give the herbs greater efficacy, he said a few Islamic prayers and magical incantations. Serge prospered from the attention and by the end of the summer was completely healed.

Being sick makes one want to head home, which in this case meant Belubus, where people often greeted my arrival with "Sudah pulang" (you've come home). So we left Padang the day after Serge's fall, despite entreaties to stay longer. We had planned to spend the night in the tourist town of Bukik Tinggi so that En could go ahead and help Wik get our rooms ready. But now we headed straight for Belubus, arriving unannounced after dark.

I knew from experience that whenever she expects guests, Wik works hard preparing food and cleaning the house. Treating the guest like visiting royalty is the Minangkabau way. On such occasions the Minangkabau observe a strict form of etiquette called *baso-basi*, which makes them among the most polite and gracious people I have encountered. But for baso-basi to operate effectively, guests must do their part by sending advance notice of their approximate time of arrival. Going straight to Belubus broke with the baso-basi that was owed Wik, for she could not welcome us as she would like.

Bowed by pain and unable to sit upright after the three-hour trip, Serge lay down on the old, familiar pea-green sofa in the living room after we walked in, greeted by Agoes's excited cries. Serge, who anywhere else would have sat down politely in a chair despite his writhing pain, obviously had come home. Certainly Wik, Endri, Eggi, and Agoes's father, Pak Edi, understood.

It was now about seven o'clock, just after Magrib (evening prayers). Although to Westerners life in Belubus might seem difficult because people live in sparsely furnished wood or brick houses without running water and have a diet of rice with a little fish or meat, I had gotten used to this kind of living and always felt at home. It helped to have our own two little rooms with a washroom, which I had added to the family house in 1987.

With Serge ensconced on the sofa, we busied ourselves cleaning our rooms, which were never used during our absences. It is common in the Minangkabau extended family household for rooms to be reserved for a specific woman and her family. Nine months of accumulated dust and dirt had to be swept and scrubbed before we could settle in—Serge to start healing and I to grapple once again with Minangkabau culture. During this visit I would begin drawing on my accumulated knowledge and experience to interpret adat Minangkabau as it is lived in Belubus.

The house that became our home in West Sumatra had been built decades before by Wik's maternal aunt, Ibu Idar. In 1982 when Pak Boestami first brought me to Belubus, and for many years thereafter, it was Ibu Idar who greeted me at the door. Throughout my stay Ibu Idar cooked wonderful Minangkabau meals and guided me through the culture of daily life. She was my mentor and friend, an older sister who mothered and nursed me through some difficult times. By accepting me into her home Ibu Idar guaranteed my acceptance in the village. She was the matriarch of Eggi's matrilineage, an important female leader in the village, and widely respected and honored in neighboring villages. Like the famous Bundo Kanduang, the semimythical queen of the Minangkabau, she would always give the right advice, whether about how to conduct a ceremony or how to deal with an errant family member.

Ibu Idar was a small woman of about five feet, beautiful like all the women in her family, with finely chiseled features in a perfectly round face. She was a widow with one grown daughter, Elli, who had married

Ibu Idar's house, 1989

her Belubus sweetheart and gone to live with him in eastern Sumatra (Riau province) where he worked as a government physician. Ibu Idar never remarried, despite numerous proposals, because she preferred to devote herself to her family and to the village. When she died of a stroke in 1990, the village mourned a respected elder and I lost a dear friend.

Ibu Idar's polite speech and good relations with villagers exemplified the Minangkabau concern for *budi*, or propriety in human interaction. She had a quiet, selfless, delicate way of interacting with those who came to the house, her hands in perpetual motion as she listened and responded to the problems brought to her while she prepared food or was engaged in some other household task. Another valued characteristic was her religious dedication to Islamic prayer five times a day beginning at 4:30 in the morning. She was the ideal Minangkabau woman.

Ibu Idar shared my heart-wrenching experience of parental loss. In 1987 news reached me in Belubus that my mother was dying in a nursing home near Philadelphia. During the next few weeks before I returned to the United States, Ibu Idar and I prayed nightly, side by side, for God to wait before claiming my mother's soul. Joining our prayers was Angku Rancha, Ibu Idar's spiritual leader, a devoutly religious man who lived in a small prayerhouse by the river and whose life seemed to be dedicated solely to God. When I returned the next year, I told Ibu Idar and Angku Rancha that our prayers had been answered: I had arrived in time to be with my mother during her last days.

From Ibu Idar I learned that a parent is never really lost, if one recognizes the signs of their continuing presence. She often talked about her long-deceased father, and together we studied the texts in which he recorded his *ilmu*, his deep knowledge, and especially his *ilmu gaib*, his special understanding of the unseen world of spirits and healing practices. I learned that Ibu Idar's father was a famous practitioner and teacher of ilmu gaib as well as a renowned leader of a local Islamic order. Studying his ilmu, and learning some of the ancient Minangkabau prayers mixed with Koranic references that he passed on to his daughter, I began to understand how the Minangkabau melded the animistic past with their Islamic present.

Ibu Idar's accounts of occasions when her dead father manifested himself led me to understand the importance of ancestors, especially those who had made a special mark in their lifetime. Once I felt her father's presence when Ibu Idar and I were praying at his grave site. A loud noise came from the roof as if something was falling from the heavens. Ibu Idar did not need to explain. I understood the look she gave me and her reverent stillness as she knelt by his grave during the next few minutes.

Eggi was born in 1987, just before the news reached me about my mother. I felt touched and greatly honored when Wik and Ibu Idar gave her my name. Our common name exemplifies my vision of anthropology as a partnership in the discovery of life lived in different ways.[3] Earlier that year, Ibu Idar had brought a very pregnant Wik to live with her. Wik had been living in a *pondok*, a flimsy hut she and her husband had built on clan land. Ibu Idar wanted to give Wik a more permanent home for raising her children. Eggi was born a few days after my birthday, which I celebrated quietly with my son Eric, who was visiting me in Belubus. I saw the two birthdays as milestones, one marking the passage of life, the other its beginning. My sensitivity to life's passages came both from the concern I had about my mother's decline and from the joyous way in which Belubus women celebrated their children's life cycle. They marked birth, marriage, house building, and the ascension of males to ancestral titles with ritualized celebrations called *pesta adat*. One knew that there was a pesta adat somewhere in the village by the streams of women, colorfully dressed and bearing elaborate arrangements of food and flowers on their heads, walking slowly and regally to or from a wedding or birth ceremony. Women never attend a ceremony without bringing food and later returning home with baskets filled by their hosts.

Although Eggi was born while I was in Belubus, she was named only after I returned to the United States. My name was chosen as a way of keeping me in Belubus, Wik explained later. "You always come and go," she said. "We get used to calling your name when you are here, Ibu Peggy, and then you are gone. This way your name will always be with us in Belubus." It was Ibu Idar, who first suggested my name. "If the big Ibu Peggy leaves," she told Wik, "we still have the little Peggi." At first they called her Peggi, but then nicknamed her Eggi, reasoning that when I returned it wouldn't be right to call out "Peggi" and have both Peggy *besar* and Peggi *kecil* (big Peggy and little Peggy) respond. When Eggi started school and needed a more formal name, Wik's sister, Ibu Ida, a local schoolteacher, decided it should be Peggi Sandi. It was when I saw how Eggi signed her name on school compositions that I realized the family had never seen my name in writing. Today, Eggi is called Peggi at school, but in Belubus she is known as Eggi.

Ibu Idar died in early 1990 about six months after her mother, Umi, passed away. The two women were buried in adjoining graves next to Umi's mother, Railah, on the land of their common ancestress. The graves, conspicuous in the dense green of the tropical foliage because of their sky-blue tiles and the well-tended path visitors take when paying their respects, vividly symbolize Minangkabau matriliny—related women, mother and daughter through the generations, joined in life and death on common ancestral land.

After Ibu Idar died I became very close to her sister, Ibu Wel. The two sisters were most unlike. If Ibu Idar was the morally superior Bundo Kanduang, devoting her life to family and religion, Ibu Wel was the fun-loving, earthy, barefoot contessa, famous for her beauty and the string of husbands she acquired and divorced. When I left in 1995, she was being courted by a sixth candidate just after her divorce from husband number five, who ran off with a woman the age of his daughter by another marriage.

Whenever I wanted to talk confidentially to Ibu Wel, she and I would go out to her fields and gardens beyond the village. After a morning of weeding, we would sit down and gossip while slaking our thirst with the juice of a young coconut she cut. There she would talk without reserve about anything and everything, letting me into a side of Belubus life not readily revealed. This is the side which includes ilmu gaib (magical knowledge) and the curse of the ancestors visited on those who break the most sacred taboos.

It was in her garden that Ibu Wel confided her desire to remarry. I gave her my blessing, knowing that the decision would ultimately be made by her daughters. When a woman reaches a certain age, her daughters have

Graves of Railah, Umi, and Ibu Idar (grandmother, mother, and daughter) on clan land, 1995

considerable say regarding her decision to marry. As it turned out, Ibu Wel's daughters, Os and Ida along with Wik, disapproved of her plan to remarry. They wanted her to act like a proper senior woman and look after her grandchildren by taking on the role of family matriarch vacated by Ibu Idar.

Ibu Wel agreed to their request and didn't remarry. Upon my return the following year, she explained her decision with the motto "Abu di atas tunggul": Like ashes on a burned tree stump, husbands blow away quickly with the wind. Even in the most solid of marriages, husbands and fathers are torn between their loyalty to mothers and sisters and their allegiance to wives and children. A good husband who provides for his wife and children is honored and treated like a king, but if he doesn't behave properly he may be asked to leave. In the case of a second or third marriage, grown children may make life so uncomfortable for their new stepfather that he has no choice but to run off.

During the years when Eggi grew from an infant to a budding teenager of twelve, our relationship went through many stages. Unlike many small children in the village, she was never afraid of me with my white skin. Nor did she behave like so many other young children who, fascinated by foreigners, come close and touch them only to fly away like a fright-

Family photo at Ibu Ida's house-building ceremony in 1985. Wik holds Adis, second from left in top row. Ibu Ida is at my right, Ibu Idar at my left. Umi, the senior woman in the family, is at the far right next to her son, Datuk Llano.

ened bird. She accepted me as part of her family, albeit not the usual sort of family member. She often played beside me as I worked on the computer, reaching up to look at this strange and wondrous instrument when she was little or, when she was bigger, gazing over my shoulder trying to decipher the words on the screen.

Every year upon my return Eggi was usually the first to greet me. When she learned to write she was the one who sent me letters. Whenever I called the family on a friend's phone in Payakumbuh, she was there to say hello. Each year we renewed our acquaintance in our customary walks through the village in the late afternoon. As she grew older these walks became a daily routine. Eggi, with her soap opera outlook, taught me to see much that was hidden from plain sight—pointing out, for example, bushes and trees underneath which certain clandestine lovers had been caught in the act. When we were not greeting people or catching up on village gossip, she would tell me about her friends or about school. Often we would stop at a food stall to eat fried bananas and chat with villagers in the late afternoon as women came out after they had bathed upon returning from their fields.

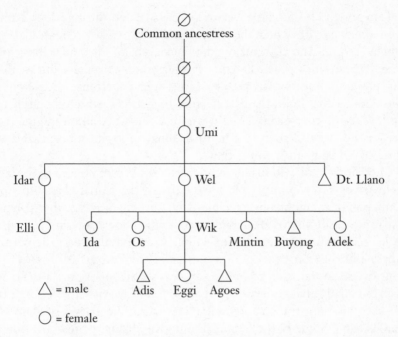

Fig. 1. Diagram of Eggi's immediate family tree. This diagram does not include all of Eggi's immediate family members, nor does it represent the complete family tree.

After Ibu Idar's death, Wik took over the running of her household in the absence of Ibu Idar's daughter, Elli. Wik also inherited the job of caring for my needs when I was in Belubus. During these years I grew very close to Wik and her sisters, Ida and Os. Along with Elli and Dt. Llano, Ibu Idar's brother who lived with his wife in eastern Sumatra, these women handled all economic and social affairs affecting the *paruik*, the extended family of matrilineally related kin (literally, "one womb").

In 1985 we all posed for a family photograph at a ceremony for the construction of Ibu Ida's new house. Most of the main characters of my story appear in this photograph. The diagram of Eggi's immediate family tree (fig. 1) shows the kinship connections among them.[4]

With the help of the women in Eggi's family and other women of Belubus, I sorted out the elaborate life cycle ceremonies so important to Belubus social life. In doing so I began to comprehend what the Minangkabau mean when they refer to their matrilineal social system as a matriarchaat. This book is an anthropological memoir of my quest to understand matricentered meanings and social forms in West Sumatra through living in Eggi's village.

I am grateful for the time I spent in Eggi's village, during which I drank from the cup of life which the villagers called *adat ibu* (women's adat) and which contains the customs of adat matriarchaat. How adat ibu works, what it means for women, and how it is hegemonic in village life are three big pieces of the overall puzzle. How men contribute to upholding women's adat through their dedication to adat law, which they call *adat limbago*, is another piece. I begin where I embarked upon my quest, in the coastal city of Padang trying to acclimatize to the conceptual structures of Minangkabau world view.

I hope this book will inspire readers to visit West Sumatra to see it for themselves and to sample the hospitality of the Minangkabau people. Unlike many societies made famous by anthropologists, the Minangkabau are easily visited. You don't need jungle boots, camping gear, multiple vaccinations, a Land Rover, supplies of food, the requisite permissions, and the constitution of a hardened adventurer. All it takes is a tourist visa and a ticket to Padang by way of Singapore or Jakarta. You land in Padang at a modern airport and obtain a tourist visa. A bus or taxi whisks you from the airport or Padang to the heartland of alam Minangkabau—home of the famous Bundo Kanduang, who adorns tourist brochures and state ideology proclaiming Minangkabau ethnic identity. Here you can stay in a modern hotel or arrange a tour from Bukik Tinggi, the central tourist city in the heartland. Wherever you go, you will be warmly welcomed. No doubt you will be given elementary lessons in adat and plied, as I was, with stories about the Minangkabau matriarchaat and its origins on the slopes of Mt. Merapi.

"NATURE IS OUR TEACHER"

CHAPTER ONE

Adat Matriarchaat as a World View

Alam Minangkabau [is] the world . . . supported by the two sacred pillars, namely Islam and adat. . . . [Today] the desire to maintain primordial identity is not diminished. . . . Whatever economic changes that have taken place so far, there has always been an inclination among Minangkabau to safeguard their matrilineal social system. It is a sacred system; it has been religiously legitimated.

Taufik Abdullah, "Islam, History, and Social Change"

L iving in Eggi's village I came to understand that the centripetal maternal ties of village social life have a significant impact on the nature and quality of life. Since husbands go to live with their wives, it is men who experience the separation and loss that women face at marriage in so many other societies. Staying in place, daughters connect women to one another and to the ancestral land cultivated for generations by their maternal relatives. The web of female-oriented relationships tied to land, household, and clan produces an aura of accommodation and cooperation that colors the emotions, thoughts, feelings, and actions and suffuses life with joy. I saw this mood in the etiquette of daily life, in the politesse, humor, strength, and agency of the women I knew, and in the nurturing attitude of men. The same zeitgeist permeates the Minangkabau understanding of the body of customs known as adat Minangkabau.

When I landed in Indonesia in the capital city of Jakarta in July 1981, all I knew about the ubiquitous word *adat* was that it was used all over Indonesia to refer to local custom. I spent a week in Jakarta arranging for a research permit and talking with Taufik Abdullah, world famous for his articles on adat Minangkabau. Pak Taufik is a native Minangkabau who earned a Ph.D. at Cornell University. He lives in Jakarta where he works in LIPI, the government-sponsored research institute to which all foreign scholars must apply for a permit to do research. In his office we had a long talk about adat Minangkabau. He gave me many of his papers, and I followed his thinking thereafter. Years later he told me that he came from a village outside Payakumbuh, not so far from Eggi's village. His influence on my thinking about adat as a matricentered philosophy has been profound.

Upon arrival in Padang I was met at the airport by Pak Moechtar and Ibu Ita, staff members of the Padang Museum sent by Pak Boestami at the request of Suwati Kartiwa. While waiting for Suwati to arrive to take a tour with me through the province of West Sumatra, Pak Moechtar and Ibu Ita escorted me all over the city. They echoed what would be a constant refrain that first summer. If I wanted to understand the Minangkabau I should study adat. I gladly put myself into their hands and began my education.[1]

From the start my teachers made it clear that adat is not the whole of life but operates in conjunction with the dictates of Islam and the laws of the nation-state. "Adat, religion, and government guide our lives," they told me. "Together they make a unity, the three-stranded rope of our lives that cannot be unraveled."

A few days into the first week Pak Moechtar excitedly told me that he had arranged an interview with the foremost adat leader in Padang, Idrus Hakimy Dt. Rajo Penghulu.[2] From Pak Idrus came my first lesson in the meaning of the three-stranded rope. One strand is adat, the indigenous code of which the matriarchaat is a part. Another is Islam, which entered West Sumatra centuries ago, most people think sometime between the fourteenth and sixteenth century. The codes promulgated by the Indonesian nation-state, formed in the 1960s after three centuries of Dutch colonial rule, constitute the third strand.[3] Much later, after living in Belubus for some time, I began to understand how villagers manage to negotiate these sometimes contradictory codes with relative equanimity.

There is a fourth code which I discovered only after making the transition from visitor to family member. This is *ilmu gaib*, or magical knowledge. After I began studying ilmu gaib with a number of practitioners *(dukun)*, I learned that Pak Idrus was an expert at blending the arts of ilmu gaib with Islam. Although he readily answered my questions about ilmu gaib, he never volunteered information, the way he did when lecturing to me about adat and Islam. Like others, he probably feared that this neophyte foreigner would misconstrue his devotion to Islam if she discovered that he sometimes relied on ilmu gaib as well. State ideology places a heavy emphasis on Islam, so not surprisingly most people talked at first about Islam in conjunction with adat. But as we shall see, ilmu gaib plays a central role in my story, on a par with adat and Islam in upholding the matrilineal system in the modern Minangkabau world.

Adat and Islam in Minangkabau Thought

No one who studies adat in West Sumatra goes without hearing something about Islam. Most of the adat experts I interviewed referred to one of two proverbs about how adat is related to Islam. Those who believe that adat shares an equivalent status with Islam say something like "Adat is based on religion, religion is based on adat." Those who hold that Islam is the perfection of adat, handed down by the godhead, present a somewhat different version: "Adat is based on Islam, Islam is based on the Holy Teaching." Either way, one gets the point. Islam and adat are granted sacred status in the official version of Minangkabau world view.[4]

The prominent role given to Islam in this matricentered culture is at first puzzling. How does one explain the seemingly benign coexistence of matrilineal practices and patrilineal Islam? As Pak Taufik puts it, "How could a matrilineal society such as the Minangkabau become one of the most thoroughly Islamized ethnic groups in the Malay World?" (Abdullah 1985:141).[5] Abdullah answers by referring to the Minangkabau historical tendency to accommodate paradox and antithesis. He suggests that the matrilineal principle survived because of the "genius of Minangkabau to synthesize contradictions harmoniously" (Abdullah 1985:141). Minangkabau history bears him out in offering many examples of how the matrilineal foundation accommodates patrilineal influences.

To take the most well-known historical events, in the fourteenth century a partial centralization of the Minangkabau kingdom was brought about by Adityawarman, a Javanese-Minangkabau king, who tried to impose patrilineal succession. At the same time or somewhat later, perhaps in the sixteenth century, Islam entered West Sumatra, bringing with it education, literacy, and, on the spiritual side, a state of mind rather than a religious dogma. This changed in the nineteenth century when the Padri War pitted Islamic fundamentalists seeking to purify adat of "pagan practices" (such as matrilineal inheritance) against adat leaders endeavoring to accommodate Islam while retaining traditional practices.

In response to the Padri War, Dutch colonialism penetrated the heartland region taking the side of adat leaders. Dutch intervention helped end the war. One casualty of the struggle was the demise of the famous Minangkabau kingdom of Pagarruyung, whose influence during the European colonial era extended throughout central Sumatra. This is the kingdom that the famous queen mother Bundo Kanduang reportedly ruled.

The war had the effect of preserving the matrilineal principle, which prospered after the accommodation of adat and Islam. Much later, in the middle of the twentieth century when Indonesia became an independent nation, the third strand, which people in Belubus alluded to only by the word *government*, became part of daily life. The rope metaphor was cited on numerous occasions to indicate that the Minangkabau were as loyal to the national government as they were to adat and Islam. One man even twined strips of bamboo together to show me how three makes one. Despite such lip service to national unity, and despite the obvious fact that people must follow the dictates of national civil and criminal law, I heard much more about adat and Islam as forming the ideological core of daily life.

Abudllah believes that the historical accommodation of adat and Islam worked in favor of matrilineal adat by raising the matrilineal principle to divine status. According to Abdullah, whatever the impact of the myriad historical and modern influences on Minangkabau society, the Minangkabau desire to maintain their matrilineal identity never diminished. With respect to adat and Islam, he cites one writer who said that the two are "not like the combination of 'water and milk' but like the union of water and oil in milk" (Abdullah 1966:3).

In an interview Pak Idrus explained how the accommodation came about. We met in a simple house on a busy Padang street, the home of the older of his two wives. Living with her were several of their grown daughters, one of whom is married and whose husband, Bahrizal, acted as interpreter.[6] We talked for most of one afternoon on the subject of adat and Islam and women's position in adat.

Pak Idrus said that when Islam entered West Sumatra adat leaders sought ways to mediate between adat officials and fundamentalist Islamic leaders who wanted to purge adat practices. To accommodate adat and Islam they devised a unique solution. The matrilineal principle was placed in the most sacred of the four adat categories devised by the original lawgivers, the category called "adat that is truly adat," along with the basic principles of Islam. Both were given the status of natural law handed down from the godhead, which meant that neither could be abolished. There could be no contradiction between matrilineal adat and patrilineal Islam because both are sacred. In his own words:

> The practices of adat go together with the practices of Islam. Many are overlapping and the same. The reason that adat is quite strong in our villages is because it is supported by religion. In adat the possessions go to women. In Islam possessions go to men and women. But actually the two things are not contradictory. In adat there are two kinds of possessions—clan and individual. Clan possessions go to women, from one woman to another. Individual possessions—the things a husband gets together with his wife—go to their children.

Like Abdullah, Pak Idrus feels strongly that there is no mystery about the accommodation of adat and Islam. He said that the women-centeredness of matrilineal customs is supported by the teachings of Islam because much that appears in adat also appears in the Koran and the holy teachings of the Prophet Mohammed. As an example he mentioned the teaching that "Paradise lies under the feet of mothers" and the tradition that tells of the Prophet's praise for the mother:

> A man came to God's Messenger and said, "O Messenger of God, who is the most entitled to the best of my friendship?" The Prophet said, "Your mother." The man said, "Then who?" The Prophet said, "Your mother." The man further said, "Then who?" The Prophet said, "Your mother." The man said again, "Then who?"
>   The Prophet said, "Then your father."[7]

Underlining the sacred importance of women in Islam, Pak Idrus concluded on this rhetorical note: "Why was Adam sent into the world by God? To accompany Eve. So Eve is just as important as Adam. Women play a very important role. Without women life would be impossible. So for these reasons women are given more privileges."

The easy accommodation between adat and Islam was apparent to me in the early weeks in Padang and later in traveling throughout the province. Daily life is marked by the call to prayer from the loudspeaker of the village mosque, which can be heard from most houses five times a day beginning before dawn. I have been wakened many times by this call; in one village I awoke first to the howl of a local dog who learned not only to fine-tune his call to the nasal chant intoned over the loudspeaker but to anticipate it as well, a little like the cock crowing before dawn.

Despite the seeming ubiquity of Islam, most people I knew were not Islamic fundamentalists, nor did Islam rule all aspects of their daily life.[8] Today, women wear the usual sarong or dress seen throughout Indonesia, and only a few cover their hair completely. As I saw it practiced in Belubus, I came to understand Islam as a spiritual state of mind and a basic cultural premise translated into ways of relating to others. Some followers, of course, are more devout than others, but Islam is not always the fundamentalist religion that we in the West hear so much about.

The Female Ethos of Adat

In addition to talking about adat and Islam, Pak Idrus had a great deal to say about the position of women in adat and the importance of etiquette guiding Minangkabau social relations.

> The main core of adat philosophy is good deeds and kind-heartedness. Democracy and thoughtfulness for the feelings of others is very important. Adat teaching is oriented to human morals and feelings. You do not accuse someone directly. You do not criticize directly. You do so with proverbs. It is very rude to point out mistakes directly. There should be no force in decision making. There should be mutual understanding. In Minangkabau democracy there is no room for rivalries. Differences of opinion are regarded as normal—consensus arrives through discussion. About differences of opinion there is a proverb: Crossing wood in the hearth makes the fire glow.
>
> One of the mottoes of adat says that you have to like what other people like. You have to practice what others like. You may not practice what would hurt others. For example, if I want to do something in this house, I have to think of how each person in the house will be affected. In other words, you have to think of others before you act. If you feel it is painful to be pinched, don't pinch others.

Describing the prominent place women play in Minangkabau society, Pak Idrus explained that their importance was due to their roles as mother, educator, guardian of the emotions, and keeper of the rice house (his way of describing women's central economic role).

> Women and men are the same, but women are more respected and given more privileges. All ancestral property goes to women. The house goes to women. Women keep the key to the rice house because women are more economical. Young boys sleep in other houses (usually mosques) to show their sisters that they do not own the houses. Men feel proud because they don't take anything from their mother's house. Men who take from another's house are accused of being weak or robbers.

Pak Idrus added that women are given more privileges because people think that women determine the continuation of the generations. Whether the next generation is bad or good depends on women because children stay most of the time with their mothers. So mothers are primarily responsible for teaching children. He added that in the home "adat is taught by the oldest sister who is called Bundo Kanduang."

The maternal meanings associated with adat are evident in sensual, aesthetic, and visual signs throughout West Sumatra. Adat structures with their buffalo horn–shaped roofs, the symbol of Minangkabau ethnic identity, dot the landscape. These include matrilineal longhouses and adat council houses built for the most part in the early part of the twentieth century. More recently, in the 1970s and 1980s, the same architecture was adopted for all government buildings erected by Suharto's New Order government as part of the *pancasila* ideology of celebrating local adat while unifying Indonesia's diverse ethnic groups under one national government. The signs of adat can also be seen in the ceremonial dress worn by men and women for adat occasions. Depending on the region and the village the dress differs, illustrating the tolerance for difference.

Adat becomes most alive in the grand performances of the life cycle ceremonies organized and staged by women. This is a time when men give flowery adat speeches and women file to and fro bearing ornate trays and baskets on their heads or carrying stacks of plates for adat exchanges. In some regions the U-shaped headdress worn by women mirrors the upswing of the buffalo horn–shaped rooftops. The image of women dressed in this fashion, standing by her *rumah gadang* (matrilineal longhouse) appears as a symbol of Minangkabau ethnic identity not just in West Sumatra but throughout Indonesia. In the chapters to follow I argue that in the signs and the performance of their ceremonies women interweave the aesthetics, commensality, and social relationships of adat with its logos.[9]

Adat is also manifested when the titled male leaders of the clans gather in the adat council house to resolve disputes over the rights to the use of ancestral land. It is in the interaction and mutual support of women's ceremonies *(adat ibu)* and male dispute settlement *(adat limbago)* that I locate the Minangkabau matriarchaat as practiced and experienced in village life. Adat ibu gives local adat its aesthetic, emotional, social, and sacred center; adat limbago makes adat intelligible as a body of rules to new generations and affirms its legitimacy in a world that pulls people in many directions. Adat ibu designs a path to guide and protect individuals by weaving them into the tapestry of village social relationships; adat limbago applies the rules that lead individuals down this path and punishes transgressors.

Village and Urban Forms of Adat

In Padang, I found that adat lore flourishes primarily in books of texts, sayings, and proverbs and in the philosophical treatises of philosophers and urban intellectuals who have migrated from their home villages. In Belubus, I discovered that adat flourishes in the life cycle ceremonies organized and staged by women. I also discovered that women are referred to as "Bundo Kanduang" when they perform adat functions. When men speak adat proverbs on the Belubus ceremonial stage, they are clearly operating in a domain constructed by women. In Padang, adat exists as a memory of the past revived in flowing speeches mixed with proverbs and maxims intoned by government officials on state occasions—in which women, here too referred to as Bundo Kanduang, serve as aesthetic adjuncts seated decorously in the audience. The difference is palpable.

The urban version of adat melds adat sayings with state ideology, keeping both in circulation. The village form is inseparable from daily life and functions as the major mechanism through which adat social relationships are regenerated. Although city dwellers in Padang celebrate life cycle ceremonies, they do not live in the tight web of adat relationships found in the villages. Despite these differences, all Minangkabau agree that adat is dedicated to three basic goals: preservation of the matrilineal system of descent, the importance of Islam, and an orientation to Mt. Merapi as the place of first origin.

The passion with which the Minangkabau speak about these goals and the tolerance they show for local differences envelopes all Minangkabau people within a common world view. Throughout my travels in West Sumatra I heard the saying "Wherever the Minangkabau live, adat flourishes." People refer to the indestructibility of adat: "Adat will neither rot in the rain, nor crack in the sun"; or taking another example from nature, they say, "Even if the river floods and the bathing place moves, the riverbed remains intact." In the words of still another proverb, "Adat will exist as long as people stand under the sky with their feet planted on earth." Although nobody specifies just what they mean when they use the word *adat* in these contexts, other than to give lip service to the basic principles at stake, the passion keeps adat alive in both its rural and urban forms.

The Matriarchaat at the Nexus of Nature and Culture

The many references to nature in adat proverbs reminded me of the Enlightenment discourse of the seventeenth century. Like Hobbes and Locke, the Minangkabau have a conception of nature and the necessity of a social contract in the transition from nature to culture. Unlike Hobbes and Locke, however, the Minangkabau weave order out of their version of wild nature by appeal to maternal archetypes. Unlike Darwin in the nineteenth century, the Minangkabau subordinate male dominion and competition, which we consider basic to human social ordering and evolution, to the work of maternal nurture, which they hold to be necessary for the common good and a healthy society.[10]

The Minangkabau construction of the connection between nature and culture by reference to maternal archetypes is most clearly seen in an account of the matriarchaat by the famous Minangkabau philosopher M. Nasroen, whose 1957 book on the foundation and principles of adat philosophy is widely cited and read in West Sumatra. Nasroen says that the matrilineal principle is very old in Minangkabau culture, coming from the time of the ancestor worship and animism that prevailed before Hinduism, Buddhism, or Islam influenced local custom. He implies that the maternal principle is older than the explicit codification of matrilineal adat which came later, as told in the Minangkabau story of their history.

Nasroen suggests that the primordial emphasis on the maternal and the development of matrilineal adat law were fused because of their fit *(cocok)* with the animistic past, in which nature constituted the model for culture. Unlike Western feminists who focus on the mother or the womb as the primordial basis for maternal meanings, Nasroen, like many Minangkabau, ascribes the primordial basis to fertility and growth in nature.

This point can be made by citing a common proverb I heard many times in West Sumatra. Nasroen cites this proverb in making the argument that the original matriarchaat stems from the Minangkabau approach to nature.[11]

> Take the small knife used for carving
> Make a staff from the *lintabuang* tree.
> The cover of *pinang* flowers becomes a winnow
> A drop of water becomes the sea.
> A fist becomes a mountain
> Growth in nature is our teacher.[12]

This proverb introduces the animistic foundation for both the Minangkabau matriarchaat and matrilineal law. When I asked people for an exegesis, they usually answered that people derive the rules of culture from observing the benign aspects of nature. As Ibu Idar said, our adat teaches us to take the good from nature *(alam)* and throw away the bad. The imitation of nature means that people learn not just from what supports life but from what destroys it as well.

According to the proverb, the good of nature provides the wherewithal for rudimentary implements needed to obtain food and shelter (first three lines). Social well-being is found in natural growth and fertility (next three lines) according to the dictum that the unfurling, blooming, and growth in nature is our teacher. As plants grow from seedlings, trees from transplanted branches, the sea from streams, and mountains from clumps of earth, people grow from infancy. Like the seedlings of nature, infants must be nurtured so that they will flower and grow to their fullness and strength as adults. Generalizing this principle, nurture is the natural law that humans should follow in devising social rules. This means that culture must focus on nurturing the weak and renounce brute strength.[13]

Many adat leaders and intellectuals write about the role of nature (conceived as teacher) in the development of adat. Pak Idrus, for example, told me, "We study everything around us: human life, animals, plants, mountains, hills, and rivers. Nature surrounds us in all the events of our lives. We learn from the good in nature and throw away the bad. The rules of adat are based in nature. Like nature, adat surrounds us." Pak Taufik cites a proverb which goes a step further to suggest that adat is sacred because it is a primordial aspect of nature.

> When nothing was existent, the universe did not exist,
> Neither earth nor sky existed;
> Adat had already existed.[14]

Because the principle of matrilineal descent is a corollary of the immanence of adat in nature and its divine potential, it too has sacred status. According to Pak Idrus,

> Matrilineal adat is in accordance with the flora and fauna of nature in which it can be seen that it is the mother who bears the next generation and it is the mother who suckles the young and raises the child. As we all know, Minangkabau adat comes from nature according to the proverb "Alam takambang jadi guru" (growth in nature is our teacher). In nature all that is born into the world is born from the mother, not from the father. Fathers are only known by a confession from the mother. Adat knows that the mother is the closest to her children and is therefore more dominant than the father in establishing the character of the generations. Thus, we must protect women and their offspring because they are also weaker than men. Just as the weak becomes the strong in nature, we must make the weaker the stronger in human life. If the mother abandons or doesn't recognize her own child, adat exists to recognize the child's descent line and to ensure the child's worldly welfare.

Adat leaders in Eggi's village expressed similar ideas. In 1985, Dt. Nago Besar, who was then at the apex of the male adat ladder, explained to me that the matrilineal system was originally devised so that children would always have a family, food, and ancestral land. Speaking rhetorically he asked, "If a child is born without a father, or we don't know who the father is, where can the child find *pusaka* (land, titles, and ancestral house) and food? Like growth in nature, we always know from whom the child descends: the mother."

Such ideas cannot be reduced to ignorance about the father's role in conception, as was commonly claimed during the nineteenth century when there was considerable speculation about a period in human evolution when women ruled. Whether they called this period the stage of mother right or matriarchy, scholars agreed that female rule preceded patriarchy in the evolution of human culture and that it was based on ignorance about paternity.[15]

The Minangkabau understand the biological basis of paternity perfectly well, yet they choose not to make protecting the blood ties between a father and his children a social issue. To do so would be antithetical to the conviction that the job of culture *(adat)* is to nurture and care for the young. While the mother-child bond can always be counted on to perform this task, the father-child link is less reliable. Dt. Nago Besar's comments suggest that concerns about biological fatherhood deflect attention from the more important emphasis on the child's well-being. This is not to say that Minangkabau fathers don't play an important role in the lives of their children. They do, but the connection of father to child is not tied to the transmission of land and houses. It is more an emotional than a material bond. Social rights are conceived so as to protect the weak. As Pak Idrus told me: "Here we elevate the weak instead of the strong. Women *must* be given rights *because* they are weak. Young men *must* be sent away from the village to prove their manhood so that there will be no competition between them and their sisters."

In village life a nurturing of the vulnerable applies not only to women and children but also to the rice cycle. The Minangkabau conceive of the rice cycle in terms of growth and well-being. The archetype of maternal nurture is the source for ideas about rice fertility and growth. The nurturing begins when the delicate rice seeds are placed in water for sprouting. Sprouted seedlings are sown in a "rice nursery" for the first stage of growth, during which time they are carefully covered for protection. Once they take root in the nursery, the vulnerable seedlings are transplanted to the cultivated rice field where they are nurtured with water and weeding.

Nurturing strength from vulnerability in the rice cycle is especially evident in ancient rice rituals, now abandoned but still remembered. Viewing a ritual performed for my benefit, I was struck by the reverence paid to the sheaf of seven rice seedlings known as "mother of the rice" and addressed as Sonan Sari.[16] This sheaf was once marked off for ritual attention because of its ability to produce a bountiful harvest. To protect Sonan Sari from evil spirits, the earth around the sheaf was ritually weeded, and various amulets were attached to the sheaf of seven. Like the human mother, Sonan Sari stood as a dominant symbol of fertility, growth, well-being, and maternal nurture. Like the child who is ceremonially nurtured throughout the life cycle, Sonan Sari had to be protected by the laws of culture. Although this ritual was abandoned after the introduction of hardier rice seeds, its symbolism elucidates once again the cultural emphasis on nurture in nature.

The theme of nurture is not reserved just for women and rice. It is also applied to the male role. Pak Idrus stressed male nurturing by citing a proverb about the fern frond.

> Fern frond, *balimbing* nuts,
> Shake the shell of a coconut,
> Plant pepper with the roots;
> Seat your child and guide your nephew,
> Think about your village people,
> Protect your village from destruction,
> And keep up the tradition.

According to Pak Idrus, and the many others who recited this proverb, each line describes a different form of male nurturing. He said that like the curled fern frond coiled around itself, a man should wrap himself around his family, custom, and the affairs of the village. Like the outward curve of the frond, he must turn outward to his village and serve as leader to his nephews and nieces, guiding them in the paths of everyday life. As a father, a man is expected to carry his children (love them, in other words), and as an uncle he must lead his nephews by the hand (educate them). When his sister calls him, the uncle comes to discipline her children. A mother will say to a naughty child: "Look, your uncle is coming. Please be good." Fathers and uncles—Pak Idrus concluded—are expected to work together to help provide financial support to the families of their sisters and wives.

The Role of Ilmu Gaib and the Ancestral Curse

Years after my first visit, I discovered that as much as they emphasize benignity in nature and refer to the sacredness of matrilineal adat and Islam, the Minangkabau also have a concept of evil in nature. This is what Ibu

Fern frond, a common symbol of fertile land near a water source and a metaphor for male roles

Idar was trying to tell me when she said that the proverb "Growth in nature is our teacher" is about taking the good and throwing away the bad.

The Minangkabau conception of evil in nature bears a resemblance to Hobbes's state of nature, the "warre of all against all." I was told that without adat human beings would be like wild animals in the jungle: "the strong will conquer the weak, the tallest will defeat the shortest, and the strongest will hold down the smallest."[17] *Jungle* here refers to nature in the raw, the world where adat does not rule. It is a world we will encounter again in the next chapter in *Kaba Cindur Mata*, a story that compares those who don't accept the dictates of adat to thieves who kill, not for the sake of stealing but because that is their nature. The implication is that without adat all is chaos.

The Minangkabau have devised a system to counteract the effects of evil in wild nature. If culture in the form of adat operates in the image of benign nature—seen in the focus on growth—ilmu gaib consists of a repository of knowledge for punishing and ameliorating the evil that produces decay and death. This body of lore includes ancient rice rituals for protecting Sonan Sari. It also includes procedures that shelter the newborn from the forces of evil flowing through the village, which might harm a child who has not yet been socialized [enculturated] in adat, a job accomplished by the birth ceremony. The conviction that ilmu gaib will protect those who adhere to adat and punish transgressors gives adat added strength in the modern world.

Ilmu gaib, as we saw, is knowledge of the hidden or unseen. *Ilmu* refers to any special knowledge, including knowledge derived from books. I am a person of ilmu because I teach anthropology. I do not, however, possess ilmu gaib. This has to be learned from a specialist, or dukun, who may or may not be a family member. *Gaib* is that which cannot be seen. In Western terms ilmu gaib is best translated as magical knowledge. There are many forms of this knowledge, and each dukun has his or her own special ilmu learned from a teacher.

The lore of ilmu gaib includes the curse of the ancestors. I heard about this curse when a man in Eggi's village died suddenly and people whispered that he had been struck by it. No one wanted to talk openly about this part of their culture, just as no one ever talked openly about ilmu gaib and its lore of black and white magic. But it was whispered that this man had been struck dead by the ancestral curse because he faked a genealogical connection to an ancestor in order to claim land not rightfully his when he was formally invested with a maternal title. After his death, it appeared that his family was also headed for disaster because the man they appointed to take on his title claimed the same rights.[18]

The curse of the ancestors must be considered sacred because it operates independently of human agency. As in Greek tragedy, where gods destroy those who transgress divine law, ancestors intervene to enforce oaths made long ago when they claimed land for their maternal line and vowed to bestow it according to adat law. Retribution in the Minangkabau case can result in the wasting away of an entire family as a result of one person's wrongdoing.

The ancestral curse operates as a cornerstone of matrilineal descent because it punishes all those who violate matriliny, especially with regard to the use or disposition of ancestral land. As such, the curse must be seen as one of the pillars of alam Minangkabau. In making this suggestion I do not disagree with Pak Taufik and Pak Idrus, who stress the importance of accommodation in Minangkabau history and the role of adat and Islam in upholding the world they call *alam*. But my aim here is to connect the notion of adat to the activities of daily life in Belubus. I want to ask: What exactly is adat as practiced in village life? How does Islam interact with adat practices in maintaining the matrilineal system? How do the codes of ilmu gaib and those of the Indonesian government support or interfere with the project of maintaining the matrilineal principle at the heart of adat? How does the ancestral curse work in today's world? Such questions must be answered in order to gain access to adat matriarchaat in village life.

Why the Minangkabau Are Not Patriarchal

To close this discussion of the Minangkabau concept of the matriarchaat in nature and culture, I want to comment on the parallels and differences between the Minangkabau vision of the state of nature and the vision promulgated by the Enlightenment philosophers of patriarchy. Where the Enlightenment philosophers grounded paternal archetypes in the state of nature, making the paternal the seed of social order, the Minangkabau turn to maternal archetypes. A long-standing tradition in Western thought views matriarchy as the mirror image of patriarchy, but the Minangkabau understanding of the transition from nature to culture shows how different the two systems are.

First, a short history of the idea of patriarchy. Although *patriarchy* was first applied to the male leaders of the tribes of Israel, the meaning of the word in modern Western thought was established in response to the controversy that raged in seventeenth-century England about the legitimate source and use of power. Carole Pateman divides the seventeenth-century discussion into two camps: the patriarchalists and the social contract theorists. The patriarchalist approach was represented by the widely influential book of Sir Robert Filmer, *Patriarcha*. Filmer broke with the biblical tradition associating patriarchy with paternal power by arguing that paternal and political power were "not merely analogous but *identical*." Filmer argued for absolute monarchy on the patriarchalist grounds that "kings were fathers and fathers were kings." Filmer's contribution to patriarchal political theory was to make the procreative power of the father the origin of political right in society (Pateman 1988:3, 19–38).

The evolution of the concept of patriarchy as sketched by Pateman can be generally applied to matriarchy in Minangkabau thought. One can see two stages in the evolution of Minangkabau thinking. The first is neither matriarchal nor patriarchal but animistic. Where Filmer associates social power and paternal power, the primordial version of the Minangkabau matriarchaat associates social power with the fertility of nature. One sees this in the proverb "Growth in nature is our teacher" and in the notion that adat is imminent in nature. Thus in this first stage of the Minangkabau construction of their matriarchaat, animism becomes the model for social power. There is no secular political power according to this schema; people live by the dictates of the divine law of nature.

In the evolution of patriarchy, Filmer's theory was short lived because of the success of counterarguments proposed by John Locke and Thomas Hobbes. These philosophers argued that all men are "naturally" free and political right can be imposed only by contract, not by patriarchal fiat. Hobbes and Locke separated paternal from political power and claimed that "contract was the genesis of political right" (Pateman 1988:3). They did not, however, include women in their notion of contract and political right. Hobbes conceived of the family as a patriarchal unit "wherein the Father or Master is the Sovereign" because "the Father of the Family by the Law of Nature was absolute Lord of his Wife and Children." In a similar vein, Locke concluded that there is "a Foundation in Nature" for the legal subjection of women to their husbands in matters having to do with "their Common Interest and Property" because "the Rule naturally falls to the Man's share, as the abler and the stronger."[19]

The second, social contract stage of the Minangkabau matriarchaat introduces protective devices such as matrilineal descent. These devices are needed because, like the Enlightenment philosophers, the Minangkabau also assume that the state of nature contains both potential chaos and the seeds of order. But where Enlightenment thought locates the seeds of order in the natural dominion of the father, the Minangkabau find analogies to the rooting, germination, and maturation of seeds. Since nurture (not dominion) is the primary social lesson that the Minangkabau take from nature, their construction of the social contract is geared toward institutions protecting the weak. Thus women, who have no rights in the Hobbesian scheme, possess rights to land and the control of its products in the case of the Minangkabau. While Hobbes and Locke saw women as needing the rule of husbands and fathers, Minangkabau husbands and fathers have no special rights derived from these roles; they fend for themselves. Only as brothers do men have rights, by virtue of their roles as protectors and overseers (along with their sisters) of rights to ancestral land.

There is another way in which the Enlightenment and Minangkabau schemas differ. According to Enlightenment thought, women are mired in chaotic nature, whereas the Minangkabau are more likely to portray young males in this manner. The Minangkabau version of primordial gender meanings associating women with order and men with chaos is reflected in the two stories I tell in the next chapter. These hugely popular stories are widely viewed as accounts of the origin of adat Minangkabau. The events of these stories take place at the center of the Minangkabau universe, the place where the people say they originated. I was introduced to them a few weeks after interviewing Pak Idrus in Padang when I was taken by my guides and teachers to the slopes of Mt. Merapi for a lesson in Minangkabau history.

CHAPTER TWO

The Divine Queens

> The main reason for writing this history of Minangkabau *(tambo Mi-nangkabau)* is that for thousands of years the pattern of Minangkabau culture *(adat)* has influenced the Minangkabau people. The matriarchal Minang-kabau are unique in Indonesia. The system of inheritance by relatives in the mother's line is followed to this day by all levels of Minangkabau society, even by the royal family in Pagarruyung and by fanatic followers of Islam.
>
> St. Mahmoed and Manan Rajo Pangulu,
> *Himpunan Tambo Minangkabau dan Bukti Sejarah*

After my interview with Pak Idrus in Padang, several of us—Ibu Ita, Suwati from the National Museum in Jakarta, Dt. Lubuk Sati (who acted as our guide), and various museum staff members— left on a tour designed to introduce me to the traditional heartland of Minangkabau culture, where the Minangkabau say their ancestors first settled and devised adat law. From Padang we traveled north along the narrow coastal highway for half an hour before stopping to pay our respects to Pak Boes and his wife. This was the first of many courtesy visits I would make to their house on my way to or from Belubus. Beyond their house, which sits just off the coastal highway, the road climbs into the mountains. The change in altitude is signaled by the deepening of the green of the rice fields and the cooler, drier air.

The rice fields diminish and narrow as we move into the foothills and then the mountains. A towering waterfall suddenly comes into view around a bend in the narrow winding road. We stop to take shelter from the tropical sun and cool ourselves in the mist at the bottom of the falls.

Climbing further, we see some little Sumatran monkeys looking for food along the road. It is an area of stunning natural beauty, with wide vistas from the cliffs that plunge down from the side of the road.

Soon we enter the first city of the *darat* (heartland), Padang Pajang. The darat is always distinguished from the *rantau*, the migration area, which refers to just about anywhere outside the heartland. The darat includes the three traditional *luak* (districts) clustered around Mt. Merapi, the cloud-hidden volcano from which the Minangkabau ancestors are said to have descended long ago. The three districts are Tanah Datar, Agam, and Lima Puluh Koto, where Belubus is located.[1]

In the heartland villages and cities one quickly appreciates the centrality of women in daily life. The traditional matrilineal longhouse, the rumah gadang with its horn-shaped roof, is common here. From our car we see women everywhere in the landscape. Female figures, bending over to plant or weed, dot the rice fields with splashes of color. Marketplaces are filled with women buying and selling, and now, during the high season for weddings, we see women parading along the roadside, dressed in the ceremonial costumes typical of the region and carrying on their heads gifts of food ornately arranged on trays or piled in baskets. From my traveling companions, I learned that women are key actors in the exchange of husbands between clans. I made special note of this custom because of the long-standing anthropological generalization that wives, not husbands, are exchanged at marriage.

Most remarkable to me on this trip is the discovery that the two public statues in Payakumbuh—the major city in the region where Belubus is located—are both of women. The statues represent female figures dressed in the distinctive ceremonial costume of this area, including buffalo-horn headdress. Both are representations of women in their ceremonial roles as Bundo Kanduang. One statue, a war memorial, depicts a woman lecturing humanity on the sorrows that war brings to a mother. The second statue, resting in a sculpted base made to look like a lotus flower, marks the site of a hydroelectric power dam. Its imposing female figure—originally white but now painted black to hide the soiling diesel fumes of passing trucks—holds in her hands the *cerano* (ceremonial bowl) that marks all adat occasions. Rising from the bowl is a lightning bolt, the symbol of natural power—another example of the merging of culture and nature in adat symbology.

Dressed similarly and carrying the cerano, women celebrate birth, marriage, and other life events. They then personify the legendary queen mother of Minangkabau history, Bundo Kanduang. I heard more

Statue of Bundo Kanduang on road outside of Payakumbuh marking a hydroelectric dam. This photograph was taken in 1981 before the statue was painted black to hide discoloring from the exhaust of passing vehicles.

about Bundo Kanduang in Pagarruyung, located in Tanah Datar near the city of Batu Sangkar, when we visited the reconstruction of her supposed palace, one of the primary tourist spots in West Sumatra. The palace is located in an area rich in history. This is where the first queen of the Minangkabau, Indo Jelito, is buried. With her sons she is said to have established the first kingdom ruled by adat law. Her sons are the most famous male figures of Minangkabau lore, Dt. Prapatieh Nan Sabatang and Dt. Katumanggungan. Along with Bundo Kanduang these figures constitute the core of the Minangkabau conception of their history.

In this chapter I tell the stories of Indo Jelito and Bundo Kanduang. Both stories associate the queen mother with the moral authority of adat and comment on the potentially subversive power of male aggression. In both the mother's role is to educate her sons in the way of adat so as to bring them under its civilizing influence. The stories constitute an ontology of the maternal and are replete with maternal symbols. Male aggression plays a subordinate role to the moral authority of the divine queen.

Reconstructed palace of Bundo Kanduang in Pagarruyung, 1995. Once a center of Minangkabau royalty, the palace is now a tourist attraction.

Tales of Two Queens

Call them unwritten law, tradition, or what you will, the tales about the two queens resonate with elements of the Minangkabau world view. The story of Indo Jelito is told in the prose form called *tambo Minangkabau*, which represents the Minangkabau imagination (and ideology) of their history. According to the tambo, Indo Jelito originated on the slopes of Mt. Merapi, where she lived in the first village with her sons and established the first kingdom under the rule of adat. Her sons are famous throughout West Sumatra as the codifiers of adat limbago, or customary law. As for Bundo Kanduang, she was the semimythical queen of the famous kingdom of Pagarruyung, a kingdom whose influence extended throughout central Sumatra in the seventeenth and eighteenth centuries. Her story is told in a *kaba* (a sung narrative drama) called *Kaba Cindur Mata*, which many people think of as like a tambo.

The events in Indo Jelito's story are set in the time of Alexander the Great, who allegedly sent one of his sons to the land of the Minangkabau, where he married Indo Jelito. But in all likelihood the events occurred about three-hundred years ago, closer to the time of the events narrated in *Kaba Cindur Mata*. Local genealogies I have consulted in the area of

Pagarruyung, and in a village where a modern descendant of Bundo Kanduang claims to rule, make Bundo Kanduang a direct descendant of Indo Jelito, several generations removed.

There are many parallels in the themes of the two tales. In both the queens shape younger males, who play the role of sons, to the dictates of adat. The youthful male energy of the sons is associated with raw physical energy, which is treated as disorderly and immature until shaped by the teachings of the authoritative mother and channeled by the activities of the mature male who follows and administers the dictates of adat. Adat is a system of rules, and its emphasis is on resolving conflict through consensus. Adat is represented as the ultimate authority, the force that modulates human passions and emotion.

In both tales, the ancestral curse plays a prominent role. In the tambo (Indo Jelito's story) the oath is the means by which clans and male titles are instituted, an act that establishes Minangkabau adat and the Minangkabau world. In the kaba (about Bundo Kanduang) the oath is administered to a gang of thieves to bring them under the sovereign law of Bundo Kanduang. In both cases the oath is sealed by drinking the water touched by the ancestral kris belonging to the queen mothers.

The words of the oath spell out the consequences for those who break the law of adat.

> On the top no leaves will sprout,
> On the bottom no roots will grow,
> At the middle the trunk will be bored by bees.

Like a dying tree, the man who breaks his oath to uphold adat will waste away and die, along with all his family.

The Tambo, the Origin of Adat, and the Matrilineal Principle

There are many versions of the Minangkabau folk history called tambo. I acquired the version presented below from one of its authors, Sutan (St.) Mahmoed, during our tour of Minangkabau historical sites in the area of Pagarruyung. I met him in one of the villages located in the area of first settlement. I chose this version because unlike the many versions of the tambo crafted to incorporate Islamic ideology, this one does not read Islam into early Minangkabau history. It is also more in keeping with the much more humble version I encountered in Belubus.

Like all tambo accounts, this one begins with the settlement on Mt. Merapi by a king, the son of Alexander the Great, who comes from Rum (Turkey) by way of India.[2] This king, whose name is Sultan Sri Maharajo Dirajo, married three women, one of whom is Indo Jelito. He established the first kingdom, Koto Batu (City of Stone), and ruled by the force of his personality in the absence of a general rule of law (Mahmoed and Manan 1987 [1978]).

When the king died there was no one to succeed him because he was a foreigner and had no maternal relatives on Minangkabau soil. Why succession must be in the maternal line is not explained in this tambo account. It is just assumed. In the introduction the authors claim that from time immemorial all Minangkabau people accepted that inheritance was to follow the mother's line. The matrilineal principle was recognized not only by the Minangkabau but by the rest of the world, they say. This idea is reminiscent of Nasroen's suggestion, mentioned in the last chapter, that matriliny is a primordial sentiment for the Minangkabau, not created or invented.

In the body of the tambo account, however, the authors switch track to say that Indo Jelito and her sons instituted matrilineal succession as law. This discrepancy can be explained by distinguishing between primordial tradition and adat rule, as Nasroen does when he says that matrilineal succession and adat became intertwined because of their mutual fit with nature (1957:34). In my view, the tambo account is a public device for elevating primordial tradition to customary law; by codifying in formal terms what already existed in practice, it defends against the intrusion by external patrilineal influences. This is a common theme in Minangkabau lore.[3]

Continuing with the story, Indo Jelito had a son by Sultan Sri Maharajo Dirajo. After the sultan died, Indo Jelito married one of the intellectuals who had come with the sultan from Turkey to Mt. Merapi, a man by the name of Ceti Bilang Pandai, with whom she also had a son. These half-brothers received the matrilineal titles of penghulu from their mother at a ceremonial ground marked by standing stones. The son of the sultan was given the title Dt. Katumanggungan. The commoner son was given the title Dt. Prapatieh nan Sabatang. The two sons drank the water touched by their mother's ancestral dagger as they took the sacred oath promising to tell the truth, be helpful, and punish fairly. After repeating the words of the fatal curse, they were told that if they broke the oath they and their family would die, like a leafless tree with bark bored by bees and roots rotting from lack of water and soil. The tambo proclaims that this oath will be valid for all penghulu from the time it was first administered to the present.

When they took the oath the two penghulu were provided with sacred objects to wear as symbols of office. Each received these objects from their mother. The authors claim that these objects, the first passed down through the maternal line, instituted the matrilineal system. However, as before, they suggest also that the half-brothers received the objects from their mother because this was the way of Minangkabau, which means because of primordial, rather than instituted, tradition.

After the sons were appointed penghulu, the two sons and their mother established another kingdom to replace the first kingdom of Koto Batu, which collapsed after the death of the king. The new kingdom was called Dusun Tuo (Old Settlement) and was led by Dt. Prapatieh Nan Sabatang and Dt. Katumanggungan. Pariangan, known throughout West Sumatra today as the first village of Minangkabau, was included in this kingdom.

After that the half-brothers traveled around conferring penghulu titles in the same manner they had received theirs. They administered the oath of office at ceremonial sites marked by standing stones and sealed the oath with the water of Indo Jelito's kris. These acts unified many villages and established alam Minangkabau under the tutelage of Dusun Tuo.

The next step was to institute a rule of law to govern the people. All the leaders met to discuss this matter. Following the Minangkabau rule of decision making by consensus *(mufakat)*, they developed the twenty-two rules of adat law *(hukum adat)*. These twenty-two rules included four types of adat, four types of *nagari* (confederations of villages), four types of words, four types of guides for decision making, four types of traditions, and two types of measures. Once these rules were accepted as the basic law of Minangkabau adat, the first four clans of the Minangkabau were established in Dusun Tuo.

Matrilineal descent is included in the first and most sacred of the four types of adat.[4] This is the category of "adat that is truly adat," mentioned in the last chapter. This category is said to be the one type of adat that will never change. Today, Islam is also placed in this category; both are considered equally sacred and neither can dislodge the other. According to Abdullah (1966:10) this category of adat is "eternal," identical with "natural law."

The Minangkabau love of flexibility and accommodation—expressed in the proverb "In different grass are different grasshoppers, in different ponds different fish, in different villages different adat" (Hakimy 1994b:110)—is reflected in the third and fourth kinds of adat, which consist of ceremonial customs and practices that develop at the local level through discussion and agreement.

The Historical Context of the Tambo and *Kaba Cindur Mata*

The events of the tambo suggest that Sri Majarajo Dirajo appears at a point in Minangkabau history when the population was expanding rapidly and local identity was threatened by a superior immigrant king. Perhaps he brought with him large numbers of retainers. Or the fame of Sumatran gold mined in the area of Mt. Merapi may have attracted immigrants and traders. Such events would have increased the local population density, expanded trade throughout the area, and increased need for agreement on common rules of behavior and standards of measurement. The time and circumstances of these events are uncertain. The immigrant king may have come from India or Turkey, as the tambo and other sources suggest, or he may have been a Hindu-Javanese ruler from the Javanese kingdom of Majapahit in the fourteenth century, although local lore and the tambo itself place the date back in the time of Alexander the Great.[5]

The historical context of *Kaba Cindur Mata* is more accessible. Numerous manuscript versions of this kaba are found in libraries around the world, many of them being written versions of the oral account in Arabic script. I rely on versions first published by A. Dt. Madjoindo in 1951 in Roman script and by Dt. Sanggono Dirajo in 1923 in Arabic.[6] According to Dt. Madjoindo there is hardly a person in West Sumatra who doesn't know the story or at least hasn't heard it. Whenever the story is performed, it attracts many people, he says. The story cannot be separated from daily life because it "lies at the heart of adat and religion, which formed the basis of government in the old Minangkabau state and a great portion of which continues to be valid and followed by people up to the present day" (Madjoindo 1982:9).[7]

In his introduction, Dt. Sanggono Dirajo says the story has been told for three hundred years. In all likelihood he is correct in this assertion. Court life depicted in the story is similar to that witnessed in 1683 by Tomas Dias, an envoy sent by the Dutch governor of Malacca to open trade relations with the Minangkabau heartland.[8] Queenship was common in seventeenth- and eighteenth-century Sumatra and Malaysia. For example, on the occasion of the death of the second queen of Acheh (North Sumatra) in 1678, Tomas Bowrey, an Indian Ocean trader, wrote, "Achin is now and hath a Considerable time been Governed by a Queen, ever Since the time that the discreet and Pious Kinge James of happy memorie Swayed the Sceptre of great Brittaine, France and Ireland" (Reid 1995:96). The historian Leonard Andaya describes letters written from the "Queens of Pagar Ruyong" to the Dutch in Malacca in his history of the kingdom of Johor (Malaysian Peninsula) between 1641 and 1728 (Andaya 1975).[9] Written early in the eighteenth century, these letters bear the mark of "Putri Jamilan," the hereditary title assumed by the queen mothers of the rulers of Pagar Ruyung and Suruasso.[10]

Another source for dating the story comes from its inclusion of Koranic themes, leading Abdullah to suggest the seventeenth or eighteenth century. Koranic symbolism in the story is consistent with evidence that Islam probably entered Minangkabau sometime in the sixteenth or seventeenth centuries (Westenenk 1918:11–13). Based on the religious allusions in the story, Abdullah hypothesizes that *Kaba Cindur Mata* belongs to the second stage of Islamization, which he says dates from the spread of religious centers in the interior of Minangkabau in the late seventeenth or early eighteenth century. This evidence is in keeping with Dias's report of Islamic officials in the area when he visited in 1683. Thus, it is probably correct to assume that the story has been told for some three hundred years.[11]

Kaba Cindur Mata and the Divine Queen at the Center

The popularity of *Kaba Cindur Mata* is widespread in West Sumatra, so much so that some call it the Minangkabau "state myth." I saw the story enacted on-stage in Padang in 1982 during a grand cultural celebration of Minangkabau ethnic identity. I also saw it enacted on a smaller scale in a village near Pagarruyung, the seat of Minangkabau royalty, the same year.

In this tale, Bundo Kanduang is depicted as the source of wisdom, the center of the universe. She is the exemplary queen mother, equal in fame to the greatest kings of the world, and resembles the divine king in Southeast Asian classical texts, who stands, as Clifford Geertz writes, "at the juncture of the divine and the human with, so to speak, a foot in each camp" (Geertz 1968:37). As such she is an Asian model for the matriarch—not as an autocratic ruler who wields power for the sake of power, but as a ruler who symbolizes the center of the Minangkabau universe and embodies the sovereign law of Pagarruyung, a law that is based on propriety and good relations *(budi)* according to adat.

Conceived as coming from "the essence of God," Bundo Kanduang and her son Dang Tuanku are, says Taufik Abdullah, "emanations rather than the creations of god" (1970:21). The sacred status of the queen is reflected in the opening lines of the kaba:

> Once upon a time, throughout the state of Pagarruyung within Alam Minangkabau, there ruled a queen whose title was Bundo Kanduang. Now this queen was

one of the original royal line, she stood on her own, equal in fame to the Kings of Rum, China, the King of the Seas, and the four-branched lineage. She wore the crown "Kulah-Kamar," she was entrusted with the magical-sacred cloth, which when spread out was as wide as the world and folded to the thickness of a fingernail. She was entrusted with the magical kris called "Medang Girai." In addition, this queen was entrusted with a magical shield, drums, and other sacred objects.

As the story is enacted, actors dramatize actions that display fundamental conceptions about right relations and the consequences of transgression. The spectacle provides a glimpse of the meaning of sovereignty in Minangkabau thought. Sovereignty is embodied not in the person of the priest-king who rules society in alliance with a warrior class at his service, as we find in Indo-European history, but in the person of the queen mother who symbolizes adat and the unity of society. This is not to say that there is no king in the story; indeed, the story opens with Bundo Kanduang teaching her son what he must know to be a proper king.

There are four protagonists in the story whose actions define the plot and who together form a quadripartite symbol incarnating Minangkabau sovereignty. Bundo Kanduang is depicted as the "eternal" queen of time immemorial who lives in Kampong Dalam, the innermost village. Her son, Dang Tuanku, participates with his mother in divine essence. He is in line to become king, a status his mother prepares him for. Together, mother and son dedicate themselves to maintaining an orderly world through the rule of law *(adat)* and associated institutions.

As the story progresses, Cindur Mata and Putri Bungsu take their places at center stage along with the queen mother and her divine son, demonstrating that the institution of sovereignty also depends on physical and reproductive energy. Cindur Mata's raw energy and magical skill, acquired from Bundo Kanduang, defeat hostile forces to save the kingdom. He is ambiguously described as the son of Bundo Kanduang's servant. Yet, he and Dang Tuanku are described as "two persons with one soul," and some versions of the story suggest that the two young men are half-brothers (Abdullah 1970:18).

Putri Bungsu is Bundo Kanduang's niece, daughter of her brother who rules in a nearby land. At the opening of the story Putri Bungsu is betrothed to Dang Tuanku and is referred to as the successor to Bundo Kanduang. As such, she is as intimately tied to Bundo Kanduang as Cindur Mata is tied to Dang Tuanku. In different ways the four individuals embody the human and divine elements that vitalize and regenerate alam Minangkabau at its center.

Cindur Mata is the most finely delineated character in the plot. Throughout the story he is described in the same terms as any energetic young man might be in the villages today. Instructing her attendant to bring Cindur Mata to her, Bundo Kanduang describes him as young and playful: "If you want to find Cindur Mata, go to where the music is being played and there are dancers dancing, in short where there is merriment. And if he's not there, look where there are people playing games, flying kites, or riding horses, among the children of the wealthy and highborn at play."

Cindur Mata is brought to the queen from the rice field where he is flying his kite. His raw animal energy in the service of culture is suggested by the observation that as he enters the palace all the animals play their various instruments to celebrate his arrival, "the monkey on his lute, the civet cat on his viola."

The plot of the story revolves around Bundo Kanduang's response to the news that her brother has broken the marriage contract in which they agreed that Putri Bungsu would marry Dang Tuanku. Bundo Kanduang is particularly incensed by the news that her niece has been betrothed to a neighboring king. Breaking a marriage contract is a very serious transgression against adat. At first Bundo Kanduang is furious and wants to go to war against her brother to punish his transgression. Thinking the matter over, she chooses instead to overlook his transgression and follow the rules of adat with respect to her niece's upcoming wedding to the foreign king. Following the rules of adat means sending Cindur Mata to her brother's land with wedding gifts. By following this course Bundo Kanduang's actions are consistent with all that adat represents—politesse, goodwill, proper form, and striving for *tali budi* (good relations) even in the face of her brother's transgression.

In following this course, Bundo Kanduang represents the single nature of adat. Her brother and other males in the story are represented much differently. They tend to exhibit a more dualistic nature defined both by the order of adat and the chaos that results from transgressing its dictates. Thus, they both follow adat and break its rules.

Dang Tuanku acts as the younger male double of Bundo Kanduang, and Cindur Mata embodies the active male element who uses force in the service of the queen. His power comes from the magical weapons and animals he receives from the queen when she sends him off to attend the wedding of Putri Bungsu in her brother's land. Bundo Kanduang gives Cindur Mata her magical horse for the journey and, for his protection, her magical buffalo, an animal of enormous strength. As it turns out he uses the queen's buffalo and weapons not just to protect himself but to subdue a gang of thieves on the borders of Pagarruyung, where chaos and disorder rule.

The account of Cindur Mata's meeting with the thieves provides a strikingly harsh picture of the barbarity of male dominance. The description of the world of the thieves illustrates in no uncertain terms what life would be like without adat. It would be a male-centered world, entirely absent of women, ruled by death and destruction. The men who inhabit this world are as ugly and unappetizing as anything that can be imagined. Unruly and uncontrolled, they do not steal out of need but merely to extract men's souls from their bodies. They know no restraint and will kill anyone regardless of his station in life, religious or otherwise. They can withstand any hardship and torture including the most fearsome of weapons. Their skin is so thick that even iron cannot pierce it. One of the thieves is described as eating iron pots, scratching his back with a chisel and his head with a saw. The speech of another is hardly human. He utters a weird sound, like corn cooking in a skillet. The list continues as each thief is likened to the worst aspects of nature—rough, gargantuan, lazy, and fierce, with absolutely no human attributes.

As he enters their territory, Cindur Mata is seized by a "great premonition" of imminent danger. Transfixed by fear, knowing that he may be their next victim, he turns toward Pagarruyung. Clasping his hands he cries out, "By your leave, Bundo Kanduang, by your leave, Dang Tuanku, who are made governors by God, who are wise in the ways of life, such is the fate that has befallen me, such is the fix I am in, I feel I can't find the means to go on. Pray to God for me, that I may be secure and protected, freed from this great danger."

Mustering all the magic he knows and gearing the magical horse and buffalo for a fight—for magic and raw power are his only weapons in this killing field—Cindur Mata proceeds onward. Soon he is confronted by the chief of the thieves, who demands that he give over the horse and buffalo. Incensed, Cindur Mata replies, "Why should I leave my horse, leave my buffalo, what's the idea? If you want to buy, I'm not yet ready to sell, if you wish to beg, I do not yet wish to give, it's not yet alms-giving season!"

Furious, the thief yells to his gang, "This is a conceited little brat, who thinks he's so smart! Surround him!"

Cindur Mata takes out the sword given him by Dang Tuanku and begins swinging as the thieves rush him. They fall on him but he is invincible—like the orange tree that is hard to climb, whose trunk cannot be mounted, smooth as butter. The thieves only succeed in killing one another as Cindur Mata jumps like a jack rabbit out of their way, here and there, right and left.

After doing battle in this way Cindur Mata commands Bundo Kanduang's magical buffalo to charge the motley crew. "Hey Binuang," he calls to the buffalo, "why are you such a layabout when we're in such a fix. Show your bullishness so we may be freed from this danger!" Whereupon, Binuang tosses his horns, swings his tail from side to side, and leaps forward like a whirlwind, casting up the red earth, breaking thick branches from the trees, so that the whole forest shudders.

The great buffalo becomes crazed with battle, as if possessed by the devil—biting, terrorizing, or killing the thieves. In the face of this superior strength, their leader finally recognizes who they are up against. They have not just met their match, they have met their king.

"Perhaps this is the raja of Pagarruyung," the chief of the gang says to his men, "who cannot be opposed, whom it is not permitted to contradict." "Let us bow to our leader and beg his pardon."

With this gesture the gang of thieves give their allegiance to Pagarruyung. Turning to Cindur Mata, their leader says, "Forgive us, our lord, in life and death, for better or for worse, we surrender our bodies and souls! Whatever you command we will do, forgive us and grant us your pardon, we beseech you."

At which point Cindur Mata makes them swear the sovereign oath of Pagarruyung and submit to the law of Bundo Kanduang. His words spell out the consequences for those who operate outside this law. He begins by painting a state of nature in which men are ruled by their lust:

> The *adat lembaga* of the world is such that an elephant moves because of his tusks, a tiger jumps because of his stripes, and humans are motivated by their lusts. Now, Datuk, it will be for you just like this: from this day forward you will never steal again, you will never do injustice again, so that travelers may be at ease. Make a promise with God and say that you will never do this sort of thing again! If you act like this again may you be destroyed by the oath you take *(dimakan bisa-kawi)*, fall to the sovereign oath of Pagarruyung, rootless below, with no sprout above, circled in the middle by bees. (Madjoindo 1982:53)

Hearing these words, the thieves vow never to rob again, sealing their promise by drinking the water touched by the magical kris of Bundo Kanduang and swearing by the name of God. Thus the oath, the same as described in the tambo, is sealed by drinking the water of the queen mother's kris, as it is also in the tambo. The moral of the story is obvious. Without the autochthonous queen to educate and guide them in the way of adat, men are not just unruly and ungovernable, they are murderous. Women symbolize adat; men symbolize natural man transformed by culture: by the "sovereign law of Pagarruyung" as embodied by the queen.

The Minangkabau Model of Queenship

Bundo Kanduang and Indo Jelito are iconic mothers in Minangkabau world view, purveyors of an ethos of peace and accommodation. As we shall see in future chapters, the icon incorporates contemporary expectations of senior women in villages, who in their ceremonial capacities are referred to as Bundo Kanduang. The meanings most evident in these stories are the equation of women with culture, the equation of undomesticated male energy with chaos, the theme of the ancestral mother who punishes male transgression, and the belief that senior women stand as emblems of protection, knowledge, justice, and order.[12]

In *Kaba Cindur Mata*, sovereign power is represented by the figure of the autochthonous queen who stands alone, rooted in place, equal in fame to the kings of the world, a queen who is of the "original royal line." Usurpation is not part of her plan; mediation and the peaceful synthesis of opposites is her way, in keeping with the adat principles she upholds. She is a female sovereign who deploys the raw power of animals to serve adat and who educates young males so that they can take their place alongside her as the embodiment of adat. Neither she nor her sons rule independently of adat. Adat is like the divine law of Greek tragedy such as seen in *Antigone*. In Sophocles' play the law of tradition opposes the human law of individual will and personal aggrandizement. Like the actions of Antigone, who appeals to the divine law of Zeus, the Minangkabau believe that following the dictates of adat results in peace, prosperity, and plenty.

This paradigm can be contrasted to the model of power conceived as hierarchic and wielded by force, such as seen in the functions Georges Dumezil assigns to the Indo-European priest-king and Marshall Sahlins delineates in his analysis of the divine kings of Polynesia. According to Sahlins, power in Polynesia is not an intrinsic social condition but "an usurpation, in the double sense of a forceful seizure of sovereignty and a sovereign denial of the prevailing moral order." Power flows from the outside and is based on force:

> The king is an outsider, often an immigrant warrior prince whose father is a god or a king of his native land. But, exiled by his own love of power or banished for a murder, the hero is unable to succeed there. Instead, he takes power in another place, and *through a woman:* princess of the native people whom he gains by a miraculous exploit involving feats of strength, ruse, rape, athletic prowess, and/or the murder of his predecessor. (Sahlins 1985:80–82)

The plot of *Kaba Cindur Mata* poses the same dualities Sahlins frames in connection with his account of divine kingship in Polynesia, for example, *gravitas* (order) versus *celeritas* (transgression), altruism versus self-interest, mutual agreement or persuasion versus power by force, culture versus nature, and democratic governance versus autocracy. The Minangkabau resolution of the tension posed by these dualities is different, however. The queen chooses synthesis rather than usurpation or struggle. Through her actions and moral example the opposing dualities are resolved, melded. This resolution symbolizes the ethos of accommodation and synthesis that rules Minangkabau adat.

Maternal Nurture as a Paradigm of Social Power

The characteristics associated with queenship outlined in this chapter—including maternity and motherliness—represent an ideal type of "matriarchal" model. This model does not replicate in female dress the cosmological father of the Old and New Testaments, nor is the paradigm of power reflected in the actions of Indo Jelito and Bundo Kanduang a mirror image of patriarchy. The power of the Minangkabau queens is not the power to subjugate but to *conjugate*—to knit together and regenerate social ties in the here and now and in the hereafter. Seen in these terms, female power cannot be defined in terms of female dominance and male subordination. Rather, one finds interdependence and autonomy in both male and female domains, and maternal nurture constitutes the wellspring of social power.[13]

Bundo Kanduang delegates power to the young male to protect himself from males who operate outside the adat social order. As the extension of the mother, Cindur Mata is part of the maternity/motherliness strategy that is deployed to wrest the thieves from the state of nature into the realm of the queen's culture, symbolized by adat. A similar deployment of force, illustrating a variant of this theme, figures prominently in another well-known story the Minangkabau tell about themselves.

This is the story about how the Minangkabau got their name. Minangkabau means "victorious buffalo," after *minang* (victorious) and *kabau* (buffalo). The story refers to a legendary fight between the Minangkabau and the invading Javanese for sovereignty in the area. The Minangkabau won the fight by a ruse. Instead of fighting the militarily superior Javanese, the Minangkabau requested that the struggle be decided by a buffalo fight. The Minangkabau tell the story of how they won the fight with great glee.

The Minangkabau were victorious over the Javanese not because they had a strong buffalo, but because they had a hungry baby buffalo with imitation horns strapped to the head. The Javanese had a big bull buffalo with horns a meter long. When the Minangkabau led the baby buffalo onto the field, it rushed at the other not to fight but to get milk. It didn't care whether the male buffalo was his mother or not, it wanted milk. The big buffalo took pity on the baby buffalo and licked it. Then the baby butted the big buffalo in the stomach, as baby buffaloes do before they suck at their mother's teats, and with its fake horns gored it to death.

The metaphors of this tale are all too obvious. Seeking to dominate the Minangkabau, the powerful, patrilineally oriented Javanese are tricked by the weaker, matrilineal Minangkabau. This story turns nurturance into superior strength in political conflict. It is another example of how the weak can become strong. The victorious baby buffalo defends local autonomy by figuratively "milking" the raw power of the Javanese bull buffalo, a ruse that exchanges the physical strength of the patrilineal Javanese for the moral power of the matrilineal Minangkabau. In this manner the hegemonic focus on maternal nurture is placed in dialectical opposition to paternal force (the male dominion of Hobbes and Locke).

According to local explanations of this story, the fight between the Javanese and the Minangkabau buffalo was in part a struggle over who would inherit land and ancestral titles when the area was colonized in the fourteenth century by the invading Javanese prince, known as Adityawarman. In a theme reminiscent of the tambo story told above, the struggle is about whether property and titles would be apportioned according to the matrilineal or patrilineal principle. To this day the same opposition is discernible in the way some Minangkabau villagers spoke to me with disdain about the "patrilineal" Javanese. No doubt, this "othering" of the Javanese has operated over the centuries as an ideological bulwark shoring up Minangkabau ethnic identity as matrilineal and matriarchal.

The tambo description of the codification of matrilineal descent as part of adat law can also be interpreted as a defense against invaders. Faced with an advanced legal system, which may have been brought by Adityawarman in the fourteenth century from the more advanced Javanese kingdom of Majapahit, the Minangkabau devised their own legal system consisting of the twenty-two rules of the tambo, replete with local male leaders to counterbalance the leadership imported from afar. This would have been a way to protect primordial principles and ensure local autonomy according to Minangkabau ways. The development of a code of rules at the center also had the effect of bringing outlying villages under the umbrella of adat. I elaborate these suggestions more fully in the next chapter from the vantage point of Belubus, which along with the other villages of alam Minangkabau is oriented to Pagarruyung and Bundo Kanduang.

DISCOVERING BELUBUS

CHAPTER THREE

Looking toward Mt. Merapi

Oh, Balubuih
The flower, the trunk, the source of our life
The place where we gather together
The shining jewel of the Four Cities
The child of Sungai Talang, our mother city.

Opening lines to Randai Saedar Jenela, composed in Belubus

The Minangkabau say that anyone who has tasted their food or experienced their hospitality will always return. Their charm definitely worked on me. I fell in love with the Minangkabau people. It was a heady experience living in this woman-friendly society. I returned not just to learn but to escape from that part of American culture which is not always kind to women. It is no accident that during the years I visited West Sumatra I wrote two books on violence against women at home.[1] I was emboldened to speak out because living in West Sumatra taught me how violence against some women affects all women. I felt the difference to the roots of my being. Life in a nearly rape-free society where women have autonomy and pride reminded me of Cicero's characterization of the Eleusian mysteries. According to Cicero, the initiate at Eleusis learns "how to live in joy, and how to die with better hopes" (Foley 1994:71). I have little idea of what Cicero meant, but I can say that living in West Sumatra gave me an enhanced sense of joy and hope.

On my return in 1982, Pak Boes introduced me to Belubus and Ibu Idar. Aware of my desire to understand Minangkabau culture through its history, Pak Boes felt that Belubus was the ideal place for me to visit. In 1981 he had declared Belubus a center for the restoration of historical remains because of the numerous standing stones in the area. Although in Belubus the stones are known as grave stones *(batu mejan)* or "raised stones" *(batu tagak)*, archeologists and museum staff thought of them as menhirs, part of the megalithic tradition found all through Indonesia and Southeast Asia. The people of Belubus say that the stones belong to the "Hindu-Buddhist" past, the time of *adat Jahiliah* (the so-called pagan, pre-Islamic past).

The stones were always located on clan land and seemed to mark an ancient burial and meeting spot. What little lore I heard about them reminded me of the stones mentioned in the tambo where men took the oath of office upon being granted penghulu titles. My initial impression about the Belubus stones is that they may have been erected when adat, codified by Indo Jelito and her sons, spread from the slopes of Mt. Merapi to the hinterland. Since this expansion probably took place before the spread of Islam, the stones can be taken as evidence of the pre-Islamic past.

Pak Boestami decided to build a small museum in Belubus on one of the megalithic sites. This activity brought researchers into the area from Jakarta to conduct a survey of the megalithic remains. Because Ibu Idar's house was the place everyone stayed, it was natural for Pak Boes to take me there. Thereafter it was assumed that as a guest of the museum I would stay with Ibu Idar. Over the years, as I spent more and more time in Belubus, Ibu Idar's house became the place I called home.

One enters Belubus through its sister village, Guguk Nunang. These two villages and two others, Sungai Talang and Kaludan, comprise the adat village structure known as a nagari (see fig. 2). The word *nagari* is of Sanskrit origin, and some writers suggest that the nagari structure was imported from India at the time of Alexander the Great. Others say that nagari was the name given to the village-states founded by the Hindu-Javanese colonists who reportedly migrated to the Minangkabau area and settled on the slopes of Mt. Merapi in the fourteenth century.[2] But no one is quite sure about this, especially with respect to dates. Nevertheless the nagari system is important to understand because it was probably the system either already in place or put into place when the historical events associated with the tambo occurred. The nagari system is also important because of the passionate commitment male adat leaders show today to restoring it after the Suharto government replaced it with the national *desa* system of regional control in the 1980s.

According to the nagari system, Belubus and its sister villages are attached to the "mother village" of Sungai Talang. The relatively new settlement of Bukik Apik is called a daughter village of the sister villages.

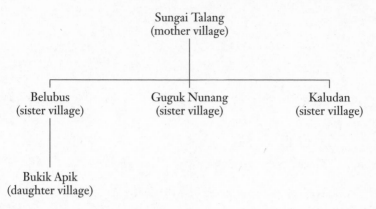

Fig. 2. Village structure of Nagari Sungai Talang, also known as the Four Koto (villages)

As the oldest settlement—and thereby the mother by adat reckoning—Sungai Talang is the center for adat affairs affecting the nagari as a whole.[3] It is also the place to which disputes are referred when they cannot be settled in the villages where they arise. This conflation of origin with centrality defined by maternal symbolism is common in alam Minangkabau. Like the common ancestress who originates the maternal line, or the senior woman who sits at the center of the adat house knitting the fishnet of social relationships, the oldest village is at the center of nagari affairs.

The people of Belubus still live by the nagari system for adat affairs, even though it was supplanted by Suharto's New Order government in what was known as the Village Law, enacted in 1979.[4] This law instituted the desa system, which played havoc with the local adat classification of villages. It was meant to impose a common standard for grouping Indonesia's villages under the oversight of the regional government. The desa system split Nagari Sungai Talang into two separate desa units, dividing the mother village, Sungai Talang, from three of its daughter offshoots. This means that now Belubus (pop. 1140), Guguk Nunang (pop. 848), and Bukik Apik (pop. 828) are administratively part of the division called Desa East Sungai Talang, while Sungai Talang and Kaludan are now part of Desa West Sungai Talang (see fig. 3).

Adat leaders in the villages of West Sumatra are not happy with the desa system because it partitions the organic realm over which the rules of adat limbago apply and creates a dualistic encoding of the social universe. For example, when the people of Belubus perform functions related to their citizenship in the nation-state of Indonesia, they have Desa East Sungai Talang in mind. When men settle disputes over the dis-

Fig. 3. Belubus in the desa structure. Asterisks indicate adminstrative centers in the desa system.

bursement of matrilineal land and titles or inaugurate a new penghulu, adat limbago takes over and Nagari Sungai Talang defines the social universe. Male adat functions are more affected by the desa system than those of females because women's ceremonies exist in a context of family and marital ties that are not compromised by the desa system. Male adat leaders decry the new system because it diminishes the motivation to hold nagari-wide adat meetings and leads people to look more readily to the local desa office to settle land disputes rather than turning to the adat council of penghulu.[5]

In 1999, the year after Suharto stepped down from power and Abdurrahman Wahid was elected the third president of Indonesia, the adat leaders in West Sumatra lobbied for the reinstatement of the nagari system. In December 2000 I received a letter from En, carefully typed on the typewriter I bought for him when he visited me in Philadelphia, reporting that the governor of the province of West Sumatra announced that the nagari system would be reinstated in 2001.[6]

Maternal Archetypes in Belubus Culture History

Assuming that the key to the Minangkabau matriarchaat would be unlocked through studying Belubus history, I concentrated at first on the standing stones. But this decision did not prove to be very fruitful because nobody wanted to talk about them. Despite their obvious presence in the village and all around Nagari Sungai Talang, whatever lore was once associated with the stones seems to have been wiped from memory. In time, however, I gained enough information to piece together a general, largely speculative, outline of the history of Nagari Sungai Talang.

From various sources—rice lore, local origin narratives, stories about particular stones, and the patterning of the stones on hilltops and flatlands—I concluded that in the region of Lima Puluh Koto, where Belubus is located, one can speak of two key periods before the Padri War and the accommodation of adat and Islam: the time of the ancestors and the period of the codification and adoption of the twenty-two adat rules.

The people of Belubus have two notions about the origin of Nagari Sungai Talang. Some talk about an origin in India long ago; others, on the slopes of Mt. Merapi. With respect to the Indian origin, many of the older people of Belubus know by heart the ancient prayer addressed to Sonan Sari Padi, the mother of the rice. The words of this prayer place the origin of rice below the hill known as Sarandib (an ancient toponym for Ceylon).

> Oh, my dear, respected Padi,
> You know the origin of rice
> For you are Adam's apple.
> You are the rice of Adam and Eve
> Planted in Hindi
> Below the Sarandi Hill.

This prayer can be compared with a proverb recited to me by a male adat leader from one of the oldest clans in Belubus. According to this proverb, not only did rice originate on Sarandi Hill, but so too did the Minangkabau people. The first line states: "Our ancestors descended from the peak of Sarandi Mountain, the one that is in the Himalayan Mountains."

The lore about an origin in India brings to mind the theory articulated by Georges Coedès regarding the Indianization of Southeast Asia. Coedès claims that the first wave of emigration from India started long before the rise of the Indic kingdoms of Indonesia. He suggests that groups were pushed out of India in the early part of the first millennium in front of the invading Aryans. According to Coedès, "the Dravidians or the Aryans, entering India from the northwest, pushed the aboriginal populations into eastern and southern India; these peoples spread to Southeast Asia, where they brought about a sort of pre-Aryan Indianization." The "characteristic traits of the pre-Aryan civilization" listed by Coedès resemble the social life found throughout the area of Lima Puluh Koto, including the villages of Nagari Sungai Talang. These include "cultivation of irrigated rice, domestication of cattle and buffalo, rudimentary use of metals, knowledge of navigation . . . the importance of the role conferred on women and of relationships in the maternal line . . . belief in animism, the worship of ancestors and the god of the soil, the building of shrines in high places (Coedès 1968:8–9).

Regarding the emphasis on the maternal line, I encountered interesting stories about the first ancestress in areas surrounding Belubus. In a village not far from Belubus, I heard a story about the ancestress who made her home in an egg. This woman was brought out from the egg into society by males who migrated into the area and designated her as the first clan ancestress. Today her grave is visited by pilgrims seeking magical power or assistance.

In another village I heard about a woman, the mother of wild pigs, who ruled over the jungle and forced humans to show reverence and respect for her jungle domain. In still another area, I heard about the first woman, who lived in a cave and bore the ancestors of the area. All these ancestral archetypes are represented as the impetus for the ordering of human social life according to set rules and taboos.

With respect to Coedès's comment about shrines in high places and ancestor worship, the megalithic sites in Sungai Talang are revealing. The distribution of sites and local lore suggest that the early settlers located their dwellings on ridgetops before moving to flatter land. For example, I heard the following story about the first settlement in Sungai Talang, located on a hill called Bukit Dataran Tinggi (High Flat Hill).

> On top of Bukit Dataran there is a cave called Gua Rimbabuakan where the people once lived. On the slope of the hill there is a "stone that shakes" (*batu mengigil*) when people are sick or the rice is diseased or someone dies unexpectedly. People take rice to the shaking stone to pray for rain. They direct their entreaties to Datuk Soyieh Panjang Janguit (Dt. Soyieh Longbeard). This Datuk is known throughout Nagari Sungai Talang as a holy man. He lives on the four hills that flank Sungai Talang: Bukit Parasi (the hill that rises over Belubus), Bukit Balo, Bukit Dataran, and Gunung Bungsu. Dt. Soyieh can be seen riding a white horse from hill to hill.

In Belubus Dt. Soyieh is said to ride in the hills with a young female spirit named Ranjani. He is reputed to have a white flowing beard and to wear white robes and, sometimes, a white turban. Dt. Soyieh's religious affiliation is pluralistic. His clothing is Islamic, yet the rites of propitiation at stones associated with him place him squarely in the tradition of ancestor worship.

On the steep slope of Bukit Parasi, the hill that towers over Belubus, is a huge stone outcrop that is considered sacred. People call it Batu Manda (Leaning Stone) because this is the place they "lean" their requests with the hope that the ancestors will grant them. Close by is a saddle-shaped stone where Datuk Soyieh comes to rest on his white horse when he visits the sick, should they seek his help through the local dukun.

Nearby are additional stones with large and small holes, called *batu lumpang* and *batu dakon*. An archeologist from Jakarta suggested that such stones were employed in ceremonies to propitiate ancestors.[7] From stories I heard from friends, Bukit Parasi still serves this purpose. Although fewer people make the pilgrimage to Batu Manda nowadays, many remember bringing offerings for the ancestors in recent times. Some say they make the trip at least once a year. The importance of ancestor worship is also reflected in the cultural meanings attached to the two mountains that dominate the Belubus skyline. All of the traditional longhouses *(rumah gadang)* face one of them, and all the stones face the other.

The Belubus Version of the Tambo

Whenever I cross into Nagari Sungai Talang on my way to Belubus and see the familiar shapes of Mt. Merapi and Mt. Sago, my awareness of coming home quickens. The mountains rise majestically into view as the road descends into an expanse of rice fields near the village of Guguk Nunang, at the border between the Four Koto and the adjacent nagari. When I see Mt. Merapi I am reminded that one comes home not just to one's village and nagari but to alam Minangkabau as well.

The male adat leaders of Belubus say that adat and alam Minangkabau originated in the village of Pariangan on the slopes of Mt. Merapi, the area of the tambo events cited in the last chapter. One gets a sense of the breadth of alam by the length of time it takes to get from Belubus to this village, about three hours by car. A local version of the tambo is recited by adat leaders in Belubus during ceremonies. The account is not nearly as complex and elaborate as the tambo summarized in the preceding chapter. Its importance is seen in the frequency of its recital. The opening lines are likely to crop up almost anytime in a ceremonial speech, either to provide a poetic filler when the speaker runs out of things to say or to alert listeners of the obviousness of his assertions.

> How do we light a torch?
> With the scrap of the thorny *talong* plant.
> Where did our ancestors originate?
> From the top of Mt. Merapi.

Each time I enter Nagari Sungai Talang, I look to see if the summit of Mt. Merapi is covered in clouds, as it often is. On a clear day my eyes

Matrilineal property with Mt. Merapi in background, 1985

sweep the broad, flat top of Mt. Merapi, broken on one side by two narrow, jutting peaks. From one of the peaks I can sometimes see smoke rising, reminding me that Mt. Merapi is a volcano. It is on Merapi, I was
told in Belubus, that the legendary immigrant king of the tambo landed
his boat when water covered all of this part of central Sumatra, save for
this peak, which was then the size of an egg.

In the Belubus rendition of the tale, this king is a *rajo usali* (original
king). Much is written about this king in the canonical tambo accounts,
but in Belubus little else is known other than that he and his followers
came down from Mt. Merapi and established the village of Pariangan,
the place which most Minangkabau cite as the first nagari village republic to be established in alam Minangkabau.[8] An account of how the first
settlers wandered around and established villages constitutes the core of
the tale as told in Belubus.

Evidence of the local significance of Merapi is reflected in the adat rule
that the longitudinal beams of the rumah gadang run parallel to the
mountain. In most cases the entrance to the houses also faces Mt. Merapi, but this is not required. What is essential is that the longitudinal
beams not be perpendicular to Merapi. To point the beams toward the
mountain would be "fighting" it, Ibu Idar explained. The timbers must

Line of matrilineal houses *(rumah gadang)* built with longitudinal axis parallel to Mt. Merapi, 1985

instead lie parallel to show respect. Those who build their houses so that the longitudinal axis points toward the mountain experience many problems in life. Fighting with the mountain creates conflict. Family relations, for example, will not be peaceful. Ibu Idar spoke disapprovingly of her sister's house: it was built against Merapi and parallel to the road, which explained why Ibu Wel had so many husbands and sometimes quarreled with her children.

There are other traces of the tradition codified by the tambo in adat practices in Belubus. Just as Indo Jelito was guardian of the first kris, the women of Belubus store the ancestral kris in their chest to be worn by the man who inherits the penghulu title of their lineage. Just as the first penghulu titles cited in the tambo were established at standing stones, local lore claims that the menhirs on the bottomlands of Nagari Sungai Talang mark spots where local titles were first established. A third example: people in Belubus recognize that those who break the oath associated with the establishment of these titles will be subject to "the curse of the ancestors." The meaning of the curse is clear in Belubus: if a title holder breaks the oath he took to uphold truth *(adat)* and exercise power fairly, he and his family members will waste away and die, like a tree that withers.[9]

The Mystery of Mt. Sago

Mt. Sago is also pregnant with cultural significance. All the planted stones in Sungai Talang, in Belubus, and indeed throughout Lima Puluh Koto point toward Mt. Sago. No one has any idea why. One clue, according to the archeologist who mapped menhir sites for Pak Boestami, is the mountain's name. *Sago* is the local version of the Sanskrit word for paradise *(sarugo)*. Mt. Sago thus represents the home of the ancestors, the place to which the spirit flies after death.[10]

This is not a far-fetched idea, since the archeological excavation of a few of the standing stones in Belubus revealed that one of them marked a grave. The skeleton was placed so that the face pointed toward Mt. Merapi while the menhir and the feet pointed toward Mt. Sago. This orientation indicates that the burial is pre-Islamic because the positioning of modern corpses points the face toward Mecca.

So why do the adat houses show respect to Mt. Merapi while the menhirs, which are always located on the same clan land as the adat houses, point toward Mt. Sago? Although Ibu Idar had a ready answer for the orientation to Mt. Merapi, she was stumped on the question of orientation to Mt. Sago. One can only speculate. If a good life is ensured by facing Mt. Merapi, the center of the first Minangkabau kingdom, perhaps a good afterlife is ensured by facing Mt. Sago, the home of the ancestors. If one's life must be lived in a focused universe, perhaps the same can be said for one's afterlife. This possibility is suggested by the present-day alignment of graves with Mecca. Perhaps in the pre-Islamic era Mt. Sago was the center for ancestor worship. This would place Mt. Sago in the time of the ancestors while Mt. Merapi, the home of the first queens, can be associated with the period of royalty.

Minangkabau Historical Periods

Looking at the whole picture—local lore, the patterning of megalithic sites in the Lima Puluh Koto area, and the stories told in the last chapter—I conclude that there are two discernible periods of history related to the origin of Minangkabau adat and the matrilineal principle. The first period is marked by ancestor worship and animism, from which the matrilineal principle was constituted. The second period may have been associated with the incursion of a foreign notable into the area of the alleged first village, Pariangan. This period is suggested by the events told in the tambo.

Line of menhirs facing Mt. Sago, 1985. Batu Manda is in the background.

The first period is defined by unwritten tradition, which the adat philosopher Nasroen associates with the earliest manifestation of the matriarchaat. The second period gives the principles of the first legitimacy through the codification of common standards. The synergy between the two cultural strata—one assuming matrilineal descent as a given, the other giving it the legitimacy of law—is consistent with Nasroen's argument that the matrilineal principle derives from the time of ancestor worship before Hinduism, Buddhism, or Islam influenced the codification of local custom. In Nasroen's view, the Minangkabau matriarchaat survived because of the "fit" between a primordial principle and the codification of adat. This view suggests that matrilineal descent was not invented on the slopes of Mt. Merapi; rather it was legitimized there.[11]

I conclude that the tambo, as conceived both in Belubus and on the slopes of Mt. Merapi, is a discursive rendering of historical progress and technological development. It is an account of a transition from the wholly animistic to the more legalistic. It marks a break from a relatively small-scale society to the unified world of alam Minangkabau, which extended its influence across central Sumatra through the institution of royalty.

There is general agreement that the institution of royalty on the slopes of Mt. Merapi united the nagari village republics under one adat and created the entity known as alam Minangkabau. As Abdullah says, however, "kingship never functioned as a governing institution in Minangkabau proper." The nagari were never ruled by representatives of the king; they remained under the guidance of the penghulu. At most, the royal centers served as the court of final appeal for the independent, democratic-leaning nagari republics. Abdullah concludes that the institution of royalty was more "a sacral equilibrium power than a ruling institution," a kind of "Great Tradition" as opposed to the "Little Tradition" represented by the nagari (Abdullah 1966:4–5).

Although Indianized, perhaps by several waves of immigrants mixing with a local population, the Minangkabau never became an Indic state. Life in the nagari villages is best seen as a *bricolage* of past and present, blending the time of the ancestors, royalty, and Islam with the sensibilities and tastes of the modern, while remaining firmly rooted in the basic principles of matrilineal descent—the core of adat or "the true adat." These principles were handed down by the ancestors, whose capacity to punish their descendants guards the ramparts of matrilineal adat to this day.

CHAPTER FOUR

Diversity in Daily Life

Ranjani heals through Inam. It works like this. When people are sick or someone in their family is sick, they go to see Inam on the nights when she sees patients. Inam lies on the floor and covers herself with a sarong. Ranjani enters her and speaks directly to the patient. It's Ranjani's voice you hear, not Inam's. The night that Ranjani came to the house, it was because she was asked to come to look at our child who was sick. She then goes back to Inam and tells the parents what they must do to make the child well. Sometimes when you go to Inam looking for Ranjani's help she is not there. At the end of fasting month she often goes on pilgrimage to Mecca. She is able to get there quickly because her spirit flies fast.

Ibu Idar, 1987

As I made the transition from studying stones to studying people I understood how adat, religion, and government are interwoven in daily life. The day begins between 4:30 and 5:30 A.M. with the call to prayer from the village mosque. The first sounds of people stirring in the houses are heard. After bathing and (sometimes) praying, people take their morning coffee or tea, either at home or at one of the numerous local food stalls. At these stalls men and women buy or sell local produce, which saves them a trip to the marketplace in Payakumbuh, about thirty minutes away by bus.

Around eight o'clock, the children come out in droves. They walk along the primary road that cuts through the village, dressed in the school uniform required by the national education system. The youngest go to the school near Ibu Idar's house. Preteens go to the middle school in the adjacent village of Guguk Nunang, and teenagers go to the high school

63

in a larger village some distance away. After the children are settled in school, men and women make their way along the road carrying implements for work in the rice fields and gardens that surround the village. A few individuals, usually women, wait for the local bus to take them to the market in Payakumbuh.[1]

Although the great majority of villagers are farmers, no family is fully self-sufficient. Everyone depends on cash for buying clothing, household items, and food to supplement the rice diet. For some, cash is hard to come by. People scramble for money in various ways. Some men and women work as farm laborers, a few men work in construction or as skilled laborers, and some women make clothing. Men and women alike engage in numerous small businesses ranging from buying local farm produce and selling it in distant markets (men only) to selling sweets and snacks made at home (women). On holidays, women and some men go to the riverbank to set up small food stalls catering to fishermen and Sunday visitors.

Those few who work as government employees—be they teachers, bureaucrats in the office of the *kepala desa* (local mayor), or employees in the nearby city—are assured a steady source of income. The office of the kepala desa is across the road from Ibu Idar's house. He is an elected official who serves as a link between the villagers and the state and national government. People go into his office to lodge civil complaints, pay taxes, or get the necessary signatures and official stamps for births, marriages, divorces, and other transactions of civil society.

No one can live in a village without some sort of orientation to the local adat structure. Just as villages are connected to other villages within the universe of the nagari, individuals are also connected to the adat structure. Families are tied to other families by the clan structure of the village. Every village has four major clans, each with its minor lineages. Membership in a local clan is necessary for village social relations. No one can get married without being sponsored by a penghulu, which means belonging to a village clan. Those who move from one village to another must be formally adopted by a local clan. This is what happened long ago when the ancestress of Eggi's matrilineage (*paruik*) was brought to Belubus by a distant male relative to inherit land in the absence of female descendants of his maternal line. Thus, each individual is tied by adat to land, family, lineage, clan, village, and nagari.

When life's intractable problems pose a special burden, people consult a dukun. Depending on his or her expertise, the dukun can heal sicknesses, counteract black magic, resolve love problems, help women through pregnancy, cure mental illness, retrieve stolen items—the list goes on. During my stays in Belubus, the most famous dukun was living in a village on the road to Payakumbuh. This woman, named Inam, worked with the help of Dt. Soyieh and his female counterpart, Ranjani. My experience was mostly with Ranjani and not Dt. Soyieh.

Of all the codes animating life in Belubus, women's ceremonies occupy center stage. Adat and royal traditions come into full view as lines of women parade proudly through the village on their way to or from a ceremony. Dressed in full adat regalia, they are a colorful sight—rice farmers transformed by the ceremonial activity into queens for a day. Male adat leaders tell me that in their ceremonies women "fulfill" the law of Bundo Kanduang. When men perform their ceremonial tasks—speaking in a highly formalized, rhetorical style on the ceremonial stage or applying the laws of adat limbago to a dispute settlement in the adat council house—they act as the modern descendants of the legendary adat lawgivers, Dt. Prapatieh nan Sabatang and Dt. Katumanggungan, sons of the first queen, Indo Jelito.

Touring Belubus

The diversity of life is reflected not just in the daily schedule but in the layout of the village as well. As one enters the village from its sister village, Guguk Nunang, the mosque appears immediately on the right. Like every village in West Sumatra, the mosque is the largest structure. It is set back from the road across from a rather large pond where men wash before entering to pray. Although Bukit Parasi looms over the mosque with its huge "leaning" stone for propitiating the ancestors, no one thinks of ancestor worship when they go to the mosque. With the exception of certain occasions such as sanctifying a marital union or praying for the soul of the departed before burial, the mosque is largely a preserve for men. Like many mosques in West Sumatra this one shows signs of the historical blending of adat and Islam. Looking at it from the road one catches sight of the buffalo horn–shaped roof of the structure covering the drum that calls the people to prayer.

The working harmony of adat and Islam is repeated in the placement of the government-built adat council house near the mosque, a location found in many Minangkabau villages. Like the office of the kepala desa, the adat council house is built in the style of the rumah gadang, the matrilineal longhouse. Unmindful of tradition beyond the sweep of the buffalo-horn roof, these buildings face the road, which means that their longitudinal axis fights with Merapi. There is a certain logic in this arrangement. Although the national government is sympathetic to local adat, the sympathy is only skin deep. Facing the commerce of the road rather than following the dictates of adat, these structures are in keeping with Indonesia's race during the Suharto years to become one of the fastest growing developing economies. Capitalism and national unity reduce adat to a thin veneer in keeping with the national ideology of unity in diversity.

Further down the road from the mosque on the same side is the small museum, built by Pak Boestami in the middle of the largest of the menhir complexes in Belubus. While all the stones in this complex point toward Mt. Sago, the museum faces the stones. Its longitudinal axis, however, parallels Mt. Merapi, and it was built according to the wood-and-post construction dictated by the adat of house building. At night snakes representing the spirits of the ancestors are said to circle the stones. I was told that if I wanted to meet with the ancestors or the local spirits, I should sleep in the museum. But I never did.

Beyond the museum is the primary school, where all children go for their early school years. A few houses down the road one comes to Ibu Idar's house. This house is built in the colonial Dutch style on clan land with money given by Ibu Idar's husband. It sits somewhat back from the road with a front yard for parking cars and drying newly threshed rice. The house shares a compound with the house belonging to Ibu Elli, Ibu Idar's only daughter. Also on clan land, this house was built with money supplied by Ibu Elli's physician husband.

Across the road from Ibu Idar's house, one can see a row of rumah gadang erected by the Caniago clan, the first clan to settle in the area. All of these houses face Merapi and are built in the appropriate manner. The same is true of the other rows of rumah gadang constructed on clan land by the original migrants to Belubus. Although these houses are now rarely built, they stand out in the village as a symbol of adat. There is a remarkable contrast between these houses, signifying Minangkabau matrilineal identity, and the majority of the houses of Belubus, which follow the old colonial style or a more modern one. Yet in all the houses the contours of daily life are the same.

Attached to many of the houses are the *warung*, or food stalls. There are some twenty warung in Belubus. Although men and women hang out in different warung to gossip and exchange the news of the day, the warung are not strictly segregated because most are run by women who erect them on clan land for entrepreneurial purposes. If the matrilineal household is the place where women hold forth, the warung are places where their husbands retreat to visit with comrades. They sit around playing cards or dominos, smoking, engaging in verbal duels, or just

Woman selling items in her food stall, 1996

chewing the fat for the sheer pleasure of it late into the night. When he was not in the fields or caring for the family buffalo and other livestock, Pak Edi spent most of his time in the warung run by his sister down the road from Ibu Idar's house. He usually came home after we had retired. He would come in, take a bath, and eat quietly in the kitchen away from all of us. He never ate, as Wik often did, in our presence.

Adat Matriarchaat and the Clan System

When one first meets a Minangkabau, conversation usually gets around to two basic identifying features—mother's birthplace and mother's *suku* (clan). Knowing a person's suku is essential because generally speaking it is forbidden to marry someone of the same suku (unless the individuals come from distant villages). Since common suku names are found all over West Sumatra, if one meets up with someone of the same suku, in another village or anywhere in Indonesia, theoretically one could expect to be welcomed as a distant relative.

Reminiscent of the institution of the system of *suku berempat* (four clans) in the first kingdom of Dusun Tuo, the villages of Nagari Sungai Talang follow the basic four-clan pattern, as do villages all over West

Sumatra.[2] This does not mean that there are only four clans in the village, however. It only means that there are four major suku in each village under which minor suku are grouped.

The four major suku in Belubus are Payobadar, Caniago, Bendang, and Kotyanir. Only these suku can install a *penghulu pucuk* (suku head). These are considered the original suku, whose members were the first to settle Belubus. Members of the minor suku are usually family groupings or paruik (descendants from "one womb"), which are either offshoots of the main suku or comprised of individuals who migrated to the village and over time were allowed to form a separate suku.

Kotyanir, the suku of Eggi's matrilineage, is also known as *Kampong Empat Ibu* (Village of the Four Mothers). I was never able to ascertain what this meant, beyond noting that it seemed to refer to a prior time when women were heads of villages and villages consisted of related maternal lines, at least in the case of Kotyanir and its three sister suku: Jambak, Salo, and Pitopang. The *Empat Ibu* may refer to the original ancestresses of Kotyanir.

Each suku (major and minor) is composed of the extended family units (or matrilines) called *paruik* (wombs). This group has its own penghulu, males whose titles descend to nephews. Every paruik has a genealogical tree *(ranji)* that begins with the original ancestress. Such a record of genealogical connections, traced through women, is essential for resolving disputes over land and male titles. Each female who is born into the paruik inherits property, house, and *harta pusaka* (ancestral objects). Those males who inherit the title of penghulu through the matrilineal line have the responsibility of protecting harta pusaka for the female members of the matrilineage. Theoretically, this man manages the family holdings with his sisters. Practically, his control is often more ceremonial than actual, especially if he lives outside the village.

The genealogies from the oldest suku of Belubus go back as many as thirteen generations, which means either that Belubus was settled in the early seventeenth or eighteenth century or that its present suku structure was initiated at that time. All of the charts show a common ancestress who originated somewhere else, usually from Sungai Talang, the mother village of Belubus. The ancestresses of Eggi's matrilineage are said to have migrated to Sungai Talang long ago. One of these women was brought to Belubus by a distant male relative to continue the line there.

It is not unusual for women to take up residence in a village and after undergoing the proper ceremonies and payments to become members of one of the matrilineal clans, acquiring the rights, duties, and responsibilities of clan membership. Eggi's ancestress (six generations removed)

Ibu Ida bringing bananas from Umi's matrilineal longhouse to her house-building ceremony, 1985

was brought to Belubus by a male relative to continue his mother's line because there were no other surviving female descendants of her line. Being a migrant to the village after other clans had been established, this woman and her descendants were distinguished from the original settlers called *orang asal*, which meant that they did not have access to as much land. They also had a lower status. For example, male members of Eggi's paruik could not take on the title of penghulu pucuk. Like all members of an established matrilineal line, however, they had a penghulu title that was passed from one generation to the next.[3]

Another indication that Eggi's extended family is not one of the founding clans is the placement of Umi's rumah gadang. Although built according to the style of the smaller rumah gadang in the village and facing Mt. Merapi, Umi's rumah gadang stands alone. It was built for her by her first husband, Ibu Idar's father and stood alone until 1985, when Umi's granddaughter, Ibu Ida (Ibu Wel's oldest daughter), built a modern house. Unlike her mother's house, Ibu Ida's house was built with its longitudinal axis facing Merapi, like Umi's house. The grave site Umi shares with her mother, Railah, and Ibu Idar is also located on this plot of land.

When I arrived in 1982 Umi was the oldest surviving member of this branch of Kotyanir clan. She was in her late seventies and was being cared for by Ibu Ida. As Umi's strength diminished, Ibu Idar presided as both leader and family matriarch. After Ibu Idar died, Ibu Wel took her place. As of 1999, Ibu Wel handled most affairs along with her daughters, Wik, Os, and Ida. Ibu Idar's daughter, Elli, exerted her influence, coming to the village once a month from her home in eastern Sumatra. Umi's son, Dt. Llano, still plays a role in clan affairs even though he lives in eastern Sumatra, but only in the more important ceremonies such as marriages. He was always consulted by his sister, who would travel to eastern Sumatra to bring him news of an impending engagement for his approval. Over the years he continued to come to the village with his wife and would usually stay at her family home in Guguk Nunang. This pattern of touching base is typical of the role of the penghulu with respect to his sisters and maternal kin.

Mixing Islam and Ilmu Gaib

At the edge of the village one encounters a complex of buildings charged with meaning for Belubus history. The buildings include a small mosque and a large prayerhouse. The mosque houses the sacred grave site of Ibu Idar's father, who is known throughout West Sumatra as the *syekh* (prophet) of Belubus or Nabi Ulah. There are a few other buildings, all looking a bit run down. Among them is the syekh's house, where Dt. Llano, Ibu Idar, and Ibu Wel spent their early years. They lived here with the syekh and his other wives and children.

The site is widely known in West Sumatra and receives visitors to this day, some of whom come to pray to the syekh with some special intention. Others come to pay their respects and study with the current syekh, one of his sons.

Syekh Muda, as he is best known, was born in 1878. After traveling to Mecca as a young man he became a famous Islamic preacher and healer. He established a prayerhouse *(surau)* in Belubus early in the twentieth century, which made Belubus an important religious center. His reputation spread as far as Malaysia, and his prayerhouse became a magnet for people seeking spiritual or physical well-being. The prayerhouse was a place where people fasted and prayed for forty days and forty nights to become members of the branch of the Islamic religious order he established in the village. Today, his prayerhouse still attracts pilgrims from afar.

Being famous, Syekh Muda was much in demand as a husband. He was a good catch, and many a mother sought his hand for her daughter. In all he had seventeen wives, but never more than four at a time according to Islamic marital law. These liaisons produced twenty-nine children.

Ibu Idar's mother, Umi, was reputed to have been his favorite wife. She bore him three children. The oldest, Ibu Idar, was the seventeenth of the twenty-nine. Dt. Llano's was Umi's middle child, followed by Ibu Wel.

Umi's aunt, Naimin, was also married to the syekh. Naimin was the granddaughter of the ancestress brought to Belubus. After Naimin's premature death, Umi's mother, Railah, ordered Umi to marry the syekh. Formerly it was common for a younger woman to be married to the widower of another woman in the family. Such a marriage was called "changing the sleeping mat," meaning that when a wife dies the husband simply moves his sleeping mat to another room in the house. Since Naimin had no female children, her property was transferred to her sister Railah and her female descendants. At the time of Umi's marriage, she was sixteen and Syekh Muda was thirty-eight. Marriage of a daughter to an older wealthy man was every mother's dream in those times.

Syekh Muda was a potent cultural innovator in Belubus. Although he died in the 1950s, some thirty years before my time in Belubus, many people with whom I spoke referred to him as their teacher in the affairs of adat, Islam, and ilmu gaib. Being of the generation that brought Islam to the village, Syekh Muda provided a model in his teaching and healing for the synthesis of these seemingly contradictory codes. His life and thought give testimony to the interweaving of adat, ilmu gaib, and Islam in village life.

In addition to his Islamic credentials Syekh Muda was a well-known dukun and specialist in adat lore. He sought to identify himself with Datuk Soyieh by riding a white horse and wearing white robes. According to Ibu Idar he adopted white because it is a sacred color. Syekh Muda was widely acclaimed for his expertise in the ilmu of Islam. He gleaned his knowledge from Islamic officials, adat leaders, and dukun and recorded it in a little book, of which there are several copies in the village. Written in Arabic script, this book includes old Minangkabau sayings on adat, Koranic references on the arts of healing, and mantras in the ancient Minangkabau language. Most of the men and women with whom I talked about these subjects studied with Syekh Muda. Ibu Idar was one of them. She spent many hours teaching me the healing mantras he recorded in his book and explaining the ins and outs of the magical knowledge needed for the birth ceremony. She also introduced me to the realm of ilmu gaib.

The Realm of Ilmu Gaib

Signs of the practice of ilmu gaib and belief in spirits are ever present if one knows where to look. Walking through the village, for example, one sees an infant wearing an amulet, a certain kind of leaf placed over a doorway, a banana leaf stalk stuck in the ground; or one learns that the spirits of the bathing place are being propitiated during a birth ceremony. But not all villagers do such things. People feel ambivalent about ilmu gaib because of the influence of fundamentalist Islam in the nineteenth century in connection with the Padri War.

In Padri times agreement was reached between the forces of adat and Islam to purge the more blatantly "pagan" practices, such as cockfighting, gambling, and black magic. However, as Americans know all too well, prohibition merely pushes cultural obsessions off the public stage, it does not end them. Today people still engage in practices that might be associated by the more doctrinaire with pre-Islamic customs of "pagan adat" *(adat Jahiliah)*. Although cockfighting and the practice of black magic have by all accounts been abandoned, one still hears about both (but never in Belubus). More accepted is the use of white magic blended with Islamic prayers. But like all magical practices, white magic relies on ilmu gaib. It is probably fair to say that the less doctrinaire in most Minangkabau villages treat ilmu gaib as part of the Minangkabau way.

To see ilmu gaib being practiced, one needs only to visit Inam, a practitioner of traditional healing, whose house near Payakumbuh fills on certain nights from dusk into the early morning. Although there are several well-known dukun who live in Belubus—one woman and three or four men—none are as active as Inam, who received thirty to forty visitors on the nights she worked, usually twice a week. Inam acquired her special powers from Dt. Soyieh, who came to her when she was living in eastern Sumatra as a young woman. Dt. Soyieh manifested himself when she was seeking herbal remedies in the jungle. He was wearing a white robe and turban and sported a white beard. He notified her that he and his daughter, Ranjani, would be her spirit helpers, which meant that one of them would possess Inam in order to heal those who came seeking her help.

I remember well when Ibu Idar introduced me to the world of the spirits and ilmu gaib. It was in May 1985. One night I awoke sometime between two and four in the morning to the sound of water splashing outside my window, as if someone were bathing in the nearby well. Half asleep, I wondered who it might be. I had always been told not to bathe after Magrib (about 6:30 P.M.) because the spirits of the well might run off with my soul and cause me to fall sick. I listened to the sound for some time to assure myself that it was real and not a dream. It sounded like the familiar splash of water poured from a bucket, the closest one gets to a shower in Belubus. Two people were bathing, it seemed, one after the other. I listened for words but, hearing none, drifted off to sleep.

Inam, a *dukun*, healing through Ranjani, 1989

The next day I described what I heard to Ibu Idar. Her reply was totally unexpected. During my first four years in West Sumatra, I heard people talk a great deal about the practices of Islam but little about the world
of spirits. I knew vaguely that there was such a world—I had interviewed
a few dukun in other parts of West Sumatra—but I didn't yet understand
how magic and religion sometimes came together. Because I knew that
Ibu Idar had studied with her famous father, I assumed that she had abandoned all belief in spirits. So I was unprepared for her answer.

"Oh, Bu," she said. "What you heard were *orang gaib* (spirits) taking a
bath. They sometimes come to the house. They are harmless, don't be
afraid. If we are good, they don't bother us. They like to come on Thurs-
days, the night when the ancestors walk. Sometimes my father comes and
knocks on the door. When I open the door and there's no one, I know
he's there."

The candor with which Ibu Idar explained all of this to me, and her
subsequent accounts of meeting her long dead father on Thursday nights
either at the house or at his grave, made me feel that I had entered a new
understanding and consciousness of the Belubus reality. It seemed to me,
and maybe to Ibu Idar as well, that by making themselves known to me
the spirits had opened a door.

After I crossed the threshold of ilmu gaib I learned how Inam heals through Dt. Soyieh and Ranjani. Inam works lying down under a blanket. It is not she who speaks in response to the those who come seeking help, but Ranjani or Dt. Soyieh. These two ask questions of the individual who comes to Inam and then make a house call to diagnose the illness and prescribe the appropriate medicine. I understood how this healing method works a few years later when I had a visit from Ranjani.

Late one evening, about 10 P.M., I was sitting in the front room, the only room in the house that faces toward Mt. Merapi. Hearing a tapping at the window, I looked out to see who was there. No one was at the window, but the tapping continued. After a few moments of this, I got a little spooked and left the room.

The next day, I told Wik and Ibu Idar about the sound. They knew immediately what it was.

"That was Ranjani," they explained. "She came at the request of Inam to check on our sick child, to see what was wrong with him."

When I heard the tapping at the window, I was deeply immersed in writing my field notes and had forgotten that members of the family had left to seek her help in healing a young boy who had come to live at the house with his mother. The boy had all the symptoms of the flu. He had gone swimming in the heat of midday at one of the nearby wells. When asked, he admitted that while there he had seen a small snake. Everyone then knew the cause of his illness.

The people of Belubus share their bathing places with local spirits. Long ago the spirit and human worlds struck a bargain about sharing the well. Humans promised to bathe only during some parts of the day and otherwise leave the well to the spirits. This little boy had broken the pact and was suffering the consequences. The snake was the sign of the spirits' displeasure.

It is not unusual for the people who visit Inam to be turned away in their quest for healing because neither Ranjani nor Dt. Soyieh shows up. The first time I visited Inam's house on a healing night, the spirits made a big fuss, refusing to enter Inam because of my presence. Later, after the spirits got to know me, my presence was no longer offensive. On one of my visits, Ranjani's absence was explained by the fact that she had gone to Mecca for the Holy Month. People are less clear about Dt. Soyieh's religious affiliation. Some say he died before Islam entered West Sumatra, others that he is a devout follower of Islam.

Most people don't question the happy accommodation of ilmu gaib and Islam, nor do they think of it as unusual. The only individual who raised questions about Inam and her clientele was an Islamic official in the village who claimed that half of the villagers believed in the old ways and half followed Islam.

The Unity of Women's Ceremonies

In the life cycle ceremonies, women manage to draw all the strands of the diverse past into one grand statement. As women give the imprimatur of adat to birth, marriage, house building, and installing a new penghulu, they weave many themes together. Adat, Islam, nature, beliefs regarding the spirits, and homage to the ancestors are orchestrated into one glorious symphony of modern and folk themes.

The spectacles range from high fashion and the politesse of baso-basi during the day to bawdy songs of love, romance, and sex at nighttime. Adat, Islam, and ilmu gaib are blended in the Koranic prayers and flowery adat speeches accompanied by the adat foods consumed commensally, almost ritually, in the presence of a dukun. It is the job of the dukun to ward off evil when a marriage is celebrated, or to propitiate the spirits of the house when there is a birth.

The ceremonies are integral to the routine of daily life; making a living, raising a family, and staging the appropriate life cycle ceremony are all inseparable. Women who neglect adat ceremonies in raising their children become the subject of gossip. Children who are not properly introduced to the spirits at birth risk their wrath. The naming ceremony stamps Minangkabauness on the newborn and weaves them into the tapestry of village social and spirit relations. Weddings knit the adat social tapestry that enfolds the young by drawing the maternal and paternal clans of bride and groom into a social network that lasts till death. Because women's ceremonies weave the pluralism of daily life into a coherent adat fabric, we find in them the famous accommodating tendency so important to Minangkabau character and culture. More than any other activity in Belubus, women's ceremonies took me to the heart of adat matriarchaat.

III

CELEBRATING LIFE

CHAPTER FIVE

Discovering Adat Ibu

The women had been working together for several days, first gathering bananas and then making *silomak* (sticky rice) for the birth ceremony of Ibu Ida's new baby. Now they were cooking goat curry. They were in high spirits, laughing, joking, gossiping. In answer to my serious questions about what it all meant, Ibu Wel explained, "This is our adat *(adat awak)*. We follow adat *(awak beradat)*." Ibu Emmy shouted out, "The adat here is from the ancestors of long ago." Ibu Nur chimed in, "A good relationship between clans depends on women."

Field notes, June 1995

I must confess that I stumbled by accident onto adat ibu, the name women have for their practice of adat. Women never talked about adat the way the men did, nor did they display book knowledge of adat. I never heard anything from women about Indo Jelito, the tambo, or the historical meaning of Bundo Kanduang. Had I stopped for a moment to take a hard look at the amount of time women spent in the *practice* of adat, I would have spent more time observing adat ceremonies. Women are doers more than talkers. Their preferred way was to show me adat, not to answer my questions. In response to my questions, they sent me off to see the penghulu of the village. At the most, some women recited ancient rice prayers and healing mantras they once used. I understood, however, that they recited these prayers and mantras out of nostalgia, not because the prayers had any relationship to the present. Eventually I concluded that what women practiced, they did not talk about; and what they talked about, they only rarely practiced.

It took me some time to realize that the adat lore I was hearing from men did not reflect social relationships in the push and pull of daily life. Social relationships are activated not just by the words of adat but by its performance as well. Although men take the stage to speak the words of adat, women put them on that stage.

My education in women's adat began in the summer of 1995 when a group of women took me under their wing and decided to show me how they prepared for ceremonies. I had just arrived in Belubus after an absence of some five years, during which time Ibu Idar died and Agoes was born. En had sent me a telegram about Ibu Idar's death, but I did not receive it. Finally, the news had come in a letter from En. The story was tragic. Soon after I left in 1989, Ibu Idar had a minor stroke followed by a major one in which she was reduced to silence and near immobility. Her daughter, Elli, came to Belubus to take her to her home in Riau province, in eastern Sumatra, to be examined by a doctor. Ibu Idar pleaded to stay in Belubus, but to no avail. Had she stayed in Belubus, Ibu Idar would have died with all her close friends and relatives ministering to her, staying with her around the clock, praying for her soul, rubbing ointment on her body. She would have died resting in the bosom of her family, secure in the knowledge that she was welcome on earth and in heaven. Instead she died in the most modern of ways, alone in a hospital.

Her body was brought back to Belubus, where people paid their last respects. They came not just from Belubus but from all the villages nearby. Greatly honored in death as in life, she was buried alongside her mother and grandmother in plots cleared on clan land. When I returned in 1995 my first act was to visit her grave to pay my respects. As I sat by her grave in the stillness, I thought of the times she had told me about visiting with her dead father. I felt she was very close.

On returning to the village, I found Wik in charge, acting as a manager of Ibu Elli's rice fields and caretaker of the house. As before, we were welcomed like family. The only difference was that Wik cooked our meals. She was a wonderful cook, having learned the best of Minangkabau cooking from Ibu Idar. Agoes had been born the year before, and Eggi was eight.

Walking through the village soon after my return, I passed a house compound where a group of women were cooking for a birth ceremony. I saw Ibu Wel among them, and we greeted one another in the usual way.

"Apa kabar," I called out. "Bagaimana?" How are you? How's it going?

Shouting and laughing, telling jokes as they worked, dressed in brightly patterned sarongs wound tightly around the waist and wearing the usual rubber thongs, the women were an inviting sight. There were about twenty of them, of all ages, engaged in various activities: cooking rice over an open fire, shucking coconuts, cutting the meat from the shells, grating it, and making coconut milk for the obligatory goat curry cooked for ceremonies.

"Hai, Ibu," Ibu Wel called out. "Come and see what we are doing. This is our adat *(adat awak),*" she said, emphasizing *our adat.*

I didn't feel the need to ask any questions, nor did I get out my notebook and pad. Pointing to the food they were cooking, Ibu Emmy said, "Ibu, we follow adat *(awak beradat).* It is the adat from the ancestors of long ago." Finishing the thought, Ibu Nur added, "A good relationship between clans depends on women." As they spoke the women within hearing distance clucked appreciatively, adding their agreement.

I understood the women's message as telling me in a polite, but friendly way that I had overlooked this realm of adat. The occasion they chose to tell me this—their busy preparation of ceremonial foods—was instructive: women didn't talk about adat because for them adat is a way of life. Adat can't be reduced to a code, in the way that males conceived it in response to my questions.

This encounter marked a crucial turning point for me. It came as a note in a bottle telling me that although the ethnohistory track I was following might yet prove useful, I had missed a rich realm of daily life. After staying with them during the remaining days of their preparations and attending the elaborate ceremony that followed, I realized that village ceremonies not only embody adat but form the core of village social life.

Without properly conducted ceremonies, I learned, a human being is not considered fully Minangkabau, cannot get married, and, if a male, cannot take on a hereditary title. Likewise, a house cannot be properly built, and errant husbands may never return to their wives. People who move from one village to another cannot celebrate a birth or a wedding in the adat way without first undergoing a ceremony inducting them into a local clan. Ceremonies are thus part and parcel of the reproduction of adat social structure.

The women who shouted out to me were senior women helping a young mother prepare to receive as many as two hundred guests for her newborn child's birth ceremony. At all ceremonies senior women of the hostess clan hover in the background doing most of the work, aided by in-married women and friends. The woman sponsoring the ceremony, a mother or grandmother, uses her own resources; sometimes she sells gold jewelry she has kept locked away. Through ceremonies a woman educates her children in the way of adat as she inserts them within a social network. She also cushions them from the possible evil that may come their way from spirits, jealous villagers, or, in the case of a wedding, magic sent by spurned suitors. When acting in this capacity senior women are often referred to as Bundo Kanduang.

Women's Ceremonial Role

In the years following this experience I spent the bulk of my time following men and women as they prepared for and participated in ceremonies. I learned that through life cycle ceremonies women wrap their children in the mantle of adat social relationships. Watching women perform adat, I realized that they had little interest in the logos of adat. Classifying adat, talking about adat, and reciting adat lore was the province of men. Women's work lay in the practice of adat. The closest women got to codifying or classifying adat was to divide it into two kinds: *adat kecil* (little adat) and *adat besar* (big adat), the distinction depending on the number of people involved and the extent of the social relationships activated.

Adat ibu is shaped by unwritten tradition. For women, adat ibu is eternal and unchangeable, part of being a mother—a way of thinking and acting, a world view that organizes a woman's existence and dictates the ceremonial cycle. As Wik told me, "If children stop listening to their parents and women stop holding and attending ceremonies, adat will be lost. But that will happen only when the world ends and Doomsday is upon us." From such comments, I understood that adat is much more than what I read in the books and learned from interviews.

A well-known proverb, which I heard all over West Sumatra, expresses the archetypal role senior women play on the public stage of village life:[1]

> Bundo Kanduang is the butterfly of the traditional house
> She is the one who owns the key of the clothes chest and the jewelry box
> She is the center where the threads of the fishnet meet
> She is the finery of the village
> She is sovereign through her dignity
> The one who is greatly honored
> The one to whom we take all our problems
> The one who receives our last wishes when we die[2]

The butterfly metaphor in this proverb has aesthetic and social meanings. In Minangkabau weaving and house carving, the butterfly symbolizes the senior woman in full adat regalia—finely dressed, laden with gifts, the conveyor of good fortune and goodwill. In this guise she is Bundo Kanduang, our own mother who is the dominant symbol of the common good. The butterfly is also associated with the central pillar of the traditional house, which is the oldest pillar because it is the first erected. Thus center, origin, and maternal symbol are joined, an association frequently found in Minangkabau symbology.

Owning the key to the clothes chest and the jewelry box carries aesthetic and social meanings. This is a subject that many women discussed with me because it has material implications for the lives of their daughters. In addition to implying finery, clothes and jewelry are part of the sacred pusaka (ancestral) objects so important in ceremonial displays and safeguarded for passing from one generation to the next. The jewelry represents a woman's economic acumen in her ability to translate rice and garden surpluses into gold as an investment for a daughter's future. It is money in the bank for cashing in when funds are needed to stage a ceremony, especially a wedding. The savings may also be called upon for buying livestock—bulls, cows, or goats—as a form of investment. The clothes in the chest are the adat costumes woven with fine gold or silver (in wealthier households) and handed down from mother to daughter to don for special adat ceremonies. The chest is also the place where the ancestral kris is stored for use by the males who inherit the ancestral title on ceremonial occasions. Thus, the chest represents the material repository of adat as it is passed from one generation to the next.

The idea that the senior woman of the household is "the center where the threads of the fishnet meet" evokes the image of this woman as hostess to the many guests that flow into her house. Because the ceremonies are so public, sometimes with most of the village attending, it is easy to see how women's activity weaves the threads of the social tapestry. Women do this on a regular basis, not just in staging their own ceremonies but through helping one another. The proper conduct of ceremonies ensures orderly peaceful relations among the members of clans who are related by marriage ties. The Minangkabau always prefer *budi* (refined social interaction) to *kuasa* (power and self-interest). It is not as if self-interest doesn't exist, for it definitely does. How it is handled is what counts in the performance of adat ibu.

Whatever the situation might have been in the past, today Minangkabau women are in charge of most activities related to the ceremonial expression of adat. Although men know the speeches and women don't, it is women who set the stage and put the men on it at the appropriate moment. Some women are the directors and stage managers, others play a front-stage role as honored guests who bring ceremonial foods. These roles are determined by family ties to the hostess. While relatively few men know the appropriate speeches that must be delivered at the appointed time, most women know the recipes for ceremonial food and the requirements for the ceremonial food exchanges. Women as well as men must be counted as experts in adat Minangkabau, albeit in different realms.

The ceremonies are so complex that it was impossible for me to record all the details through participation alone. Yet when I asked women to fill in the blanks later—to tell me, for example, who had given what—I got nowhere, except with Ibu Idar, who had the fine points firmly etched in her mind. Busy with their work or enjoying each other's company, the women would either change the subject or provide the barest outline of what subsequent observation showed to be a complex sequence of non-random events, which changed only according to finances and clan status.

In the absence of spoken texts—verbal recipes for ceremonial events—I started making a photographic record of each ceremony beginning with the invitation and preparations. If I didn't understand something, I would take the pictures to the women who sponsored the ceremony. After the excitement and stress of a large ceremony, they were glad to sit down and think back over it, especially if I left the pictures behind so that they would have a record for their scrapbooks. As I sat quietly with them of an evening, they explained the rationale for the activities, food exchanges, various displays, dress codes, and whatever else baffled me. Presently I realized that the different types of ceremonies followed a preset plan. Birth ceremonies were marked by one set of procedures, marriages another. The commonalities across ceremonies were as interesting as the differences.

If I could reproduce, here in this book, the smell and taste of Minangkabau food or the sounds of traditional music, I would do so. Instead I shall try to re-create the preparations for a ceremony, the ceremony itself, and the entertainment in which female bards brought to the village sing deeply felt songs educating men about life—entertainment lasting long into the night and often until dawn lights up the Sumatran sky.

Lexicon and Intentions of Ceremonies

The cultural importance of women's ceremonies is reflected in the complexity of their lexicon. First, there is a special word for a ceremony—*pesta*, which means party or festival and applies to all ceremonies except for the death ritual. The scale of celebration depends on the wealth and status of the family. A common denominator of the more festive occasions is the practice of *baalek*, which means to hold a pesta adat. The procession of women bearing offerings of food atop their heads to and from

Women working together preparing for a birth ceremony, 1996

a ceremony is called *baarak*. *Baalua* refers to the adat speeches given by men during adat ceremonies. Today, although only a handful of men are fluent in the practice of baalua, everyone recognizes its importance in maintaining adat.

Women refer proudly to baalek and baarak, saying, "This is adat awak, our adat." The verb *beradat* means to do things in the adat way. One must dress in a certain way, cook certain items, bring certain offerings to the pesta, give certain items in exchange, and treat certain relatives with proper respect. The goal is not just to uphold adat but to show proper respect for the living and dead. Communal effort in adat ceremonies encourages village well-being and good relations between the clans. No one wants to be talked about as one who shirks responsibility to children or to relatives by marriage, the focus of all ceremonies. Such a person faces chaos, and the children are sure to go astray.

The primary rule guiding all ceremonies is expressed in the form of a proverb: "Adat diisi, limbago di tuang" (Adat is filled with contents, the custom is fulfilled). This enigmatic explanation for anything that happened during a ceremony was recited by men and women alike. It refers to all that must be accomplished in a ceremony for adat to have its *intentions* fulfilled.

There are two basic intentions of every ceremony. First, there are acts and foods designed to stamp a consciousness on the subject of the ceremony, be it the newborn, the newlywed, the man receiving a penghulu title, or the couple building a house—to mention the most common occasions. All ceremonies, large or small, share the basic intention of shaping those who have entered a new stage in their lives according to the dictates of adat. The shaping is accomplished by means of words, foods, clothing, and flowers.

The second intention, more apparent in the larger ceremonies, is to weave the individual into a web of adat social relations through a ritual exchange of words and foods. When men exchange the appropriate adat words and women the appropriate foods in the larger ceremonies, adat is fulfilled. The exchange marks key social relationships that are prominently on display as women of the guest clans bring food to a ceremony, leave it with people there, and depart with their baskets filled by the women of the host clan. Men are involved in marking social relationships through the words they speak on the ceremonial stage. Certain men have the job of speaking to certain other men, an interaction which is observed by all in attendance. The marked relationships are always between members of clans tied by marriage.

By marking clan social relationships through the exchange of food, the ceremonies keep these relationships alive and functioning. Four types of relatives are ceremonially marked in the preparations and subsequent exchanges. These four classes of relatives enfold the newborn and the newlywed in a web of cross-clan ties.[3] Theoretically, the four types of relatives could be members of the four clan groupings, the suku berempat. Thus, ceremonies bring the structural schemata of cross-cutting, clan-related social ties into public view.

Since there is always the potential for members of the different clans to come into conflict over land and movable property, women's ceremonies provide a forum for the public display of goodwill and sociality. Good relations enhance the appropriate climate for settling interclan disputes in the adat way rather than in national courts, which is always an option. My experience in Belubus taught me that the adat way is always preferred and that those who betray adat by going to court risk their prestige and social status. So we see that in matters of social conflict, women's ceremonies uphold the adat way. How all of this works in the context of the birth and marriage ceremonies is the subject to which I now turn.

CHAPTER SIX

Eggi Becomes Minangkabau

Wik came back from the clinic today bringing her baby girl. Ibu Idar told me that there would be a birth ceremony to *malapeh pantang*. She explained that *malapeh* means "freedom" and *pantang* means "forbidden by taboo." The birth ceremony frees mother and child from the taboos associated with birth. The ceremony consists of several rituals, she said. There is the first bath *(turun mandi)*, giving the first food and drink *(memberi makan dan minum)*, the Islamic birth ceremony *(kekah anak)*, and the naming ceremony. Also associated with birth is taking a trip to the dukun to acquire amulets for mother and child, which are worn to ward off evil spirits.

Field notes, 1987

Wik gave birth to Eggi in a nearby clinic and then moved into Ibu Idar's house with Pak Edi and their son, Adis, after living in their pondok. It is somewhat unusual for a young couple to live in a garden hut; most new brides live with their mothers. Wik told me that because she had "run away" to marry Pak Edi, she preferred living in the hut away from the family. Her decision to move in with Ibu Idar was in effect a reincorporation into the family, which is what Ibu Idar was seeking for her. It is not uncommon for a young woman who has run away to get married to return home after a child is born.

Because in the years prior to Eggi's birth I rarely saw Wik, I knew her only slightly when she moved into the household. Interacting with her was extremely difficult because whenever I came into her vicinity she would flee like a frightened bird. In the interest of developing some sort of relationship, I learned to speak to her briefly and only when necessary, deflecting my gaze quickly so as not to exacerbate the debilitating shyness she felt in my presence. After a month of this I felt we had made little progress. Thus I was surprised to learn upon returning the following year that her daughter bore my name.

Eggi's birth ceremony took place in August, a few weeks before I left. Ibu Idar made the distinction between little and big adat ceremonies when she told me that Eggi's would be a little ceremony. Compared to many other ceremonies I attended, it was indeed small. Only the immediate family was present, whereas as many as two hundred people might attend the bigger ceremonies.

The birth ceremonies demonstrate that being born within the sheltering nurture of the paruik does not alone make one a Minangkabau, nor does it protect the newborn from the dangerous forces that inhabit the village bathing place and glide through the air from other villages. Birth is a time when everything must be done right according to adat in order for the mother and child to grow strong. When all the rituals are completed and the child has acquired its protective amulets, several important hurdles have been surmounted: the spirits who live in the bathing places have been placated, the child has been named in the adat way, and proper thanks have been extended to God. These measures free mother and child to go about, unhampered by the unseen forces that attack the weak mother and the vulnerable infant. Most important, the amulets protect the newborn from the illnesses caused by spirits, especially the *palasik*, bloodsucking vampires believed to emanate from certain other villages. Some of the more modern mothers, however, forego the amulets unless their infant gets sick.

The first step is to choose the appropriate day for the ceremony, for otherwise disaster may fall on the family and the newborn. Family members consult the astrological schedule prepared by Ibu Idar's father. Many people in Belubus have a copy of this schedule or if they don't they get it from someone who does. This chart is faithfully consulted not just for the timing of ceremonies but also for the best time to depart on important journeys. I have frequently used it to decide when I should leave the village to return to the United States. Choosing the day for departure in this way made a little ritual out of parting, which Wik especially seemed to appreciate. The date and time is announced in advance and the whole family congregates to say good-bye. The feeling that we are in tune with the path of the stars charted by Syekh Muda made it easier on all of us to *berpisa* (separate) until the following year.

The path of the stars, as the schedule is called, is based on Islamic astrology, which Ibu Idar's father had studied with famous Islamic scholars both in Mecca and in West Sumatra. Islamic astrology is the study of the movement of the stars and the planets to understand how they affect daily activities and events and the character and personality of individuals. For example, certain days are bad because "much money will be lost," while other days are acceptable because "there is much to be gained."

After much thought and consultation between Wik and Ibu Idar, August 25 was chosen as the right day. This date was then discussed with the rest of the family, including Pak Edi. Such discussion *(musyawarah)* and mutual agreement *(mupakat)* is common in the affairs of daily life.

Men and women play very different roles during the ceremony, as do the mother's and the father's families. The mother and her female relatives orchestrate the event, choose the day, invite the guests, and prepare the food. The father's family prepares the special foods that will be fed to the child. A male dukun is called in to perform the first feeding. He sits with the father and other male guests, husbands of female relatives of the child, to perform this task. The central role of the father is reflected in the fact that after the child is fed two or three mashed grains of rice from a banana-leaf plate, he eats the remainder.

The job of feeding the infant cannot be carried out by anyone. It must be done by someone who is adept at uttering appropriate Islamic prayers and adat mantras over the food fed to the child. Ibu Idar's father, Syekh Muda, was a man of this caliber. Today there are few men in the village who fill this role. The only two I knew were both students of Syekh Muda.

With one exception, every birth ceremony I observed was officiated by Dt. Nunang, one of the better known dukun in Belubus. Dt. Nunang has an ethereal quality, common to dukun in West Sumatra. He is a thin, wiry, intense man whose abilities at ilmu gaib are well and widely known. His specialty is healing people with *demam*, fever due to soul loss. He heals demam by sending his own soul out to bring back the soul of the sick. Sometimes his soul makes lengthy trips to strange places.

My favorite story about Dt. Nunang tells of a soul-finding excursion when his shoes ended up in one tree and he in another. Once, upon my arrival in Belubus, he came excitedly to the house to tell me that he had visited my home near Philadelphia while I was away. I was intrigued by the accuracy of his account of what my house looked like and its location: "Your house has big trees all around it," he told me. "It is near a stream."

On another occasion he described events that took place on my journey that year to Belubus: "You were in a big city and a man was arrested and handcuffed by the police," he said. I had in fact witnessed an arrest in San Francisco that year on my way to Belubus. It was the only time I had ever seen someone arrested on the streets. I have no explanation for Dt. Nunang's visions; all those he shared with me were correct.

Over the years I watched him perform the first-feeding ceremony many times, and nothing much changed. Although he studied with Syekh Muda, he said that the ingredients were handed down from the ancestors. Ibu Idar confirmed this. The purpose of the ceremony, she said, was to introduce the baby to the food and ways of the ancestors.

The ingredients are very simple. They are all taken from the chicken coop and the family garden. They must be carefully selected. According to Dt. Nunang, one of the most important qualities of the foods selected is their ability to speak. This quality of the foods imbibed by the child suggests that the whole affair is a throwback to the animism of ancestral times. The ingredients are a young coconut, an egg, a sprig of red pepper, a *pisang manis* (a sweet banana), cooked rice on a leaf of *pisang batu* (another type of banana), and a piece of gold. Dt. Nunang explained that the right coconut, egg, red pepper sprig, and so forth must be carefully selected to find only those that fit *(cocok)* with the intention of adat. Finding the right item requires questioning many candidates.

When I asked him how coconuts, eggs, and bananas could speak, he explained, "Oh Bu, everything that lives in nature can speak. But, you must believe in the power of nature to speak before trees, leaves, coconuts, or rice will talk with you."

I nodded my head in agreement, thinking of the many stories I had been told of Dt. Nunang's special powers.

To illustrate his point, Dt. Nunang took some leaves of a *pisang batu*, "king of the bananas." One of these leaves would be selected as a plate for the rice that would be fed to Eggi and then given to Pak Edi so that father and child might share the first meal. Addressing the leaves as he would a person, Dt. Nunang said, "Kau, Siadaun?" (Are you Siadaun?).

Siadaun (the leaf) answered, "Saya sipuluik" (I'm for sipuluik), which meant that it was appropriate only for wrapping sticky rice, not for using as a plate on which to place the child's first rice.

"Kau, Siadaun?" Dt. Nunang asked another leaf.

"Saya sipuluik," came back the same answer.

"Kau, Siadaun?" he repeated to the next leaf, showing that one had to search long for the right candidate.

Finally, he got the right answer.

"Nasi bana" (correct for rice), this leaf answered.

The leaf that gives this answer is saying that it does not have a "hard head"; it is not stubborn but soft enough to be used as a plate for cooked rice. Otherwise it has to be warmed to make it pliable, such as is done when wrapping sticky rice. The implication here is that the child who is fed from a pliable leaf will have a flexible personality in life.

Dt. Nunang continued his conversation with the candidates for Eggi's first-feeding ceremony. He placed various sprigs of fine-looking, long red peppers *(lado)*, some young coconuts, a few bananas, some eggs, and a piece of gold on the table at which we were working. I understood that properly administered with the appropriate prayers, these items would baptize Eggi into full Minangkabauhood.

To the young coconut, Dt. Nunang told me that one must ask, "Are you full?" which means that when a small hole is made in the top of the coconut the water shoots straight up. This is important because if Eggi had her first taste from such a coconut, she would surely want to plant many coconuts in her garden.

"Are you odd, like a coconut? Closed like a bottle?" he asked the coconuts.

When I asked why coconuts are "odd," Dt. Nunang explained that all coconuts are odd because the contents wrap the water rather than being immersed in water as is the more normal case in nature. If the coconut is closed like a bottle, it means that drinking its water quickly quenches one's thirst or lowers one's fever.

To the banana candidates, Dt. Nunang asked: "Manis? Sudah masak?" (Are you sweet, already ripe?)

To the eggs: "Lomaknyo?" (Are you delicious?)

Dt. Nunang explained that the egg is given to the newborn so that it knows about the importance of eggs in addressing the ancestors or spirits of holy places.

Ibu Idar, who was sitting nearby as we talked, added that the egg signifies the practice of *bernazar*, the visiting of sacred places such as a parent's grave or a standing stone to pray for a special intervention. If the wish is granted, the person promises to do something in return, such as come back with an offering. Giving an egg is the smallest of such offerings. In Belubus there are several sacred spots, marked by stones, to which people once went to pray for an intention, promising to come back with an egg if the intention was granted.

The most important is the question addressed to the red pepper.

"Podenyo?" (Are you hot?)

This is a key question because the main dish of the Minangkabau on a daily basis is rice with *sambal lado* (a sauce with red pepper) or *cabe* (red pepper ground with onion, garlic and a little lemon juice). I have eaten rice and red pepper for breakfast, lunch, and dinner. No day is complete without rice and cabe or lado.

It is the job of the class of relatives called *bako*, maternal relatives of the father, to acquire all items for the child's first feeding and bath. Bako are key to a child's life. At birth they feed, bathe, and fuss over the child born to the son whom they have given away in marriage. In Eggi's case, among her bako relatives only her father's sister attended the ceremony. Eggi's father's mother and family were living far away.

Because his maternal relatives were so far away, it fell to Pak Edi to prepare the appropriate items for Eggi's first feeding. With the help of Ibu Idar, he also selected the items for Eggi's first bath, which is also the job of the father's maternal relatives.

In the large ceremonies, the female bako relatives bring the items for the first bath and first feeding. One of the women, usually the paternal grandmother, carries the items for feeding the newborn on a *dulang tuo* (brass ancestral tray inherited from mother to daughter) covered with a cloth of white lace. Flanked by many bako women, she carries the tray balanced on her head. The use of the tray indicates that adat is very heavy in the birth ceremony.

Ibu Idar told me that Pak Edi's sister and mother would take Eggi for the first bath. I didn't observe them do this, however, so I don't know if it actually took place. Here is what Ibu Idar said about the first bath.

> Once they have arrived at the house and eaten, the bako women take the baby to the house well or spring where the family bathes with the items for the first bath. For this trip the infant is wrapped in a long piece of batik cloth brought by the bako. Usually the infant's paternal grandmother carries the infant and another bako relative takes the dulang tuo on which the items for the ceremony have been brought. Still another holds an umbrella over the child to shelter it from the sun. The mother of the child stays at home as only bako relatives are involved in this trip. Many children run along with the group, because they look forward to eating some of the items that will be left for the spirits. At the spring, the infant is washed with a special medicine by the dukun. This medicine consists of water in which a little uncooked rice has been placed. It is carried in a small gourd called a *labu caciak*, which holds sacralized water. The items are left at the well for the spirits and the children to make them happy. This includes a red flower called *bungo perindu*, a banana called *pisang godong* (big banana) cut into three pieces; *botia* (popped sticky rice, which the children particularly relish), *tebu* (pieces of sugar cane), and *bareh rendang* (uncooked rice fried with no oil).

Ibu Idar left the job of explaining these items to Dt. Nunang. He said that the name of the red flower is based on the root *rindu*, which means "longing"; the flower reminds the family that bako will always keep the child in mind. This flower both summons the spirits to eat the offering and is left as a sign that the child will be much in demand. Dt. Nunang likened the popped rice, a symbol of opening up, to the growth of the infant's thoughts; it expresses the wish that the child be intelligent in school and in business. He said that the fried rice symbolizes the wish for the infant to always have a sweet smell in life, like perfume. The same is true of the sugar cane; it makes the baby sweet and beautiful. The banana is cut into three pieces as a symbol of the three most important principles that will guide a child's behavior: adat, religion, and government.

These foods and the flower are left in the banana-leaf plate beside the bathing place of the house. Someone addresses the spirits, either Dt. Nunang or the paternal grandmother, to this effect: "We bring our child so that the spirit owners of the bathing place will know that our baby has been brought." The bako also tell the spirits that this is the child of their child, at which time they mention the father's name. With these offerings the person whose ilmu gaib is believed to be efficacious, a person like Dt. Nunang for example, can order the spirits not to bother the child.

The children of the family follow the trip to the bathing place with great excitement because they get to eat the items gathered for the first bath, as long as a little is left for the spirits. If the ceremony is performed at the house, as sometimes happens, the children gobble everything up, forgetting about the spirits altogether.

I have seen the first bath being given only twice. It is not as necessary to go to the spring because many families now have deep wells dug in their houses. Nevertheless, in all the birth ceremonies I observed, the family went through the motions with the ingredients mentioned above. People still believe that it is necessary to pay lip service to the spirits in this way before the birth taboos restricting the baby's movement can be lifted and the mother and child can leave the house. People also hold firm to the belief that the child who grows up the wrong way or is frequently ill has not been properly protected from the spirits of the well.

Adat Symbolism in the First-Feeding Ceremony

Once the first bath is completed, everyone gathers for the first feeding. The guests of honor for this part of the ceremony are always the infant's father and the husbands of the other women in the family. Almost all of the husbands of the women in Eggi's immediate family were present for Eggi's first feeding. In addition to her father, Pak Edi, Ibu Wel's husband was present, as was the husband of Ibu Os, her aunt. So was Dt. Kosek, Ibu Ida's husband. A few other in-married husbands of more distant relatives were also present—for example, men from the clan of Ibu Elli's husband. It is clear that while the first bath is given by bako women, the first food is given by bako men.

As a rule the child is held by the paternal grandmother or by the father's sister for the first feeding. Pak Edi's sister was in attendance, but Wik held Eggi.

Everyone sat on the floor with the meal spread before them. Dt. Nunang sat next to Wik and Eggi, who was tightly wrapped for the occasion in the batik cloth supplied by Pak Edi's sister. All the ingredients for the ceremony were placed on a mat before Dt. Nunang: cooked rice on the banana leaf, banana, egg, lado, young coconut, and a gold ring.

Before beginning, Dt. Nunang put his hand on Eggi's forehead and recited the Islamic call to prayer, heard over the village loudspeaker five times a day. Throughout the feeding, Islamic prayers and adat mantras would be uttered as each piece of food was touched to Eggi's mouth.

He then picked up the banana leaf on which there was a mound of cooked rice. He recited a prayer in Indonesian to the rice. Using the familiar form of address for both the rice (in the plural) and the child (in the singular), he said, "Our dear Rice will be given to our dear Child," and then, to the rice, "Please separate so that the hunger will be appeased."

In this prayer he asked certain grains of rice to separate from the rest. The grains must separate in clumps of three, five, seven, or nine. These grains have magical power and represent the soul of rice: Sonan Sari, the goddess or mother of the rice.

Once the prayer was recited, the grains responded by separating into a clump of seven. The seven grains answered, "I am the one who can make hunger vanish." It was actually the soul of the rice that responded, not the rice itself. No one but Dt. Nunang could hear it because it was uttered by the *roh yang gaib* (invisible sacred spirit) of Sonan Sari.

After Dt. Nunang identified the seven grains of rice, he mashed them in the plate with a bit of banana and a dash of egg yoke. The banana skin was peeled from the banana in four pieces. Various explanations are given for why it is cut into four, but all refer to the importance of the number four as a symbol for adat. If the banana is peeled into three pieces this is supposed to represent the three codes that guide life: adat, religion, and government. Usually Dt. Nunang peeled the banana into four strips.

Once the banana was peeled Dt. Nunang mashed a tiny bit of the fruit with the grains of Sonan Sari. Then he added a bit of boiled egg yoke to the mush, so that Eggi would understand bernazar, the practice of going to sacred places to pray for special intentions.

Before giving her the mashed mixture, Dt. Nunang dipped the sprig of red pepper into the coconut water and dripped a few drops into her mouth. Then he rubbed a bit of the mashed mixture of rice, banana, and

Eggi's first-feeding ceremony, 1987. Wik is holding Eggi as Endri looks on. Datuk Nunang is feeding Eggi mashed rice, banana, and egg.

egg on her gums. When she moved her lips and cheeks, showing that she had swallowed the coconut water and chewed the food, he gave a sigh of pleasure, saying, "Sudah" (It's done). Eggi had accepted the Minangkabau way.

The grand finale came with touching gold to Eggi's lips while reciting still another prayer. This gesture was meant to instill the proper way of speaking: choosing one's words carefully, speaking infrequently, and thinking before speaking. The gold was wrapped in batik, showing that the mouth too must be wrapped. One must speak prayerfully and with respect, always remembering Allah. Touching the mouth with gold keeps the mouth small, the words short, the attitude polite, in conformity with Minangkabau etiquette. Like the proverb "Nature is our teacher," people should choose the good rather than the bad from the thoughts that well up within them, being careful to speak only the good, just as they must be careful to take only the good from nature and discard the bad.

After this was accomplished the leaf with the rice was handed to Pak Edi. I was told that eating the remains of the rice is a symbol that the father will die before the child. Yet my impression was that giving the father rice that his mother had brought to the ceremony drew an analogy between father and child and made the child part of the paternal family.

Eggi's father, Pak Edi, is given the rice that has been blessed for Eggi to eat after Eggi has her first taste of rice, 1987.

The emotion that the infant's paternal grandmother and other bako relatives showed in the other birth ceremonies I attended demonstrated the strong ties men and women feel for the offspring of their sons.

Naming Eggi

After the first-feeding ceremony finished with a lengthy prayer delivered by Dt. Nunang, the naming ceremony got started. We all took up our pens and put our choices on a little piece of paper for Wik and Ibu Idar to consider. A lengthy discussion ensued. The names came from around the world. Eggi's aunt, Os, suggested Sri Bulan, a Hindu name, which Wik liked but Ibu Wel didn't. Dt. Nunang gave two Arabic names, Na'jzul Sinin and Na'jzul Muhsinin. I suggested the name Linda, which Eggi's older brother, Adis, liked. I chose this name because it is the name of my niece and many people in Belubus have a similar name (Lina). Other names chosen were Mariana, Julie (chosen by my son, Eric, in honor of his sister, Julie), Zulhijah, Gusniarti, Salma (chosen by En because he had a younger sister with this name who had died), and Luu'd

Erna Sari (chosen by Ibu Ida's husband). Another name that Wik considered was Sri Bungo, for flower.

Until Eggi was finally named, sometime after I left Belubus, she was called *gadis*, which means "young girl." Upon my return to the village, Wik and Ibu Idar didn't tell me her name right away. When I asked, they told me somewhat sheepishly, fearing perhaps that I would take offense. To me it was the greatest honor I could receive as an anthropologist, and I told them so.

Plurality and Harmony in the Birth Ceremony

What struck me most about the birth ceremonies I observed over the years was the repetitive quality of the acts and the plurality of the meanings they manifested. It is obvious that birth is a time for constructing a mold into which the child must fit. Food presses the child into this mold. The mashed banana mixed with rice introduces the child to one of the most enduring pairs in Minangkabau food symbology. Banana and rice eaten together symbolize the all-around Minangkabau practice of "sticking together." The banana is the symbol of male fertility, the rice of the nurturing mother.

The separation of the grains of rice into the magical number seven introduces Sonan Sari into the child's palate. The calling of the spirit of Sonan Sari into the modern birth ceremony connects past with present in a very special way. In ancient rice rituals believed to have been imported from India, Sonan Sari Padi Aku is the name for the soul of rice or for the rice goddess who stands in the middle of the rice field and ensures that the harvest will be bountiful and safe from pests and pestilence.[1]

The other foods of the first-feeding ceremony evoke different themes. The egg, symbol of bernazar, conveys the importance of propitiating and honoring the ancestors. The juice of the young coconut is not just reminiscent of the importance of cultivating coconuts but makes a statement about Minangkabau character. Like all else in human life, character should be carefully wrapped in adat, just as the milk of the coconut is wrapped by the meat and husk of the coconut. The banana leaf on which the rice is placed, and from which the father eats, is taken from the *pisang batu*, the "king of the banana," a symbol par excellence of male fertility. The red pepper is also characteristic. It's hot taste is always cooled by the bland but (to the Minangkabau) always beautiful taste of rice. Finally, gold is rubbed on the lips to make the child aware of all that speech means to the Minangkabau.

Thinking back on Eggi's developing character as I watched her inter-acting with her mother and with me from year to year, developing from infant, to child, girl, and young adolescent, I realized how the birth cere-mony provides a model of and for proper behavior. Children do not nat-urally fit into this model, but everyone works on encouraging them to do so. Eggi's temperament sometimes showed the virtues of golden speech and other times not. I saw this tension in her personality increase with the growing consumerism that better times brought to village life in the 1990s.

Thinking about the multivalent meanings of the birth ceremony, I was often struck by the seeming contradiction between appeasing the spirits of the well and going to the mosque to pray; speaking to leaves and co-conuts while praying to Allah; imbibing hot and cold simultaneously; meshing the foreign with the local. People saw no contradiction in these practices. Before Dt. Nunang sent his soul out of his body to bring back the souls of others, he recited Koranic prayers along with old Minang-kabau prayers. Even Syekh Muda, known far and wide as a holy man, mixed the ancestral with the religious.

As I watched Minangkabau men and women move seamlessly in and out of what others might see as the contradictory realms of adat, reli-gion, and ilmu gaib, I understood that for them there was no paradox. If there was a conflict, it existed only for the outsider, not for those who from childhood had been wrapped in a bricolage of meanings handed down from one generation to the next, in which harmony and balance ruled life. As Ibu Idar told me, "These are the ways of the ancestors."

The love of meshing past and present, royal and ancestral, religious and animist, foreign and local is part of the ethos of accommodation and symmetry that defines the Minangkabau soul. Accommodation and sym-metry are also at the core of Minangkabau social organization. It is evi-dent in the exchanges through which affinally related women celebrate children born to couples they have united in marriage. Harmony and balance are achieved through incorporating all interested parties, so that everyone plays an important role in a child's upbringing. From the mo-ment of conception, nothing is left to chance. Harmony has to be worked on constantly, it does not come naturally.

Adat requires people to take the good from nature and throw away the bad. Just as people construct the lessons of culture by observing growth in nature, as Ibu Idar said, they also learn by observing the processes of decay. She had a similar explanation for why gold must be rubbed on the mouth of the infant. The gold helps the growing child and young adult to select good rather than bad words. The same reason was given by Dt. Nunang for why one must select the foods for the first feeding ceremony so carefully. Like finding the right words, it is necessary to find those objects of nature for which there is a special fit *(cocok)* with the intention of adat.

The importance of the bako, the paternal relatives, in the birth ceremony can be understood in this light. Their love and care for the child of their son is part of the good of nature, so it is celebrated ceremonially. While the matrilineal system ensures that mother and female children are never in want of land, the bako system ensures that children are supported by a network outside the matrilineal clan. As much as they depend on the women of their matriclan, children rely also on the women of their father's matriclan. Maternal love is not limited to those of the matrilineal descent group; it extends to the children of males. The fruit that grows from the joining of two clans must be nurtured by the women of both. This attitude makes mothering as important as descent from a common ancestress. The heart of adat matriarchaat, one can conclude, lies not only in matrilineal descent as a means to protect children but also in the extension and sharing of mothering across clans.

CHAPTER SEVEN

Exchanging Husbands and Bananas

Ibu Idar had an interesting explanation for the key role bako relatives play in all ceremonies. "The relationship with bako is extremely tight," she said. The ceremonial respect paid these relatives ensures that the traits of the bako pass on to the newborn. Her rationale for this statement was based on the observation that a child comes from sexual union and from "God." "One-half of the child is formed by the mother, the other half by the father," she pointed out. "Adat ceremonies recognize this dual source of the child by uniting the two families for the sake of the child."

Field notes, 1987

Ten years after Eggi was born, Ibu Ida, Wik's sister, gave birth to a baby girl just before I arrived in the village. Ibu Ida was the oldest of Ibu Wel's children, already past forty when the baby was born. She had three children, two boys and a girl ranging in age from eleven to twenty-one.

The birth ceremony she planned was definitely a big adat affair. Her husband, Dt. Kosek, was a member of one of the oldest clans in the village, which meant that many people had to be invited in keeping with the family's adat status in the village. In addition, Ibu Ida was a teacher at the local school, which added to the public scrutiny of the event to be staged.

These considerations affected the choice of the day. When the new baby was about fifteen days old, I heard Wik question her older sister about the date for the ceremony. "Uni," Wik said, using the term of address for an older sibling, "have you recovered from the birth? What about the ceremony? Are you ready?"

"Later, Wik," Ibu Ida responded, calling Wik by her name, as is the custom between older and younger siblings. "In a month. We want to invite all the teachers from the school," she explained, expressing her own wishes but using the usual *we* instead of *I*.

Wik had broached the subject of the ceremony during the school holiday. Ibu Ida was saying that they could hold the ceremony anytime after July 21, the first day of school after the summer vacation. She suggested Friday, July 25, because on Fridays the men come home from their fields at noon for Friday prayer. A Friday date would also make it easier to enlist the services of Dt. Nunag to lead the prayer for the ceremony. He would surely be available on a Friday, Ibu Ida said.

But Wik thought that particular Friday was not a good day. She had consulted Syekh Muda's astrological schedule for the timing of ceremonies and found that July 25 was a day of *banyak kicuh mengicuh*, much deceit and swindling. If the ceremony was held then, items in the house might be lost, people's jewelry stolen, and so forth. The date that fit all the criteria, including its being a school day so that the teachers could attend, turned out to be July 22, a Tuesday, which would be *sempurna kerja apa saja*, a perfect day to accomplish any intention. This date was then discussed with the rest of the family, including the baby's father, Dt. Kosek.

The next step was to invite the guests. The first to be invited are the bako. Especially important are the *induo bako* or *bako kontan*, who are the father's immediate maternal relatives: his grandmother, mother, female siblings and cousins.

The Role of Bako

I wasn't prepared for the importance of the paternal side in this strongly matrilineal society anymore than I was prepared for the role that the spirits played among a people who pride themselves on their devotion to Islam. With hindsight one might say that it is wholly consistent with the Minangkabau ethos of balance and accommodation for the father's close maternal relatives to play a dominant role in a child's life at birth, marriage, and death. But serendipity, not logic, led me to this conclusion. What struck me the most was the discovery that bako women play a major role in a child's life, especially with respect to adat. From birth to death it is the responsibility of bako to provide the child with whatever he or she needs to follow adat. The batik cloth that wraps the newborn for the birth ceremony, the clothes that bride and groom wear for their wedding, and the white cloth that wraps the corpse for burial—all are supplied by bako. The connection to bako is so close that they can ask to have the corpse buried on their ancestral land (but this request can be refused by the maternal relatives if they choose to bury their dead).

Bako kontan—the paternal grandmother, aunts, and female cousins—are the first to arrive at a ceremony and often the last to leave. In the large adat ceremonies they walk together in a stately manner to the ceremony, colorfully attired in the latest fashion. They carry the symbols of adat, bring adat foods, and go home with adat gifts given them by the women of the child's clan.

I heard a number of explanations for the importance of bako. A mother who gives her son in marriage to another clan wants to remain on good terms. Together with his sisters, sons will oversee the disbursement of usage rights in clan land. A mother never forgets that her son has two roles: father to his children and brother to his sisters. The best way to ensure a balance in these competing roles is through the ceremonial institution of respect and the recognition of mutual obligation between intermarrying clans.

As for the mother of the newborn, she is encouraged to treat the father of her child like a king, especially if he is a good husband and provider. She extends this courtesy to her husband's maternal kin because she knows that they will lobby on her behalf if she treats him well. If nature and inalienable land rights provide the glue that binds maternal relatives, the paternal element adheres because of ceremonial customs.

The ceremony gives public recognition to the lifelong commitment of the paternal side to the child's interest. This commitment is partly due to the long-standing marital bonds tying members of husband-giving and husband-receiving clans.[1] Having been tied by marriage once, the two clans will be tied again. A good relationship is part of a tradition that unites intermarrying clans in which the flow of grooms continues through the generations.[2] A good connection between the clans is also considered necessary for the child's welfare. As a male adat expert told me, "Ceremonies maintain a good connection between families united by marriage; if something happens to the father or the mother, the child is never forgotten."

The invitation for a big adat ceremony follows fixed rules. Women invite women, men invite men. In addition to the all-important bako relatives, neighbors and friends are invited, usually by word of mouth (in the case of a marriage ceremony, printed invitations may be distributed). Relatives living in other locations are also informed. For example, Wik made a special trip to invite the wife of the grandson of a *mamak* (maternal uncle) living in another village. She called this grandson an *anak*

Woman bringing bananas for a birth ceremony, 1997

pisang (child of the banana), as he is a descendant of a male lineage member, in this case a mamak (or penghulu). Since she is bako with respect to this grandson, the relationship is called *bako anak pisang*. Close relationships with anak pisang are always maintained because they are ideal marriage partners, no matter how far removed.

Usually, the close mamak of the family, such as Dt. Llano, informs the rest of the mamak in the suku. Since Dt. Llano was living in eastern Sumatra, Dt. Kosek, the baby's father, informed Dt. Llano's assistant, a man with the title of *gindo*, who then informed the remaining *ninik mamak* (penghulu or senior males in the maternal family) including Dt. Penghulu Besar, the head penghulu *(penghulu pucuk)* of Kotyanir, the clan of Eggi's maternal relatives. It was Dt. Kosek's job also to invite all other males, including those in his own clan.

Preparation for Food Exchanges

Preparation for a ceremony begins days, maybe weeks, before the event. About a week before the ceremony the group of women who will work together during the preparations—women from the sponsoring clan, their friends, wives of their close male relatives *(binih mamak* and *suman-*

dan), and the child's father's close maternal relatives *(bako kontan)*—go out in small groups looking for bananas. They stop at houses, ask for bananas (or for permission to cut them) and carry back large clumps of the unripe fruit on their heads, talking loudly among themselves and calling out to other women as they pass their houses.

The air is festive; preparing for a pesta is obviously a time for fun. Throughout the preparations much laughter, talking, and joking comes from the house where the festivities will take place. The same sounds of pleasure and comradery can be heard from the men and women who gather in the rice fields to plant or harvest. Working together *(gotong royang)* and the demands of adat oil the machinery of social relations and make life less contentious.

After the bananas have arrived, women congregate to make *nasi lomak*, otherwise known as *silomak* or *nasi enak* (delicious or sticky rice). Sticky rice and bananas, the staples of all adat ceremonies in Belubus, are given to all women guests in exchange for the rice and sweets they usually bring.

The amount and quality of the items given and received depend on the closeness of the relationship. The father's close maternal relatives *(bako kontan)*, the wife of the family's penghulu *(binih mamak)*, and the wives of brothers and cousins *(sumandan)* bring elaborately decorated round cakes and large amounts of *beras* (hulled rice). They carry these offerings atop their heads either on a dulang tuo or in a *katidiang jombak* (ceremonial basket). The dulang tuo, antique brass trays handed down in the maternal line, are as sacred to the family as the family's kris, the dagger that marks the penghulu title. The katidiang jombak are less revered, but still important as a sign of adat.

Adat is stronger *(lebih barat)* for these relatives. When they leave the ceremony they are given more silomak and a large clump of *pisang batu* (banana of the stone), a sign of respect because pisang batu are more valued than other types of bananas. These relatives also take home at least one of the round cakes they bring, which extends the celebration back to their households.

For one week the women prepare—painting and/or cleaning the house, gathering bananas, cooking silomak, and the night before the ceremony cooking goat curry for as many as two hundred guests, if not more. Males play a role at the preparatory stage as well. It is the job of the maternal male relatives along with in-married husbands to paint the house, if needed, build a platform for the entertainment, slaughter the animals that will provide the meat, and perhaps set up a tent.

Part of the work of the father and the mother of the newborn is the sacrifice of at least one goat in a religious rite known as *kekah anak*, thanking Allah for giving the family a child. The sacrifice takes place without fanfare behind the house. An Islamic official known as a bilal or muezzin comes to the house and slaughters the goat by cutting its throat while intoning a prayer that the purpose is to kekah anak. If the baby has a name, it is written on a piece of paper and put inside of the cut throat while the animal dies. If the baby has no name, the name of the child's mother is written instead. This practice is understood as substituting the goat for the sacrifice of the child demanded by Allah.

According to the Islamic official, at birth a baby properly belongs to Nabi Mohammed, not its birth mother. The goat is slaughtered so as to provide a substitute child so that the birth mother can redeem her infant. The sacrifice also ensures that if the baby dies it will join its parents in heaven. Otherwise the parents and the child can see one another only as through a mirror; they cannot communicate with one another. One woman told me that once parents have made the goat sacrifice and paid Nabi Mohammed, they can meet their child in heaven face to face.

After the goat is slaughtered and offered to Nabi Mohammed, it is then butchered, and women spend the night cooking goat curry for the birth ceremony the next day. Goat curry follows a set recipe in all ceremonies. Large caldrons of goat meat, coconut milk, bamboo shoots (*pucuak rabuang*), and spices are cooked until early morning hours. The bamboo shoot is a well-known motif in Minangkabau weaving and carving, represented as the tip of a triangle and used as a border separating bands of motifs. The motif refers to the bamboo spikes villages once used as protective devices against enemies or to signify village borders.

Choosing the Proper Outfit

Before the ceremony women buy or have made an outfit for the occasion. I decided to do likewise and gathered En and Serge for a trip to Bukik Tinggi, the center of fashion in West Sumatra, to look for *baju kurung* (loose-fitting blouse and long skirt) fit for a grand adat occasion. When we returned, Wik asked me indirectly, according to the Minangkabau way, whether the trip had been a success. After Ibu Idar's death we had become very close. She had nurtured us with wonderful Minangkabau meals for lunch and dinner. I was always impressed by the quality and variety of the food she put on the table. Serge loved her cooking and exclaimed so at every meal, much to Wik's delight.

"Are your clothes ready for the ceremony?" she asked me that night as she sat near us while we ate. This was her time for visiting. She never joined us at the table, no matter how many times we asked her to do so. This common custom of Minangkabau hostesses is very much in evidence during ceremonial feasting. They prefer to serve rather than join the guest.

"Yes," I answered. "It took us four hours to find the right size in the market in Bukik Tinggi," I said. "By that time, Pak Serge and Endri were completed exhausted." I hung my shoulders, slumped at the waist, and exhaled to suggest how much the project of finding a suitable outfit for the birth ceremony had tired us. She laughed.

Her delight with the selection was evident. We had chosen a green-and-white print—the green of seedlings in the rice nursery.

"The color looks great against your white skin," Wik said. I remembered how my white skin had frightened her when we first met. Indeed there was a time in Belubus when many people kept their distance because of my color. Sometimes children would cry when their parents jokingly told them that I would carry them off to America.

The outfit I had chosen was definitely 1997 style, quite different from what women wore in 1987. Back then it would have been easy to find a suitable outfit for my tall frame. Sarongs and baju kurung were made so as to fit just about anyone. You wrapped a length of cloth (usually batik) around your waist and held it in place with a corset. Then you added a loose-fitting top with long sleeves and draped a *salendang* (long sash) over one shoulder.

By 1997 styles had become more personalized. Women still wore long sleeves and skirts down to their ankles, but they experimented with colors, materials, and cuts. Instead of wrapping cloth for the skirt, women selected colorful prints and had the seamstress make a fitted skirt with a matching top. Few wore the traditional salendang. In its place many wore a small hat hiding their hair, a style acquired from the restrictions imposed by Islam to encourage female modesty. Over this hat, which in the hot sun was like a small oven, a matching scarf was often added.

I found this bow to Islamic fundamentalism in women's dress paradoxical, given the increasing freedom of movement granted young women and the growing sexualization of the female on Indonesian TV, especially in the soaps and advertisements. However, even though I am not *orang agama Islam* (a person of the Islamic religion), I bowed to the current style by wearing a small white cap to cover my hair and a white embroidered veil to cover the cap. I knew I had succeeded with this outfit when I so blended in with the guests that Ibu Wel didn't recognize me at first. When she did, a smile lit up her face as she raised her thumb in a sign of approval. For a moment, I understood what it must feel like to be Bundo Kanduang for a day.

It gave the people of Belubus great pleasure to see me dressed like other women. For me this was a bit of a chore because it is quite difficult to sit on the floor during a ceremony in the tightly fitting clothes of a properly dressed woman, especially on a hot day. Sitting for long the way women do, with legs to one side (mine always became numb after about an hour), made it difficult to get the photographic record on which I relied for later interviewing. Nevertheless, for important family ceremonies I made the effort.

The Ceremony

On the morning of July 22, after working for nearly a week preparing for the expected two hundred guests, Ibu Ida and the women of Eggi's family were ready to receive the baby's bako relatives. I posted Eggi outside Ibu Idar's house down the road to watch for the gathering of the bako, whose arrival would begin the first bath and feeding ceremonies.

Presently groups of bako could be seen proceeding along the main road toward the house where the ceremony would be held. When Eggi alerted me that they were gathering, I dashed outside, clad in my new green and white outfit, to photograph their arrival. They were a colorful sight in their chartreuse, bright pink, red, green, and yellow outfits. With their heads covered by the then fashionable lace hats and salendang shawls of matching colors, they shone like a rainbow against the dull greens of the palms and banana trees. Somewhat oppressed by the midday heat, I marveled at their spirited talking as they made their way to the house where the mother of the newborn awaited them along with members of her clan.

One woman stood out at the center of the group. Clad in brilliant yellow-green, the color of newly sprouted seedlings in the rice nursery, she balanced on her head the antique bronze ancestral tray, the dulang tuo. All eyes were riveted on her as she walked slowly down the road toward the house. Other women joined her along the way, falling in behind with their offerings in the ceremonial katidiang jombak on their heads or hand-carried in stacked plates wrapped in white cloth.

The woman at the center was the baby's paternal grandmother. Ibu Lina (not her real name) was flanked by her daughters and other members of her clan.[3] She would be queen for the day, the other women her courtiers. They had all worked hard for the occasion cooking and preparing the foods for the first bath and the first feeding. This was an espe-

Paternal grandmother brings the items for her grandchild's first feeding, 1996. She is at center of the procession of *bako* women on their way to a birth ceremony.

cially proud day for Ibu Lina. Like Indo Jelito and Bundo Kanduang, whose devotion to their sons is reflected in the master narratives of the Minangkabau mythic past, a mother's raison d'être lies not just in working for her daughters to ensure them a secure economic base but also in preparing her son for his life's work. She devotes many years to him, bearing and raising him, teaching him adat ways so that he will be in demand as a groom, negotiating his marriage, preparing for his wedding, and now celebrating the fruit of the womb he has fertilized.

My eyes went naturally to the contents of the dulang tuo. I could just barely see them as I reached on tiptoe to see above Ibu Lina's head. She was unusually tall by Belubus standards. The contents formed a panoply of tropical colors bright against the beautifully embroidered white lace: the light green of the young coconut, the bright yellow of a clump of bananas, the yellow-white of popped rice, the bright red of several sprigs of lado pepper, the dark green of a large banana leaf, red blossoms, the pale green of sliced sugar palm, the earth colors of a folded batik cloth, and the golden glitter of a ring wrapped in white cloth.

Arrival

As the women continued their parade, other women came outside to observe or to join the procession. When the procession arrived at Ibu Ida's house, a few women came outside to greet the bako women. I noticed that most of them were sumandan (wives of male lineage members). One took the dulang tuo with its items from Ibu Lina and carried it into the house. The katidiang jombak baskets and piles of wrapped plates were taken to a specially arranged spot just beside the house and placed by two seated women. Neatly stacked around these women were many piles of bananas of all kinds along with hundreds of small packages of silomak wrapped in banana leafs.

The two women receiving the baskets were specialists in the knowledge of what to take from the containers and what to give in return. Confronted with the array of these containers, they asked only the name of the person to whom the container belonged as they began to perform the exchange dictated by the saying "Adat is filled with contents, the custom is fulfilled." They emptied the contents of each basket brought by the bako women ("adat is filled with contents") and substituted packets of silomak and clumps of bananas for them to take home ("the custom is fulfilled"). These acts of emptying and filling the women's baskets are said to satisfy the intention of adat.

The clumps of bananas that refilled the emptied baskets were the fine-looking pisang batu reserved for bako kontan and sumandan. The baskets had come filled with three cakes, two of which were removed. These cakes would be added to the display of food arranged on the ceremonial dining table on the floor of the main room. One cake was left in the basket for the woman who brought it to enjoy at home along with the pisang batu and silomak that was put into the basket.

Later other women would arrive—neighbors, friends, and distant maternal relatives—carrying hulled rice and cakes in plates wrapped in white cloth or brought in baskets. When these containers were taken from them, other kinds of bananas were substituted along with packets of silomak, usually in smaller quantities.

First Bath and Feeding

The first bath ceremony went swiftly. No bath was given, and the contents of the tray meant for the spirits of the nearby bathing place were quickly gobbled up by the children. The bathing place was near Umi's house and had been her only water source during her lifetime. In 1985, Ibu Ida had built a house nearby (paralleling Mt. Merapi, like Umi's house). Ibu Ida used Umi's bathing place for many years until she had the funds to dig a well near her new house. On this particular day, it seemed as if the spirits of the bathing place, about which I heard a great deal over the years, were for the moment forgotten.

We all then gathered for the first-feeding ceremony. There was a momentary halt in the proceedings as much discussion ensued as to who would hold the infant. I heard loud voices and one woman crying with intense emotion. Finally, all this subsided and this woman came forth to take her seat by Dt. Nunang for the feeding ceremony. I learned later that this was Dt. Kosek's sister, and the fuss had been over her wish to hold the baby as a way of healing a dispute that had frayed her relations with her brother's household. Everyone seemed happy, and the ensuing events resembled those that took place ten years before at Eggi's first feeding. The husbands of the women in the family gathered around the infant and Dt. Kosek was given the banana leaf with the rice the infant had eaten from.

The naming was also the same. Each of us wrote names on a slip of paper and handed them to Ibu Ida. There was a hush as Dt. Nunang looked at each suggestion. We all waited expectantly, hoping that our choice would be selected, but it turned out that Ibu Ida and her husband, Dt. Kosek, had agreed on a name beforehand. They chose Siti Halimah, the name of one of the wives of Mohammed. Dt. Nunang liked the name but said it would be better just to call her Halimah; Siti Halimah was too long.

After this discussion everyone ate. The room was filled with female as well as male bako relatives, the honored guests. We all sat on the floor on mats, filling the main sitting room of the house. As always, I tried to find a place where I could lean against the wall. The food was placed in the middle in many little plates. The main course was *kambing gulai* (goat curry) from the goat that had been slaughtered for the sacrifice.

After this round of guests had eaten, the festivities continued as new guests came to take their places on the mat. All day and into the night groups of finely dressed, beautiful women of all ages entered the house with their offerings, sat down to eat, and then went outside to retrieve the containers they had brought, which had been filled with bananas and silomak to replace their beras and cakes. As they left the house, each woman stopped to speak briefly to the mother, handing her an envelope with a gift of money. Usually when the mother counts up the amount the next day, she finds that she has been given just enough to cover the cost of the ceremony. The festivities often go on until about 11:00 P.M. or midnight. In this case they ended at 4:30 A.M. because Ibu Ida had chosen to bring in entertainment, two women singers and a man who played the *saluang* (a bamboo flute).[4] Nighttime is when most of the men come, usually in pairs or small groups.

After the party was over the family wrote down the names of all the people who gave money or gifts, recording the amount given by each. This was done so that when the gift giver holds a pesta the family knows how much to give in return. People always try to give the same amount, or preferably more. This practice, I was told, is also "adat awak" (our adat).

The Amulets

After its first-feeding and naming ceremony the baby is ready to go out into the world. To do so it must be made strong against the various ghosts and bad spirits that roam the land or come up from the springs. Not all of these spirits are indigenous to Belubus. Some come from other villages. This is true of the palasik, the bodiless heads that drink the blood of children, all of whom come from one particular village. On the outside the palasik look like anyone else, but they are actually bloodsucking vampires who prey on children. Parents say that the symptoms of palasik illness are a big stomach, thinness, watery eyes, diarrhea, and a sinking fontanelle.

A *tangka palasik* is an amulet worn by mother and child to ward off these creatures. Today many mothers don't bother with amulets, unless the child gets sick. Ibu Ida, for example, said that she doesn't believe in them anymore. But she added that if her baby got sick she would go to the *dukun tangka palasik*, a specialist in these amulets.

The best-known dukun in Belubus for tangka was Pak Yauni. He got his knowledge from his mother and grandmother. After he died in 1996 his daughter, who had studied with him, took his place. Pak Yauni told me that wearing an amulet protects the child and the mother against many spirits. He mentioned *jin kafir*, listing *iblis* (devils), *satan*, *hantu* (ghosts), and palasik as examples. Traditionally, the mother begins wearing the amulet while she is pregnant to guard against ghosts who cause bruises on pregnant woman.

The amulet is a little packet of various items wrapped in a black cloth and sewn with a red thread. The amulet is dangled from a *banang pincono*, a necklace woven of wool of three, five, or seven colors (it is very important that this number be odd), usually white, yellow, red, black, and blue. The necklace is likened to a broom, which is stronger if it has many branches.

The amulet is thought of as a *pagaran* (fence) *tangka* (preventive), which I interpreted to mean putting up a fence against evil spirits. Inside it are several ingredients, each with a different function. A bit of black and red cloth is to guard against *jumalang*, a spirit that has the features of an animal. *Inggu*, a plant with a bad smell, chases iblis. Black peppercorns *(lado kaciak)* are included because the smell wards off ghosts. In addition one includes a piece of white onion *(dasun tungga)*, and *jarianggau*, which looks like a wild onion and has a good smell. *Pinang kuai*, the areca nut, is specifically for palasik. These ingredients are essential if the amulet is to work.

Pak Yauni is also a specialist in giving the baby its first bath at the family spring. He told me that when he takes the baby to the spring he puts the *banang pincono* in the bucket for washing the baby, which gives tangka (preventive) to the water. Later he ties the string *(banang pincono)* around the baby's wrists, waist, and ankles. The rest of the string is used to tie the amulet packet around the baby's neck. The string and amulet cloak the newborn in a panoply of white magic, which wards off the emanations of evil ever present in the hidden world of the gaib. Secure in this armor, the newborn can grow to strength, just as the proverb "Growth in nature is our teacher" promises. Once the child is able to walk and talk the amulets disappear.

Adat Limbago of Ceremonies

Observing Ibu Ida's birth ceremony and several others helped me to understand the meaning of the enigmatic proverb "Adat diisi, limbago di tuang" (adat is filled by the contents, the custom is fulfilled). In addition to fulfilling the intention of adat in the first feeding, this proverb calls for making the proper payments in exchanges that take place during a big adat ceremony.

Explaining this proverb to me, one of my adat teachers in Belubus, Dt. Ampek, said, "When women come to a ceremony in the adat manner, they bring certain foods and in return receive sticky rice and bananas. And so the custom is fulfilled." He didn't tell me much more, nor did anyone else. "All adat ceremonies are ruled by the desire to meet the requirement of contents and filling," he repeated over and over. This was the most I could get from him about the connection between the proverb and behavior.

Dt. Ampek was one of the foremost adat leaders in the village in 1997. He had inherited his title from Dt. Paduko Sati, whom I interviewed before he died in 1987. These two men were fonts of wisdom and knowledge about the male realm of adat, always answering my questions with long disquisitions on proverbs, maxims, and sayings.

The literal meaning of the proverb which so intrigued me is easy to understand: women supply the necessary items for the ceremonial rituals (the contents). Although some of the contents of the rituals change depending on the ceremony (like the items for the first bath and feeding), others always remain the same. These are the staple items of adat ceremonies. The special adat items are brought on the ancestral tray, the staple items common to all ceremonies are brought in baskets or hand-held dishes. Upon arriving at the ceremony, the hostesses take the trays and the baskets brought by the guests. All guests go home with their trays and baskets filled so that no one leaves empty handed. The phrase *adat diisi, limbago di tuang* thus literally means bringing, emptying, and filling up the baskets with adat contents.

However, there is more to the story. On another occasion, Dt. Ampek commented: "Bundo Kanduang meisi adat" (Bundo Kanduang fills the contents of adat). By this he meant that in the big adat ceremonies the mark of Bundo Kanduang must be present. This mark is seen in the ceremonial dress with the buffalo-horn headdress worn by a mature woman in some cases and a young girl in others. The verb *meisi* in this statement is active, whereas *diisi* is passive (it means filled by something or someone). As exemplars of Bundo Kanduang, senior women are responsible for filling adat. They do so by exchanging set items, thereby embodying adat just as the legendary Bundo Kanduang did in *Kaba Cindur Mata*.

Exchange is crucial to the semantic relationship between filling and contents. There is an analogy between women's exchanges and the adat speeches of the titled male leaders that are given at all ceremonies. Sitting on opposite sides of the room, men from the sponsoring clan fill the ears of men from the guest clans with the appropriate speeches. Once the tongue of the speaker is emptied of words and the ears of the man to whom he speaks have been filled; this man speaks in return. This formalistic exchange, in which one empties proverbs from one's repertory and fills the ears of those present until all the appropriate words are spoken and heard, marks the male portion of the ceremonies.

Women's ceremonies fill adat by circulating adat foods (the contents) in a living tapestry of prescribed social relationships. Without ceremonies to fill adat, adat is an empty vessel. Seen in this way, the ceremonial expression of adat can be likened to totemic rituals drawing people together in common cause. My point here is to suggest that rituals filled with adat provide people with a sense of connection—a flag around which to rally in recognition of community. In this case community is created by following the ways of the ancestors signified by ancient meanings attached to particular foods. These are not just any foods but ones that celebrate common identity. Just as the mark of Bundo Kanduang is present in all ceremonies, so is the mark of the past in the foods prepared for exchange, especially the bananas and sticky rice.

The Flow of Husbands and Bananas

When bananas and sticky rice are given as a pair to all departing guests, not every guest is given the same kind of banana. The most special of all bananas, known as the "king of bananas" or pisang batu (banana of the stone), is given to the women who have taken a husband from the hostess clan (husband takers) and to women who have given a husband to the hostess clan (husband givers). Everyone else is given smaller clumps of other kinds of bananas such as *pisang gadang* or *pisang manis* (big banana or sweet banana). Why, I ask, give pisang batu as a special sign of respect to the wives of male lineage members and to the maternal relatives of the father?

There are several answers. First, it should be noted that in the banana hierarchy, pisang batu stands alone at the top. This banana is the fruit of the largest, most beautiful and sturdiest of banana trees. This tree grows under any conditions, unlike the more domesticated banana trees. The fruit itself is highly valued because it can be cooked in many ways—steamed, boiled, fried—as well as eaten raw. It is, you might say, the all-around Minangkabau banana. Giving clumps of the most revered banana greases marital links, always fraught with tension and ambivalence.

As I related earlier, giving pisang batu to someone is a sign that adat is *lebih barat* (heavier): more adat rules must be followed. Thus pisang batu is given to bako and sumandan (women who are husband givers and takers) because these relatives are the ones for whom adat is strictest. By coming laden with adat foods, bako relatives show respect to the members of the clan of their anak pisang (children of the banana, meaning children of male relatives). The respect is reciprocated by filling up the trays and baskets of the bako relatives with large clumps of pisang batu and silomak to take home when they leave the ceremony.

Women emptying and refilling baskets of food and cakes brought by women guests to a birth ceremony, 1997

There is another dimension of pisang batu that must be considered. This is its allusions to male fertility. Showing respect to husband givers and takers with icons of male fertility says something about the exchange of men in Minangkabau culture and about female control of male fertility.

When a husband moves into his wife's house, his maternal relatives bring symbols of his insemination in the form of sprouted coconut leaves and rice seedlings to be planted in his wife's land. The husband himself symbolizes fertility, for he is equated with the rooster that is brought to live in the chicken coop symbolic of the home of the bride. The meaning of these associations is clear. Husbands fertilize; women sit on the eggs to produce the children in the chicken coop.

Women from a clan that either gives a groom to or receives a groom from the women of the hostess clan are honored by being given the gift of pisang batu. The exchange is reciprocal, because of the special foods the husband givers bring and the prominent role the husband takers play in the ceremony. This giving and taking of a banana representing male fertility between women who give or take husbands suggests that women are the ones who manage the circulation of symbolic and real male fertility.

Maternal Webs of Social and Symbolic Significance

The big adat birth ceremony wraps the newborn in webs of meaning that can be likened to the woven fabric of ceremonial cloth worn by women on adat occasions in some villages, or to the fishnet tied by the senior woman referred to as Bundo Kanduang in the proverb "She is the center where the threads of the fishnet meet." In their ceremonies women renew a way of being in the world as they knit a social fabric for their child. As they do so, they reknit and patch the fabric where it has been worn thin by dissent between spouses or arguments between members of their matrilineal clans.

What women accomplish in adat ceremonies is no less important to the political scene than the male arbitration of disputes in the adat council house. It does not stretch the imagination to suggest that these two arenas of village life are mutually reinforcing. If women neglected the ceremonies, the ever present pull to settle disputes outside the adat system—by turning to the national system of justice, including the police or the national courts—would be much stronger.

Through their ceremonies women rule without governing. They facilitate social bonding outside the machinations of political power by bringing members of different clans together in mutual aid and in exchanges predicated on adat rules. The bonds established by this interaction become especially important when disputes arise. Emotional ties and social cooperation, energized through women's ceremonies, facilitate the men's job of adjudicating disputes according to the rules of adat and consensus decision-making.

The exchanges linking the hostess clan with bako relatives demonstrate how the ethic of balance and accommodation works to incorporate paternal ties in this matrilineal society. Because paternal ties are always mediated by women, they never turn patriarchal. Patriarchy is out of the picture because the father does not hold authority over his children; his is always primarily an emotional relationship. Male authority is confined to the roles of penghulu or mamak, the titled male or the maternal uncle. Authority in the paternal line, to the degree that it exists, is wielded by the father's female relatives, not by the father himself.

This social tapestry, so intricate and symmetrical, balances male and female ties around the principles of fertility, nurture, caregiving, and oversight. The icon of male fertility is the banana that moves among women along the same paths as husbands move in the wedding ceremony; the icon of female fertility is the immobile chicken coop where the egg is incubated and comes forth as a child of the union. Male and female nurture finds expression in the love and care for the children of their maternal line. This nurture extends outward to the children born to male members of the matriline. Ibu Idar's comment that the child is made of two parts—father and mother—means that the father's side must have a chance to feed and bathe the child at birth, even if only symbolically in a ceremonial context.

Male and female oversight is exercised by both maternal and paternal relatives. Maternal uncles look after their nieces and nephews and with their sisters oversee use rights to land. Together, paternal and maternal relatives see to it that each stage of the life cycle conforms to adat. When courtship enters the picture, the watchfulness over the young woman intensifies. No one wants their daughter improperly treated by a young man. When a marriage is mentioned, four families come into the picture. These four families—the maternal and paternal relatives of the boy and girl—oversee the marriage as soon as it is first discretely and tentatively mentioned. The concluding marriage ceremony is among the grandest of all adat ceremonies.

CHAPTER EIGHT

Negotiating Marriage

Abdul's mamak opened the meeting with a rhetorical pantun: "Sia rindu, sia rinai; sia jalo, sia tajun," which means, literally, "Whoever feels most strongly must cast the net to catch the fish," in other words, the family that most wants the marriage must pay. The bride's family answered with the amount they were prepared to pay Abdul's family. Although no one ever said so directly, it was as if they were buying Abdul.

Field notes, 1998

T he marriage game is complex, involving considerable back and forth between relatives of the bride and groom. Although romantic love is often a prime consideration for young couples, it is not important to the adults who arrange the marriage. When romance enters the picture, adults tend to be more suspicious than not. If a young man shows any sign of being too interested in a girl by visiting her too often, her family suspects that he has the wrong intentions. Her maternal uncle is sure to speak to the girl's mother, echoing the mother's own fears and lending extra weight to a mother's desire to control the rebellious daughter who thinks she is in love.

"Why does this boy visit you so often?" her mamak may ask her mother. "Does he want marriage or is he only playing? If he is only playing, don't let him come so often. It is shameful for us if the people of the village see this."

Such comments come from the suspicion that romantic interest will result in sexual union. This fear stems from the assumption, based on long experience, that a boy will break up with the girl he has deflowered. Young girls are counseled from an early age not to give their virginity to a boyfriend. It is to be saved for their husbands, their mothers tell them. Theoretically, if on the wedding night a husband finds that his bride is not a virgin, he can reject her. No one in Belubus can remember a case in which a husband left his wife for this reason, however. If a boy gets a girl pregnant, the families see to it that they get married.

Most of the older women in Belubus were married at an early age, as young as twelve to fourteen. Many have been married three or more times. Generally, their first marriage was to a much older man, arranged by their mothers because of his wealth or status. Umi, Ibu Idar's mother, was sixteen when her mother, Rai'la, ordered her to marry the thirty-eight-year-old Syekh Muda.

Since Syekh Muda's father was of the same suku as Umi, the marriage also conformed to the ideal marriage in Belubus, known as *pulang ke bako* (coming home to the father's clan). By marrying Umi, Syekh Muda came home to bako. From the viewpoint of Umi's family, she came home to the child of her mamak *(pulang ke anak mamak)*, because Syekh Muda's father was Umi's mamak.

Umi divorced Syekh Muda when he was about seventy in order to marry a man more her own age, one she had picked. In those days, even though women were ordered to marry their first husbands they usually married the man of their choice later in life.

"The first husband pays off our debt to our mother," Ibu Wel told me. "We chose who we want after that." According to Ibu Wel, when a woman chooses a husband later in her life she is guided by a combination of factors: love, passion, fate, and help in making a living.

Ibu Wel was fourteen when Umi ordered her to marry her first husband, who was then thirty-five. Before the wedding she devised a plan to flee from home—often the outcome of a forced marriage. Ibu Idar traveled several days from where she was living in another province to help her sister run away. But Ibu Idar arrived too late, and Ibu Wel fell sobbing into her arms. The wedding ceremony had already taken place the night before and Ibu Wel was no longer a gadis, or maiden. Ibu Idar stayed for a week and then went home. By that time the two young women understood that they had to make the best of a bad situation.

Ibu Wel eventually divorced her first husband and remarried three times. When her fourth husband took off with a much younger woman, Ibu Wel flirted only momentarily with the idea of remarrying because she encountered adamant opposition from her daughters. Explaining her decision to me she recited the familiar proverb "Abu di atas tunggul"—a husband is like ashes on top of a burned stump of a tree, which blow away quickly with the wind. By this she meant that if her children did not treat her husband with respect he would feel compelled to leave.

Ibu Idar's one and only marriage ended tragically. This was an arranged marriage, which was also a love match. Ibu Idar was eighteen when she married, and her husband was twenty. Ibu Idar loved her husband deeply and they had a good life together, helped by his income as a member of the military. Her heart was broken when he took another wife, who lived near Belubus. For years, her husband kept this marriage a secret, explaining his absences as necessary for military duty. It wasn't until he had two children with this woman that Ibu Idar found out about the marriage. After that her life with her husband was never the same. Wik still remembers how angry Ibu Idar would be when her husband came home from the house of his second wife. He tried to make it up to her by building her a house and buying her a car. Later, he married a third time to a woman who was the age of Ibu Idar's daughter. Again, Ibu Idar's heart was broken. Finally, her husband died after an operation on his stomach in Padang. Some say it was the food his third wife fed him while he was recovering in the hospital that killed him. Others say that it was his passion *(nafsu)* for food and women that did him in. Ibu Idar devoted herself to her daughter and to adat affairs in the village and never remarried, despite many offers from worthy men, one of whom was related to her first husband and looked just like him.

Choosing, Finding, and Buying a Husband

Today, people say that young women would never agree to marrying someone older chosen by their mothers. Yet, my experience is that mothers play a dominant role in a daughter's decision to marry. Despite the considerable lip service paid today to girls' right to find their own husbands or even run away to get married, families including the bako relatives play an important role in the task of finding a husband.

Many considerations affect the final choice. Clan affiliation is one of the prime factors in choosing a mate, with some clans being more preferred than others. Nobody is allowed to marry within their own clan. In the case of Eggi's clan, Kotyanir, marriage is not allowed among the subclans.

Families look for a responsible, hardworking man with an income for their daughter. On the male side, families seek a household for their son that can sustain him and his offspring. The preferred marriage is still pulang ke bako. This kind of marriage (mother's brother's son to his father's sister's daughter) means that the child's grandparents will be of the same clan. Because such a marriage joins two clans with a history of mate exchange and family ties, the arrangement is called "keeping the fish in the same pond."

Girls today are just as likely to marry someone chosen for them as they are to find their own husband. If a daughter indicates that she and a boyfriend have talked about marriage, her family wants to know every-thing about the boy's family—his mother, his mamak, and his ancestors. They also want to know about their situation in life, their wealth. The family asks many questions about the boy's history. Does he have a girl-friend already? Is he married? Has he ever been married? What kind of job does he have? Even if the boy passes these tests, marriage does not necessarily result, because the girl may not be ready for marriage. For example, there may be an older unmarried sibling in the family. In such cases, the girl will be asked to wait. If the family doesn't move quickly to marry off the older sibling, the relationship can easily fall apart, for the couple will be discouraged from seeing too much of each other. Some-thing like this happened to Adek, Ibu Wel's youngest daughter.

Adek's Story

In 1998 at the age of twenty-one Adek got engaged and married in the space of a few months. In the preceding years there had been some ques-tion as to whether Adek would stay in Belubus or go to Padang to find work. Finally, it was decided that Adek would stay with her mother. Ibu Wel was getting on in years and not as able as she once was to take care of the family rice fields and garden. She needed help, which meant finding a husband for Adek, since her daughters were so adamant about Wel's not remarrying.

Adek had many boyfriends over the years, but she turned them all down until she met Siwir. The two met in Belubus when he came from another village to play in a local badminton competition. After that Siwir came frequently to see Adek on Saturday nights. Siwir was the first young man Adek thought of as a possible husband. True, there had been others she liked over the years, but she wasn't ready to settle down. Now she was.

She suggested to Siwir that they begin marriage negotiations. It is not unusual for the girl to raise the issue in private conversation. Publicly, of course, her making the first move would never be revealed. In this case Siwir agreed, but said that the best time for him would be in another six months when his flock of chickens would be ready for sale. Then he would have some money, he explained. Adek agreed and her mother made this proposal to a member of Siwir's family, who also agreed. Meanwhile, Ibu Wel's main consideration was first to marry off her one and only son. Because he was older than Adek, it was important that she accomplish this step lest she offend him.

After the decision to marry was discussed with Siwir's family informally, Adek waited expectantly to talk more with Siwir. But his visits began to taper off, and when he did come to the house he seemed unwilling to discuss the subject. Then a member of Siwir's family came to suggest that the marriage be postponed, which surprised Adek because she had heard nothing from Siwir. Too embarrassed to approach him directly, Adek effectively ended the relationship by seeing other young men.

While Adek and Siwir were seeing each other, Adek met Siwir's friend Mari. Mari was invited to accompany Adek's girlfriend, who often accompanied Adek to Siwir's house. But Mari was more interested in Adek. When the relationship with Siwir fell apart, Mari started coming alone to Adek's house on Saturday nights. There were many signs of his interest. He invited Adek to his house for Hari Raya Haji, an important religious holiday. Adek came bearing gifts of cake and in return Mari's mother gave her rendang, the famous Minangkabau curried beef. It was the first time Mari had brought a girl home, even though he was already thirty years old.

Adek was surprised when Mari's older sister unexpectedly asked the young couple, "What is the nature of your relationship?" Adek said nothing, because girls generally respond with silence when asked about their feelings for a boy. Mari answered by admitting his interest in Adek indirectly. "This is the one I would like to talk about now," he said.

Adek understood that Mari wanted to be more than just a friend, that he had a deeper interest in her. Mari's sister then told Adek that members of another family wanted to visit the house to talk about marriage with Mari, although he was not interested. She asked Adek directly, "What about your feelings?"

Once again Adek was silent, indicating that she, too, was serious. Had she not been interested, she would have said something like "I'm not ready for marriage."

In response, Mari's older sister spoke about him, telling Adek that he was a good worker, going every day to the rice field and garden.

"Do you like him?" she asked Adek.

Once again the answer was silence.

The next question was from Mari's mother: "What is your mother's name?"

Adek told her. "Oh, I know who she is," Mari's mother said approvingly.

Mari's mother brought out the cake Adek had brought and asked her to cut it. They ate the cake together and then Mari took Adek home. She was happy with the rendang that Mari's mother had given her, which she carried back in her cake dish.

Later, when Mari came to the house, Ibu Wel spoke to him rather directly. "Would you like to marry Adek at the time her brother gets married?" she asked. "We can hold a joint wedding," she suggested. This would have been ideal for Ibu Wel because it meant she could cut the expense of two weddings in half.

But Mari answered, "It's better that Buyong (Adek's brother) be married first," he said. "I need to wait until I have enough money."

Signs of Mari's interest did not abate. Two weeks later, he came to the house bringing ten kilograms of cucumbers, seven kilograms of string beans, and three kilograms of red peppers from his garden for the upcoming wedding feast of Adek's brother. Ibu Wel noted the difference between Mari and Siwir's expression of interest later, when Siwir came to the wedding bearing only a small gift of money.

After Buyong's wedding, Ibu Wel felt it was time to approach Mari once again. True, he had expressed interest in Adek, but so had Siwir. She wanted to pin him down. "What is your relationship to Adek?" she asked. "Are you a friend, or do you want to marry her?"

Mari answered saying that he didn't yet know. "Wait," he said. "Then we can plan."

Over the next month, when Ibu asked again and again, Mari responded in the same manner. The point of no return was approaching. It was either marriage or breaking off the relationship. Ibu decided to broach the matter with Mari's family. She did so discretely by speaking to distant relatives first.

"Please tell Mari's family that he comes often to our house to see Adek," she said. "According to our adat, it's not good to come often for so long. We are beginning to be uncertain as to his intentions, whether they are honorable."

Mari's family told him of Ibu's concern about his frequent visits to see Adek. "What is your wish?" they asked him. He answered that he was ready to embark on marriage negotiations, which would result in the formal engagement.

This information was conveyed to Ibu Wel by Mari's older sister. She came to see Ibu Wel for the confidential, informal marriage discussion known as *marisiak*. In this discussion a tentative agreement was reached on the wedding costs. Mari's family would contribute Rp 500,000 (about $50) while Ibu Wel would bear the remaining costs. As it turned out she spent more than Rp 4 million for everything, including the wedding feast, bedroom furniture, entertainment, and rental fee for Adek's clothing. In a separate meeting with Adek's bako, Adek's father's family agreed to pay half of the cost of renting clothes. Technically, the greater cost borne by Ibu Wel might be interpreted as Adek buying Mari; however, in this case the distribution of costs was based on the economic status of Mari's family.

The next step was to report the arrangements to Dt. Llano in Riau province where he lived. Ibu Wel paid him the obligatory visit of respect to bring him into the negotiations. Dt. Llano then passed the news along to the head of the suku and the other suku penghulu. A date was agreed upon for the all important *manakok hari*, when the two families would meet to formalize the engagement and decide the date of the wedding. In accordance with the custom, the family of the prospective groom came to the bride's house.

Fifteen members of Mari's family came, including his mamak. As usual, the women of the groom's family came with the appropriate adat foods. After eating, the negotiations were opened in the usual way with Mari's mamak asking: "Why have you asked us to come today?"

Adek's mamak answered that their purpose was to continue the wedding negotiation. "We want to find the best date and time according to adat and Islam."

Mari's mamak answered, "We agree with whatever date you suggest."

After a short discussion a date was agreed upon. The marriage would take place in two months. The engagement was formalized with the *timbang tando*: the groom's family gave a kris to the bride's family to hold until the wedding was completed, and the bride's family showed gold to the groom's family, signs that both sides were equally committed and neither would pull out. Mari's family then paid the *kobek tando* (token amount indicating agreement to the marriage), which was divided among the bride's mamak. Mari's mamak gave Rp 15,000 (about $1.50) to Adek's mamak, who divided it among the other mamak. This payment sealed the engagement.

Mari's family went home with silomak and pisang in place of the cakes they brought. Uncooked rice replaced the cooked rice they had brought for the meal. The wedding plans were sealed, the couple tied, and thereby the families. Backing out by either side would come at a high cost. Adek and her mother proceeded to prepare for the final ceremony.

Wedding Costs

Wedding costs, which can be quite substantial, are usually divided among the bride and groom. Normally the groom's family pays to furnish the bedroom in the bride's house where the couple will live, but not always. The bridal bedroom is gaily outfitted because it will be a centerpiece of the wedding for all to see.

Although wedding costs are divided among the families, there is no set rule as to how much each must contribute. The deciding factors are ability and willingness to pay. Often it is the bride's family who bears most of the cost, but generally the families try to stay even. Sometimes the groom himself may be both willing and able to finance the marriage, but his family may not agree. This happens when the groom's family has another bride in mind for him. It can also happen when the groom's family is of higher status than the bride's family or when the groom has high earning power. In such cases special incentives may be given to the groom in what can be called a groom-price according to the saying "Whoever feels most strongly will cast the net to catch the fish." The family that most wants the marriage must provide more of the costs. However, I never heard this saying applied to prospective brides, only to grooms whose family either had other plans for their son or whose status was higher than that of the bride.

In other parts of West Sumatra a groom-price is routine. The price depends on the groom's earning power and status. I knew of one case on the coast in which the bride's family paid the groom's family several thousand dollars and bought a car for the groom, who was a medical doctor.

Bride-Price or Groom-Price

Considerations of bride- or groom-price in Belubus is complicated by the fact that *four* families spend money for a wedding ceremony. Although the central wedding events take place in the houses of the bride's mother and the groom's mother, the households of bako relatives are also involved: the bride and groom are dressed in the homes of their respective bako, and the bako play a visible ceremonial role in the processions and food exchanges.

One of the major wedding costs is the couple's bedroom. As a rule, the groom's family buys the furniture. This might be considered a bride-price but for the fact that the furniture will always remain in the bride's house. There are two necessary elements in the adat ceremony that might be thought of as a groom-price and a bride-price. First, when the bride comes to take the groom from his mother's house to her own, a woman (usually the wife of the bride's mamak) brings a small amount of money that is presented to the groom's mamak in a *tepak*, or ceremonial box. The name of this payment is *lantak kandang*, which literally means "fencing in the chicken coop," but no particular meaning is attached to these words. The payment is simply referred to as *uang untuk jemput suami* (money to get the groom).

In addition to this money, only a token sum, the bride's party brings a few other objects to fulfill the requirements set by adat. On the outside of the tepak a kris is wrapped in a special cloth. The kris is the one given by the groom's ninik mamak at the time of the meeting to arrange the wedding (the timbang tando, discussed above). Along with the kris there is a folded sarong and a *jas* (black jacket worn on special occasions by men). These items are wrapped around the tepak with the sash worn by the ninik mamak when dressed formally. Inside the tepak, along with the money, there must be *sirih langkok*, the proper ingredients for chewing betel in the adat way.[1]

People say that the money could be taken as "buying the groom" from his ninik mamak, but the actual amount is so small as to be inconsequential. More important, the mamak do not take all of the money; they leave one quarter of it in the tepak. As with so much else in Minangkabau, that which is given is always returned in some measure.

One final payment, made by the groom to the bride's family, could perhaps be seen as a symbolic bride-price. When the bride brings the groom back to her house for the last time, she waits outside the door while he knocks on the closed door. The door is not opened to him until he pays a token amount to the bride's mother. This might be interpreted as buying the services of the women of the house. But people in Belubus see it somewhat differently. They say it is "money to open the door, so that when the husband comes home he knows that he must bring money to support his family." Such money, they say, is necessary so that the wife will always follow her husband.

Once all is decided between the families of bride and groom, separate negotiations take place between the bride's family and her bako relatives. This discussion concerns the issues of wedding clothes and musical entertainment. As a rule, bako relatives provide the wedding clothes (always rented) and the musical accompaniment for the processions, but all this must be discussed. Another financial consideration is who pays for the entertainment. Because people like to hire costly bands or the traditional (and less expensive) saluang performers, there must be an agreement on how this cost will be apportioned. Similar negotiations take place between the groom's maternal family and his bako relatives.

Invitation: Paying Homage

Wedding preparation begin weeks before the event with the *menjelang*, or invitation. This stage is one of the most important, because if certain people are not invited in the adat way considerable friction can develop. Menjelang means literally "to call on," "to pay one's respects." Menjelang is a time for paying special homage to bako relatives and the wives of male lineage members. During the wedding these women will accompany the bride as she goes back and forth between her house and that of the groom.

Menjelang includes bringing food to the guest as part of the invitation. In the case of Adek's wedding, some two hundred individuals were invited with a visit to their houses bringing rice and rendang. Wives of the mamak *(binih mamak)* in Adek's suku and those of her male bako relatives received a bonus of specially prepared cakes. Wives of male lineage members *(sumandan)* of Adek's clan also received a special invitation. Women invite women, men invite men. Only women bring food to invitees, however, never men, who issue invitations only by word of mouth. The men who do the inviting must be of the same status as the invitee. Mamak invite mamak, in-marrying husbands *(sumando)* invite sumando, and so on.

As always, the women who menjelang (that is, bring the food offerings by way of invitation) come home with their containers refilled, usually with uncooked rice. The magnitude of the invitation stage can be understood by the amount of food used to issue invitations to Adek's wedding. Ibu Wel cooked six kilograms of meat, used up to a hundred coconuts, cooked six batches of rendang, and made six cakes. For Adek's father's family (Adek's bako) she cooked *singgang ayam* (curried chicken), cakes, and rice and sambal; she brought this food to their house for a common meal, after which they discussed their share in the cost of the wedding.

Ibu Wel also made singgang ayam for her brother, Dt. Llano, which she took to him in the eastern Sumatran city where he lives. This was the way in which she showed him the respect all mamak hope for but sometimes do not receive. Some say that Minangkabau adat stands or falls on the degree to which women in the family show respect to their mamak. The same, of course, applies to men in the family. However, it

Adek bringing Mari to her house in their wedding ceremony, 1998

is the women who have the means to show their respect through their food offerings.

All of the above procedures are carried out by women of the groom's family as well. It is as if two weddings were being planned, one for the bride and one for the groom. The maternal male and female relatives of the groom issue invitations to the same classes of relatives (bako, binih mamak, sumandan, sumando).

Wedding Preparations

After the invitation stage, preparations for the festivities begin about one week before the ceremony. The preparations are much like those described for the birth ceremony. They begin with women going out to cut bananas. Then the women gather to make the sticky rice, which will be given along with clumps of bananas to each guest in the manner described for the birth ceremony.

Another element common to all ceremonies is building the outdoor stage for the musical celebration that so often accompanies a ceremony. Males with any relationship to the bride (bako, in-laws, and maternal

Adek and Mari sitting on wedding throne in Adek's house, 1998. The bedroom is in back at the left.

relatives) come to the house to construct the outdoor stage where the music will be played.

Unique to the wedding ceremony is the construction of the *palaminan*, the wedding stage in the household of the bride. The stage where bride and groom sit is the center of attention during the wedding. It is constructed by men and decorated by women, usually women from a nearby village whose specialty is wedding stages and costumes. Without the stage and its thronelike seat, people are said to be *kurang adat* (without adat). I have heard people speak harshly about those who neglect such finery: "Minang hilang, tinggal kerbau" (The Minang part of one's identity has been lost, only the buffalo remains). It is also said that in the absence of the stage and the appropriate dress, the couple has not been properly married.

Seated on the stage and dressed accordingly, bride and groom are regarded as queen and king for the day. The stage is decorated in bright pink, green, black, white, orange, and red. Five is the minimum number of different colors, but usually there are seven. The colorful cloth with its gold and silver trim is bright and eye catching. The bride and groom are likewise extravagantly dressed in matching gold or silver embroidered costumes on a background of blue, red, or the now fashionable orange.

The stage is always set up in the household of the bride's mother. For the larger weddings, the groom's family follows suit by constructing a stage in their household so that bride and groom can be greeted by the groom's bako and maternal relatives in their home environment. Once the stage is ready, the goat curry cooked, the special foods prepared, the packets of silomak wrapped, and the bananas stacked, all is ready for the wedding day.

CHAPTER NINE

Getting Married

After everyone had finished eating in the bride's house on the second morning of the wedding ceremony, Ibu Sinar said in a formal voice, "We are here to eat, to see the chicken coop, and to look for the lost rooster."

After the ensuing speeches, one of the women from the bride's family joked about my asking when the bride and groom would finally sleep together. She said, "If you want to see the rooster enter the chicken coop, be here at two this morning."

"Shh," another woman whispered. "It's not good to talk like that."

Field notes, 1996

Awedding is not to be missed in Belubus, or for that matter anywhere in the Minangkabau world. Filled with pomp and circumstance, the wedding ceremony stands at the apex of village social life. Unlike the even grander penghulu inauguration ceremony, which draws most of the village but occurs only once in several years, many wedding ceremonies take place during the year.

A wedding is often treated as two weddings: one for the bride and one for the groom. Sometimes these ceremonies are identical, with thrones being erected in the houses of bride and groom. The couple reigns like king and queen over the throng gathered below them on the floor. They sit in dazed, shy silence, nodding briefly to the guests who deposit money in a small envelope on the bride's lap or nearby on the floor. If they are sitting in the groom's house, the gifts are given to one of the women of his family. The grand finale takes place at the house of the bride when, after several days of festivity, eating, and drinking in the houses of bride and groom, the groom enters the bridal bedroom. In Belubus all weddings are consummated here. In those rare cases that the couple take a few days to themselves, perhaps in Padang or even Jakarta, they do so only after the full wedding cycle has been completed, including consummation.

In a wedding, the motto "The contents of adat are filled by custom"—so important in the birth ceremony—applies on an even grander scale. There are many more adat contents and customs to be filled. In addition to the foods carried and exchanged by the women, men exchange money and speeches. The world expressed through adat speech in the wedding ceremony is a world unto itself, similar yet different from women's acts on the ceremonial stage: similar in weaving good relations between intermarrying clans, different in the use of words rather than food. In both there are many allusions to the royal past.

Et and Edison's wedding was a typical adat wedding. It was typical because, unlike the wedding of Adek and Mari, both Et and Edison lived in Belubus and were members of intermarrying clans. Et is a member of suku Payobadar, one of the oldest and most respected suku in Belubus. Edison is a member of Kotyanir, but not from Eggi's branch. In this case, the marriage negotiations were more equal, with Et and Edison's families splitting the costs.

Et and Edison got married in 1995. Edison first declared his interest in Et by writing a letter asking Et to become his girlfriend, to *berpatcher*. Twenty-two at the time and dreaming of going to school in the city, Et had no thoughts of love or marriage with Edison or anyone else. However, after two weeks thinking it over she agreed to berpatcher with Edison. This meant that they would appear together in public. When she appeared with Edison before the fasting month, walking with Edison to the top of Bukit Parasi to visit Batu Manda in a traditional pre-fasting celebration, everyone knew that they were a couple.

Et and Edison saw each other for three years before marriage entered the picture. For awhile she had another boyfriend, who might have been considered more desirable because of his government job. But his interest waned after he left the village, and Et took up again with Edison.

Edison's family took the first formal step regarding marriage by sending one of their in-married males to speak to Et's mother. They asked if Et was ready to get married in the confidential, informal discussion *(marisiak)*. Et's mother talked it over with Et's father and the parents agreed that it was up their daughter, which was an indirect way of showing their approval. The next step was to ask Et what she thought. When she said it was up to her parents, this was a sign that she agreed.

Et's father conveyed the news that marriage discussions were underway to Dt. Ampek, Et's mamak and the other mamak in Et's clan. The oldest woman in Et's clan, her grandmother, conveyed the news to the women in the family. At a meeting of the members of Et's family, including all spouses, Et's father announced, "Someone has come who wants to become our son-in-law." At this meeting, which Et attended, her silence was taken as a sign that she agreed.

The next step was taken by Edison's mamak, Dt. Penghulu Besar. He came to Et's house carrying sirih (betel leaf, areca nut, and lime). He opened his conversation with Et's parents by first taking the sirih from his pocket to indicate that this was an adat matter. Then he spoke in a formal tone:

"I hear that our child Edi has agreed with Et to be engaged. What does the family here think of that? Do you agree?"

Et's mother signaled her agreement by taking some sirih and chewing.

The next day, Et's mother took sirih to her mamak, Dt. Ampek, and gave it to him, saying that Dt. Penghulu Besar had brought sirih. Dt. Ampek indicated his agreement by saying that the matter should be finished quickly and the wedding held.

Continuing to weave the complex set of relationships that a marriage sets in motion, Et's mother then went to see Et's *bako kontan* (close maternal relatives of Et's father), in this case Et's paternal grandmother and great-grandmother. Once again sirih clinched the agreement.

After this, sirih was taken to all the mamak of Et's suku and their wives. Once they had all agreed, the way was open for discussing the date and determining who would pay for what.

A day was set for a general meeting, which included all the social relationships activated by a wedding: ninik mamak and their wives of the clans of both Et and Edison, matrilineally related women of the bride and groom's clans, and fathers of the bride and groom and their close maternal relatives. They met at Et's house for a common meal provided by the women representatives of all sides. The discussion began with the mamak of the two clans speaking to one another in a highly stylized manner.

The negotiation began with the official exchange *(timbang tando)* between the male leaders of Et's and Edison's matrilineal clans to seal the agreement of marriage. For the duration of the engagement period, Edison's family gave their ancestral kris to Et's family, who in return gave gold, the symbol of female ancestral wealth. If Edison should change his mind, it was said, the kris would kill him. If Et should change her mind and run away from her marriage, the gold would be used to look for her. The engagement was completed when Edison's mamak paid the nominal sum called *kobek tando*, which was divided among the mamak's of Et's clan.

The Bako Fetch the Child of the Fruit

On the morning of the first day of the wedding, Et was fetched by two women from her father's house. Both women were bako, close maternal relatives of her father. Ibu Emmy and a younger woman arrived carrying sirih in a *bokor*, the quintessential adat vessel in which people carry the ingredients for chewing sirih. As a rule, at the receiving house the women mix the ingredients together and chew them, another sign that the visit has to do with adat. In this case, Ibu Emmy simply opened the cloth covering the bokor to show its contents to the female relative who met Emmy at the door. Once the bokor is opened, the saying goes, "The intention is announced and adat is served."

The intention in this case was to escort Et to the house of her father's mother and grandmother to clothe her for the wedding ceremony. The clothes, made of royal blue velvet with silver brocade, were rented for the occasion. The costume was made according to the traditional style: a sarong topped with a long-sleeved blouse of the same material. A fake silver crown *(suntiang)* was also rented. Formerly, when central Sumatra was a source for much of the Southeast Asian gold and silver trade, the crown was of solid silver. Gold is used when the bride chooses the more common red for her wedding dress.

Et went alone to her paternal grandmother's house with Ibu Emmy and the second woman, where she was dressed by the women renting the clothes to the family, who also prepared her hair and makeup. These same women dressed some young girls in similar clothing but with the buffalo horns, to resemble Bundo Kanduang. Fully dressed, Et posed for pictures with her father, grandmother, and great-grandmother. The family ate together and then gathered for the procession back to Et's house.

Et's bako relatives had all the necessary dishes and foods laid out on the table ready for the grand procession to Et's house. Accompanied by her father, a few men playing the *telempong* (a traditional percussion instrument), her paternal grandmother and great-grandmother, and various female bako relatives, Et was escorted back to her mother's house. These were the same women who at Et's birth had prepared the necessary foods for Et's naming ceremony. Now on the same dulang tuo they were carrying different but equally necessary foods for her wedding.

Et's paternal grandmother carried the dulang tuo atop her head. For the wedding the tray must have at least twelve plates, including at least three with large round cakes. The remaining plates should contain traditional sweets, such as *silomak, galamai, sopik, wajik, umpiang, sagun,* or *kue loyang* (see fig. 4).

FIG. 4. FOODS CIRCULATED BY FAMILIES OF BRIDE AND GROOM DURING WEDDING FESTIVITIES

Bride's family → groom's family	*Groom's family → bride's family*
Prepared by bride's bako:	Prepared by groom's bako:
Singgang ayam (curried chicken) with nasi (rice)	Live rooster
Silomak kunit	Hulled rice (10 cupak)
3 cakes	Sprouted rice seedlings
Traditional sweets: wajik, silomak, galamai, sopik, umpiang, sagun, kue loyang	1 live ikan kalui fish
	2 sprouted coconuts
	Traditional sweets (same as given by bride's family)
	3 cakes
Prepared by bride's clan:	Prepared by groom's clan:
Fried curried fish	Hulled rice (10 cupak)
Fried curried small fish	
Fried curried egg	
Curried beef	
Singgang ayam	

The central food, in addition to the wedding cakes and adat sweets, brought by the bako of the bride was singgang ayam, a whole chicken curried in spices and coconut milk and served with yellow sticky rice. Singgang ayam is always made by taking the stomach and intestines out of the chicken and replacing it with the leaf of an edible tuber. The requirement here is that the chicken cannot be cut, it must be all in one piece including its head and feet. The heart and stomach remain at the house to be eaten by the bako.

Singgang ayam was also prepared by the bride's family to take to the groom's house. This gift lifts the groom to the status of son-in-law. It is also said that the gift of chicken cooked in this way honors the son-in-law, for it is a very special ceremonial food. Another important ritual food carried by the bako relatives is known as *silomak kunit*, sticky rice made with coconut milk and with saffron added to make it yellow, the color of singgang ayam. Silomak kunit is made not as "a friend" to singgang ayam but as a dessert. It is shaped into a pie-like arrangement, covered with the leaf of a banana and carried in a covered tray.

The singgang ayam carried by the bako stopped at the bride's house and then continued on to the groom's house, together with singgang ayam prepared by the bride's family. Only the singgang ayam made by the bride's family was actually eaten at the groom's house, however. The bako brought their singgang ayam back to their house for a communal meal and prayer that night with Et's father. The singgang ayam, then, is associated with the in-married male: the groom, on the one hand, and the father of the bride, on the other.

The katidiang jombak carried by bako contained cooked rice for fetch-ing the groom *(nasi untuk menjemput junjuangan)*. This rice was left at the groom's household where it was exchanged for uncooked rice. Other women from the family of Et's bako brought uncooked rice and cakes to Et's house, where it was exchanged for silomak and pisang batu. Some bako relatives went on to the groom's house carrying the food offerings; others went home after eating at Et's house.

Adat Speeches

Upon arriving at Et's house the procession was greeted by a sumandan (in-married woman) on the path in front of the house. She was carrying a bokor with sirih to greet them in the formal adat way. After the greet-ing everyone went inside for the opening wedding feast for the bride's bako. This feast, given by Et's matrilineal relatives, was specifically for Et's bako. None of the groom's family was involved.

After everyone was seated, they waited for the mamak to open the meal with *baalua*, adat speechmaking. The speech is full of flowery phrases and obscure references. Usually, the main speakers are the penghulu of the host and guest clans, in this case Et's mamak and the mamak of her bako (her paternal uncle or great uncle). Other speakers can substitute, however.

When adat speech is involved men usually sit alone in a rectangle or a circle around the room, while women wait respectfully in the shadows or in another room. Sitting across from one another or at either end of the rectangle, the mamak speak in singsong style. Everyone in the room falls into silence lulled by the rising and falling of single male voices respond-ing to one another, reminding me of Gregorian chant in the stillness of a monastic service. The male voices go back and forth in counterpoint. One intones a few verses, filling up the ears of all who listen while his respon-dent waits attentively for his turn. They begin by paying homage to the twenty-two rules of adat instituted by Dt. Perpatih and Dt. Katumang-gungan, referring to *cupak* and *gantang*, the standard measures for un-cooked rice according to adat, mentioned in the last two rules.

> Aia, Datuak,
> By the order of adat
> By the measure of cupak and gantang,
> We greet you
> With honor and respect.

The speaker continues making verbal forays down many side paths, speaking of the rule of adat that must be applied, promises that must be

Men exchanging speeches to close the meal at Et's house, 1996

kept, the truth that is "the shadow of the inner being," from which there can be no turning away. God is mentioned:

> My thanks are to God
> For the greatness of adat.

The image of adat speech as a way of tying people and guiding them—seen in the proverb which makes Bundo Kanduang the "center where the threads of the fish net meet"—is reflected in the metaphor of adat as cloth:

> Adat is like the textile
> We weave for our clothing.
> In the world
> It guides us, shapes us, protects us.
> Adat shapes our village
> Sees after our needs,
> Whether we walk or sit together
> We share the burden.
> The food has been offered
> The water has been poured
> The rice has been served

To make our life perfect.
This is my salute
My understanding returns to you.

In answer, the mamak from the responding clan says:

Si Alek
Aia, Datuak
Your words call us
Greeting us with respect.
They come to me as threads loosened from their cloth
I tie them together in my speech.
According to baso-basi
I surround them with a sweet mouth and a soft heart.
Good words are like good news
They sound so nice
Like the softness of the talempong
Like the drum whose echo responds to its own sound.
The intent of your words
Is like the feeling that will always be remembered.
Being physical it can be felt
Being inner, the words can be pondered.
We compare your words to a woven cloth
The cloth that weaves us together.
The cloth of our being is bright like the moon
With it we can go downstream.
It provides the boat and the rhythm for rowing upstream
The tools to protect ourselves
The measure of cupak
So that all will be true, according to adat.
Adat and religion are of one line
Like the penghulu who sit together
We are in harmony.
I pass it back to you, Datuak.

Answer:

Si Alek
In relation to Datuak's statement
I hear your respect.
It is like the food that has been put before us
The water that we will drink
The rice that has been placed in our midst
These are the words of Datuak.
Datuak, you are kind
If we need a scale, you provide one
If we fall down, you pick us up
If we lose balance, you catch us

> You have answered our greeting
> My heart is pleased.

The speaking continues like this, high pitched, full of emotion and meaning, emphatically expressed. Just as one wonders if it will ever end, one of the men bursts out with a heartfelt prayer, reminding the listener how closely intertwined are adat and Islam on these occasions.

> Oh Allah, oh my God!
> Please, join the two hearts of bride and groom
> Just as you tied the hearts of Adam and Eve.
> Oh Allah, oh my God!
> Please, join the two hearts of bride and groom
> Just as you tied the hearts of Joseph and Zulaiha!
> Oh Allah, oh my God!
> Please join the hearts of bride and groom just as you tied the hearts of Mohammed,
> Our Prophet and Aisyah, Our Mother.

The prayer signals that it is time to begin eating. After everyone eats, another round of speaking ends the meal.

This time, a man by the name of Pak Sulin began the speaking, representing the clan of Et's father (her bako). He is not a penghulu but is well known for being gifted in magical lore *(ilmu gaib)*. He is often asked to be present on ceremonial occasions to ward off any danger due to evil spirits or black magic that might have been conjured by someone hostile to the wedding.

Pak Sulin drew out the lines of his verses so they had a parallel rhythm and made the words rhyme as he made analogies between adat and alam.

> All that is wrongly touched is to be given back;
> All that is mistakenly eaten should be vomited.
> Touching charcoal makes the hands black;
> Stepping on turmeric makes the foot yellow.
> We must be careful to do the right thing according to the laws of nature.

Addressing himself to Et's senior mamak, Dt. Ampek, who arrived late, Pak Sulin continued in a singsong voice. "Datuak! We await your words. Please give them to us. We have been treated with food and drink. This is proper, as it should be. The problem we wish to raise is as clear as the sun, as clean as the moon. The drinking is finished, the food is completed.

Now, we would like to go home. What do you think about that, Datuak! You know how to consider the good and bad."

Dt. Ampek answered, "Have you finished speaking, Datuak? There is much to be considered; it is late, we have far to go, and much to do. We apologize for being late."

Pak Sulin responded, "We receive your apology, Datuak. We ask your pardon in return Datuak because we entered the house before you arrived. It is right to apologize; this is our adat, to show our respect for one another."

The speeches continued. Pak Sulin summarized what has gone on before Dt. Ampek arrived: "We have brought our child from the house of her bako. She has been received by your representative, Datuak. Now, we want to ask permission to go to our homes. It is a good time of the day to go home."

Dt. Ampek answered, "Yes, go home, if you are finished, if you have enough to eat and drink, please go home. If you have not had enough we ask your forgiveness."

Pak Sulin replied: "We are full, we have had more than usual to eat. Now, I ask your permission to unwind my legs to go home."

After uttering the common prayer, he stood to go home, followed by the remaining men. Pak Sulin did not join the procession as it moved to the house of the groom. Three of the men, mamak from the bride's family, followed along because they participated in the ceremony known as *menjemput junjungan* (fetching the groom). They were joined by some of the women from the house of Et's bako and more women from Et's family, including wives of male lineage members. The procession proceeded to the groom's house with more foods including the foods brought by the bako.

The Bako Fetch the Groom

Earlier in the day, Edison, too, was fetched by his bako relatives to clothe him in the manner of adat. The procedure was the same. They arrived bringing a bokor and signified their intention to take the child of their son to their house to prepare him for his wedding. Edison's outfit was the same as Et's. He wore blue with silver trim, an elaborately embroidered jacket with long sleeves and pants. On his head he wore an embroidered silver cloth wrapped in the style of hats worn by penghulu.

Edison's bako relatives prepared a different set of food offerings, ostensibly to take to Edison's house but which actually ended up at Et's house later in the day. They prepared the same tray of twelve plates, including three round cakes and nine plates of various traditional sweets. But instead of singgang ayam and silomak kunit they brought a live rooster; two coconuts for planting, *boniah* (sprouting seeds of rice) for planting; one *ikan kalui* fish from their fishpond; and ten *cupak* (measures) of uncooked rice (fig. 4). This was all taken to Edison's mother's house. The tray of cakes and sweets remained, but the rest went to Et's house when Edison was taken there.

The Bride's Family Fetches the Respected One

Most of the women participating in the procession to fetch Edison at his mother's house were either Et's bako or the wives of the mamak of her clan. They carried the most important items, whether or not they made them for the ceremony.

They brought a dish of singgang ayam with cooked rice, bananas, and silomak kunit. One of these women carried a tray of twelve types of sweets—three round cakes and nine plates of adat sweets. Other women brought various plates of food and rice, which were added to the table at Edison's house. When the women arrived at the house of Edison's mother, the women there took the foods but left some plates untouched for the bride's family to take home. In all cases, the trays and baskets were filled with bananas and silomak, as in the birth ceremony.

One item that must be carried by the wife of a mamak is the tepak, with a token amount of money, which will be given in payment for the groom, along with the ingredients for chewing sirih. Wrapped with this small wooden box is the kris left by the groom during the marriage negotiations, along with a sarong and jacket, the clothes the groom will wear to the bride's house on the final day. While these items are supposed to be wrapped with the adat sash of the costume worn by the penghulu, I have always seen only a regular piece of cloth being used to secure the items to the tepak. Such deviation from the expected is frequent. People try to follow tradition, but if they don't have the proper objects on hand they find something to substitute.

At the groom's house Et and Edison sat on the wedding throne. After the obligatory speeches to open the eating, this time delivered by Edison's mamak to the representative of Et's mamak, everyone ate on the floor below the royal couple. After the speech that ends the meal, the mamak then moved to the core of the ceremony, known as fetching the groom.

Et and Edison on their wedding throne in Edison's house, 1996

Dt. Penghulu Besar, the head penghulu of Kotyanir, Edison's suku, began by addressing the assembled mamak, who were seated in a circle below the wedding stage on which Et and Edison were seated. "Datuak Rogang, Datuak Sati, Datuak Panduko nan Panjang," he said, bowing in the direction of these datuak. "You are the three Datuak who have been summoned. We gather today, all of us for a special occasion. First, we look to the south and north, to the left and the right. We have eaten the food placed in front of us. Hai, Datuak! We can be grateful for prosperity. There is rice on our plates to be eaten, water in our glasses to drink. These are our pleasures. Now, Datuak, the speech goes home to you."

Datuk Panduko nan Panjang was the designated speaker who responded on behalf of Et's mamak: "Lai, sampai lah, Datuak, have you finished the speech? After we look to the south and north, after we look to left and right, my respects have been paid. Everything depends on Datuak."

Datuk Penghulu Besar took up the speech, asking Dt. nan Panjang, "Lai, sampai Datuak, have you finished the speech? In your speech the real words are used. They are not only complete words, but the words of our customs and traditions. So now we give our respects so that there is rice on the plates to be eaten, water in the glasses to be drunk. These are the hopes of our hopes. I give the speech to you, Datuak."

Dt. Panduko nan Panjang responded,

> Have you finished, Datuak? The right time has been chosen. The basic words are complete. The betel should be chewed. The areca nut bitten. That's all. It depends on you, Datuak. All is in accordance with your words, the real words. Customs and traditions are like growing flowers. Pusako (heirlooms) have domains defined by what is right and proper. We have regulations and we follow the rules. We have a proposal of marriage in front of us. The betel has been chewed, the areca nut bitten. The betel is for beginning the speech. The Datuak is the person who must give the speech. I pass it to you, Datuak.

A lengthy discussion ensued as the men examined the contents of the tepak and chewed betel, sealing the marriage in the traditional way. The back and forth of the word exchange continued, touching on many important adat matters in the poetic style known as *gurindam*, a rhapsodic type of free verse.

> Hai, Datuak!
> You speak with words
> But they are adat words
> Following the order of cupak and gantang
> Respectful like the pepatah of adat
> Like the patitih of cupak and gantang.
> Our meetings are based on agreement
> Grace comes from harmony
> Betrayal elicits attacks
> We will not show ill will.

He continued:

> The palm tree grows at the head of our town
> Take one piece for flooring.
> The core of the marriage agreement has come
> We apply the current adat to seal the agreement.
> All the ninik mamak upstream agree
> With those downstream.
> We have opened the tepak,
> Examined its contents, eaten the betel.
> The siriah is the flower of our desire, our wish
> The pinang is the fruit of our request.
> As to the bridegroom
> He is here and is ready.
> According to the rule of limbago
> The seed born at this moment

Examining the contents of the *tepak* before the groom is handed to bride's family for the procession to her house, 1996

Will grow bearing flowers and fruit.
Come, let us begin the procession bringing our child
From our house, to the other house.
Let us all follow the procession
Marching along the road
To cheer up mother and father
To please the ninik mamak
That is our message
We turn back to you, Datuak.

Answer:

Are you finished, Datuak?
Referring to your words
They are many,
Like the birds that sing and the corn ears that grow.
Adat words run like a labyrinth
Following the rules of speech.
Whether two or three sit together
The words seek the truth.
Round, like the water that flows in the bamboo tube
Seeking common agreement.

When words become round in agreement
The request has been met
The desire fulfilled
We have understanding.
I return the words to you.

Answer:

Hai, Datuak
Listening to your words
Peace enters my heart
My mind is at rest.
Our request has been met
Our wish fulfilled.
Come, let us take them in procession
Let us go down from this house
This is my salute to you
My understanding returns to you.

This ended the adat speeches. Having eaten the sirih, examined the contents of the tepak, and delivered their speeches, the penghulu arose, and everyone went out to assemble for the procession that accompanies the bride and groom to the bride's house.

Taking the Uncooked Rice and Tying the Husband to the House

The procession that forms is long because it includes relatives of bride and groom—mostly bako, sumando, sumandan, friends, and children. The maternal relatives (of both bride and groom) rarely take part in these processions because their duty is to remain at home to receive guests. The procession proceeds slowly; bride and groom walk near the front, flanked on either side by young children dressed as Bundo Kanduang and by women from both sides carrying food.

Added to the cakes and sweets moving in this procession are the seedlings and rooster supplied by the groom's bako (fig. 4). These items are meant for the express purpose of *berkembang*, which means to grow and expand. The two sprouted coconuts and the sprouted rice seedlings are meant for planting. Live fish, which are kept in every house for this and other festive occasions, will be added to the fishpond of the bride's clan. A large quantity of uncooked rice is also brought; half from the groom's family, the rest from bako of the groom. In exchange for all this, the women carrying these items receive the usual bananas and cakes.

When the wedding party arrived at the house they found the front door closed. Et sat outside, while Edison went up to the door and knocked. He was let in only after providing a token payment. Upon entering, he was led around the oldest post of the house. According to adat he circled the post seven times, a sign that he had become attached to the house.

The oldest woman of the house performs her part of the ceremony of arrival. She lights two small torches symbolizing the newlyweds. She passes the torches over the two baskets (katidiang jombak) three times (some say this should be seven times). Each basket holds the same amount of uncooked rice; one of them is supplied by the groom's family, the other by his bako. The bride takes a small amount of the rice and some water into her mouth. She then blows the rice grains out of her mouth, extinguishing the torches. She does so in one breath so that in their house there will be *sakato* (one word, or agreement) between her husband and herself.

That night, bride and groom sit into the wee hours of the morning nearly immobile on their wedding thrones. The music plays, people come and go bringing small presents of money, which they leave behind after they have eaten. Everyone looks in at the bedroom that bride and groom will occupy. It is lavishly decorated like the wedding couch on which the young couple sit. Young men and women come in and out. The young women leave early, but the young men stay late into the night playing cards, sometimes gambling. Music—traditional or Indonesian rock—provides the entertainment.

Looking for the Lost Rooster and Seeing the Chicken Coop

The next day, bako women from Edison's father's clan along with wives of his mamak came to Et's house to "look for the lost rooster" and "see the chicken coop" *(mencari ayam hilang, melihat kandang)*. Edison arrived on his own and the women came separately. He and Et sat together around the mat with the other guests. They ate singgang ayam and cooked rice brought by the women of Edison's house that morning.

Arriving at the house they said, "Is my rooster here? I'm looking for the lost rooster."

The receiving woman responded, "He's here, come in."

After everyone had eaten, a spokeswoman for the groom said, "We have come to look for the lost rooster and see the chicken coop. Have you prepared a nice place for him? Will you treat him well? Give him food?"

After the obligatory return speech (made by a woman from Et's house), everyone got up to look at the chicken coop (the bedroom). Satisfied, they all left. In answer to my joking question, "When will the groom get to sleep in the chicken coop?" one of the women laughed and said, "Come back at two in the morning."

I heard another woman mutter that it's not nice to talk like that. This response reflects a common dualism I find in Belubus culture. Some women and men are quite bawdy in their approach to reality, while others are extremely polite and distant. I knew enough by then to be prepared for both responses.

Asking for His Clothes and Eat, Bringing Back the Bamboo

The last act took place first at Edison's house and finally at Et's house. After looking for their lost rooster, Edison's relatives went home and waited to receive the bride and her family. They came later in the day with Edison, and once again everyone ate. After this meal was over a spokeswoman said, "We are here to eat and to take Edison's clothes," referring to his everyday clothes that he will need when living with his wife.

Throughout the meal Edison's mother was in his room packing his clothes. There was a great deal of sniffling as she said good-bye to her son, even though he was only moving less than a mile down the road. The clothes were given to Et's bako relatives. As they left they took back with them uncooked rice in exchange for the cooked rice they had brought. Edison went with them. He and Et received their friends the rest of the day at Et's house. The band hired by bako relatives played American rock, Indonesian style. Edison's friends came by and he talked with them late into the evening, well after Et retired to their room. As promised, he entered the chicken coop about 2 A.M. Everyone went home and the new family began its history.

Analogies in the Food and Speeches

The exchange of adat speeches between the penghulu on the wedding stage place the contribution of mature males, wise and knowledgeable in adat, on a par with women's ceremonial performance. The speeches anchor the young couple in the world of adat as assuredly as the adat foods prepared by women for the occasion. The words that flow from the mouths of the ninik mamak—back and forth, from clan to clan, filling the ears and satisfying the soul—are as sweet as women's food. The stately interchange between speech partners from different clans is a mark of high etiquette. Their tone is nurturing and respectful. Like Bundo Kanduang in her ceremonial capacity, in their speeches the penghulu are sovereign through their dignity, the center where the threads of the fishnet meet; they are the greatly honored ones, and hence the ones to whom we would want to take all our problems. Words capped by chewing betel taken from the tepak seal the relationship between the two clans, one giving and the other receiving the groom.

This overlapping of masculine and feminine meanings, manifested in the cooking, finery, and aesthetic displays of women and in the adat speeches of men, is typical of gender relations in Minangkabau. Men and women constitute analogies for one another. The meanings are similar but their expression differ.

The analogies in gender meanings is the most obvious in the symbolism associated with the bride's bedroom and the groom: the chicken coop *(kandang)* and the rooster *(ayam jantan)*. Female relatives of the groom bring a live rooster, fish, and rice seedlings to the bride's house. The groom implants, the bride nurtures. The cooked chicken, rice, and clothes brought by the bride's family to the groom's house suggest that women are responsible for transforming the raw energy of male fertility into the cultural purposes of adat. The elaborately prepared and presented sweets and cakes circulated among the paternal and maternal families of bride and groom sweeten the newly forged links with graceful ritual interaction.

Entertainment is provided on the evening of the main wedding day. A rock-style band or organ performance may be hired to please the younger members of the village. The more traditional saluang performance is the favorite of the older generation. The saluang performance features well-known women singers from the nearby city of Payakumbuh, who sing into the early hours of the morning accompanied by the saluang flute. Piped over the village loudspeaker, the music pervades the village. Like the daytime ceremony, the saluang performance obeys the laws of adat. It is the one time when women have their say on the adat stage. Bawdy at times, poetic, reaching deep into the emotions, the saluang performance responds to a desire to hear women pour out their souls on topics ranging from thoroughly mundane matters to sex, love, and loss.

CHAPTER TEN

Songs and the Performance of Desire

The sound of her voice, the feelings she expresses, and the haunting melody of the bamboo flute, following her in unison like a devoted lover, float through the night. Sometimes the emotion hangs heavy in the air drawing the heart to the sound. At these times, heads bow. Pak Edi lifts his hand to his forehead and buries his head. Usually reticent, a man of few words, he tells me that the songs take him far away. During the performance he draws close to us and we share the experience wordlessly. It's about 2 A.M. The female singers, sitting in the Minangkabau way with legs to the side, face the by now mainly male audience on a low, open-air stage. Their heads are bowed so as not to lock eyes with the male gaze as they sing their innermost thoughts. That which cannot be said during the day floats melodiously through the star-studded night: heartrending stories, funny or serious, of desire, separation, and loss—a child wants its mother, a mother misses her children, a wife yearns for her husband, a man returns to an empty village after many years away. . . . The tension of loss is broken by jokes about sexual dysfunction, and everyone laughs uproariously.

Field notes, 1997

Anyone can attend the entertainment on the night of a wedding. The stage is always outside the house, sometimes under a small tent in the event of rain. Chairs may be set up for visitors, but most often people sit around, sometimes on the ground. Loudspeakers pipe the music to the whole village. Generally, the organ rock performances end about midnight. The more popular saluang performance lasts until 4:30 A.M. Throughout the focus is on the female singers, usually two, who are accompanied by a male saluang player.[1]

Many authors have written about women's poetic expression in male-dominant cultures. We learn about women's laments in ancient Greek texts, the bawdiness of women on the Shakespearean stage, and the poetry of veiled sentiments from Bedouin ethnography. We can conclude that even when women are closeted from public life, allowed to express themselves privately with other women but publicly only at the event of a death, they are not passive participants in their subordination but vital agents in social life, contesting and resisting, thumbing their noses at public conventions, venting the laughter of the oppressed in their private performances.

For those who wonder what women's poetry might be like in an egalitarian, female-friendly society, the saluang performance is instructive. The heartfelt emotions expressed by the women singers about everything from children to sex are testimony to the Minang woman's sense of agency, her sexual and spiritual autonomy. In their songs women speak of male and female desire from a woman's point of view. There is no embarrassment; in song women liken unattended female sexual desire to a rice field in need of cultivation and watering, and male sexual impotence to the hoe that can no longer cultivate the field. We hear about the lovers women look for and those they avoid. But songs of love are not restricted either to lovers or to sexual performance. They cover all the basic kinship connections, with a primary focus on the connection to the mother and father.

The songs range from extemporaneous songs about people in the audience to well-known songs sung all over West Sumatra. The audience is carried along: laughter rings out when the songs are funny, sadness settles over the audience when they tell of suffering and loss, loud discussion and shouts greet songs with sexual meaning. There are also songs about the problems and difficulties of life and, inevitably, about love unrequited. In them all one finds the emotional identity of the Minangkabau.

The performance starts at about 9 P.M. There are always at least two female singers. The saluang player sits cross-legged, in the way of men, on a woven mat on the raised stage. The two women singers sit near him with their knees folded to one side. They rarely look directly at the audience, but downward, cradling the microphone.

As the night wears on the people in the audience gather closer and closer to the singers and to one another. It's cold and we seek warmth, inspired by the intimacy of the songs. A group of men play cards nearby under a light. The gambling is very discrete, the cries of surprise at winning or losing never compete with the singing. Gradually only men are left as the women drift home. A few women stay with me, but by the early morning I am alone. The hostess or her helpers appear from time to time

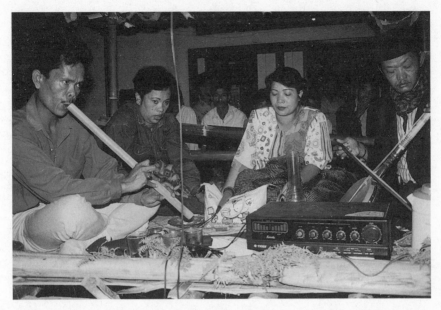

A saluang performance, 1996. *Left to right:* Pak Jala (saluang player), Gadis Suayan and Si Ai (singers), and Nijon (playing the rabab).

to serve refreshments to the performers and onlookers, who sit on the stage with the performers.

Most women go home around midnight. They have to rise early the next day to care for children, cook, go to their fields, and take care of business. If their houses are close by, they hear the songs as they drift off to sleep. Some women have told me that they don't like saluang; others are devoted to the genre and tell me of their favorite songs and singers. I was never able to understand why some women were reticent. Perhaps they were in the throes of experiencing the very emotions articulated in the songs. Or, maybe they didn't want to see their husbands gambling. The near absence of any reference to Islam may also limit attendance.[2]

The songs delve into emotions and life experiences, shifting back and forth between lighthearted themes and tales of suffering and loss. In the songs and the responses they evoke in the audience, I feel myself transported to the heart not just of Minangkabau but of a humanity that is still in touch with the elementary emotions of mother-child bonding. At these times I am confirmed in my impression that the "matristic" or "matriarchal" is not about political power but about the primordial social and emotional bonds uniting parents and children.

Men playing cards at saluang performance, 1997

This is one of the few times on the Minangkabau cultural stage when women express themselves through words. They do so in the same poetic structure of the adat verses intoned by men during the day at the ceremony itself. The difference between the adat of the afternoon and the adat of the night is striking. Whereas in the day adat is melded with Islam, in the traditional saluang performance one encounters the adat of pre-Padri times, when gambling and exuberance were no doubt more common.

During the daytime ceremony, men deliver long set verses reflecting on history and tradition. One is lulled by the lyricism of the poetry flowing from the lips of the better speakers. At night one is lulled by the *communitas* of the shared experience. The graciousness of speech and the aesthetic display of food and dress during the day yields to the emotional display at night. In both there is communal bonding. In both, men and women play their appointed roles, although women are the central actors—as stage managers during the day and the focus of attention at night.

The Performers

Knowing that saluang is my favorite form of entertainment, certain men in the village—saluang aficionados, you might say—inform En as to the latest favorite star whenever I arrive in Belubus. After checking around, talking to women as well as men, I discover that the opinion is usually unanimous. The popularity of saluang stars rises and falls like that of rock stars on Asian MTV. I am always happy to oblige requests for certain saluang singers. I do so by finding the appropriate occasion. If there is a ceremony in Eggi's family, I hire a saluang group; if not, I bring a group to the house to sing and talk, and saluang lovers soon appear at the front door to join us. Once, I brought a group to entertain the entire village. In this case the performance was staged in the yard of the local mayor. In all cases, word gets out through the food-stall grapevine that Ibu Peggi is bringing a saluang group on a certain date.

For several years my favorite group consisted of four individuals. In addition to the saluang player, there are two women singers and one male singer who also plays the *rabab*, a three-string instrument smaller than a violin but played like a cello. I choose this man because he is a native of Sungai Talang, the mother village of Belubus, and composes his own songs about villages of the Four Koto.

En arranges for the performance by visiting the restaurant in Payakumbuh where performers hang out in the late afternoon and drink coffee with their friends while waiting to be picked up for a gig. The procedure is simple. En agrees on a date with one of the performers we are looking for and he or she rounds up the others. None of the performers work in a permanent group, and there is no set leader. On the night of the performance they wait for us at the restaurant at about six o'clock. If one of the designated performers can't make it, there is always someone else who is available.

One of my favorite female singers is Gadis Suayan (the girl from Suayan). I like her because of her throaty voice and the passion with which she sings. She is a about forty-three, wears her hair very short, smokes, and always dresses in pants. She was born in Suayan, a village near Payakumbuh, famous for four songs called the Four Suayans, two of which are presented below. Gadis Suayan has been married twice and is presently divorced from her second husband. She speaks of him with great sadness and longing. Much younger than she, he left her to live with his parents in a city in eastern Sumatra. She jokes with me about being *sawah liek*, that is, an arid rice field—the title of a famous song she will sing later in the evening about a woman who lies fallow, uncultivated and unfertilized, because she has no man. The implication is also that women married to older men are also "sawah liek." This song is almost always sung; I can't remember a performance without it.

Another of my favorite singers is Si Ai, a very feminine woman who dresses fashionably, usually in a skirt and pretty top. She is also in her forties, a little older than Gadis Suayan. She is a favorite with many in Belubus because she is very good at making everyone feel at home. She sings any song that is requested; if she doesn't know it, she makes up some words to go with the name and meaning of the song. She knows many of the old classical songs. She is also the favorite of Pak Pera, a local widower who shows up at every performance to sit next to the singers. On one occasion Si Ai joked with him through out the evening about his offer to give her some coconuts, and then sang about a man who can climb a tree to reach the coconuts but can't throw them down. When Pak Pera showed up with the coconuts later in the night, she sang about coconuts in which there is no milk—a thinly veiled reference to male impotence.

Pak Jala, one of about seven well-known saluang players in the region, comes from the original Minangkabau village, Pariangan Padang Pajang. He has two wives, one in Payakumbuh and the other in Pariangan. He has made two songs from his home area popular in the Payakumbuh area. One is a song about a village near his home village. The other is one of Pak Pera's favorite songs, called Salawat Dulang.

Nijon is in his middle fifties, well known for his rabab playing throughout West Sumatra. He has performed in Malaysia, Jakarta, eastern Sumatra, and recently appeared on TV. He is a member of the Kotyanir clan from Sungai Talang and the nephew of the former head of adat in Sungai Talang, which puts him in line as his successor. Nijon chose not to take on this important title, which would make him the head of adat for the entire Four Koto because of the heavy burden of duty it implied. He lives in Payakumbuh with his second wife. His first wife was a very fine singer whom I heard on several occasions. Nijon's songs are mostly of his own composition. He does not begin singing until late in the night. The later the time, the more salacious his songs become as he mimes sexual performance while bowing the rabab. Everyone laughs and sits in rapt attention. Earlier in the evening he sings songs about places in the Four Koto. These are simple songs usually mentioning natural objects and everday events well known to villagers.

The Song Corpus

Many villages in West Sumatra are made famous by locally composed songs that performers carry to other villagers. These songs are known as *lagu pusako*, or ancestral songs. Other songs in the corpus are based on pop songs translated into the saluang idiom. The lagu pusako are learned by performers solely by attending saluang performances, because few of them are recorded. Gadis Suayan, for example, started attending performances when she was twelve or thirteen just to listen. She then studied with a saluang player by following him wherever he went just to listen. This man made her popular by including her in his group.

The lagu pusako are named after the place where they were first sung. It's hard to speak about their composers or composition because every singer adds his or her interpretation. For example, I was told that there are 120 versions of the opening song, known as "Singgalang," after the village where the saluang is said to have originated. Many of the songs sung in Belubus are from villages in the Payakumbuh area, but many also come from other areas in the heartland or from as far away as the coast.

The song corpus is huge. During one night up to four hundred songs might be sung, including the extemporaneous verses composed by the singers on the spot. The women singers say they can sing all the songs in the saluang corpus. This isn't quite true because I have seen singers either refuse to sing a song or sing it by mentioning the name of the village only and making up verses as they go along. Singers usually know which songs will be requested when they come to the village. During the night they alternate between singing songs of their own choosing and songs requested by the audience. In what follows, I present the songs that people in Belubus most often request. Examples of extemporaneously composed verses about people in the audience are also presented along with some of Nijon's compositions.

The Problem of Translation

It is impossible to translate a saluang verse verbatim. Adat verses can be likened to the small knife used for carving the intricate floral and geometric designs adorning the traditional house and rice granary; they make word carvings on the soul. Examples taken from nature issue forth in speech as assuredly as they appear in carving and in weaving. The message of adat is always wrapped in lyricism, be it melodic, poetic, or visual. In addition to the many metaphoric allusions to nature, words are chosen to caress the notes of the saluang. The female voice stays in loving conversation with the male melody. The meaning is important, but only within this melodic context.

After taking a few songs to friends who were fluent in English in other parts of West Sumatra (no one speaks English in Belubus), only to get gibberish by way of translation, I decided to translate them myself. En pointed out that before one can translate the songs one must understand their meaning, and that requires hearing them in the village context. En and I attended many performances, which I taped. He transcribed one performance using the Minangkabau language in which the songs are always sung but rendering them also in Indonesian. We then discussed the songs, sometimes line by line, with those who had heard them many times in Belubus. I also invited some singers to the house to discuss their own interpretations. The resulting translations, I am confident, have both captured local meanings and retained the original poetics.

The Opening and Becoming Familiar

Once the group arrives in the village, they have coffee and cake at the house of the hostess. The singing gets started at about 9:00 or 9:30 P.M. The ceremony in question is Adek's wedding at Ibu Wel's house. The performers sit on a small stage covered by a plastic canopy erected in front of the house facing the road. Serge and I sit on the few chairs set up for the occasion. We face the singers, and as the evening moves on there is much talking between the singers and the audience. Men and sometimes women and children sit up on the stage close to the singers. Pak Pera, especially, likes to take a place close to his favorite singer.

The opening song from the village of Singgalang eases the way for strangers (the performers) to enter the village setting gently without ruffling local feathers. To protect themselves from hostile magic, the singers ask for permission of the village penghulu to sing. They offer apologies in advance and ask forgiveness should they offend anyone by their presence or by the words they sing. With this bow to budi the singers establish proper relations with the audience by signifying their good intentions and their willingness to abide by the standards of the village. The song begins with the theme of loss and separation that will be repeated throughout the evening:

> We the children of people from far away are distraught
> We come with anxious hearts
> It's late and there is no one to receive us.
> Please excuse us
> We ask your pardon a thousand times
> We apologize to the ninik mamak.
> We bring our ten fingers together
> Bowing in apology to all
> We apologize, its getting late.
> We buy the cloth of this village

We use the proper measurement
We abide by your standards in every way.

In another verse of the opening song, the singers go into more detail about standards of measurement, likening the etiquette of the performance to the appropriate marketing of rice.

The measure we bring is brimming with rice
It is the measure of the three regions of Minangkabau
The measure for the Minangkabau world.
We raise our hands to salute you
To ask your forgiveness should we offend you
By words that go outside of adat.

Here the singers serve notice that although they may not be conversant in local adat, they are part of alam Minangkabau. By saying this they give notice that they can be trusted, which gives them the leeway to tease the audience during the evening without fear of retaliatory anger that might come their way in the form of magic.

The opening song thread is long, consisting of some six or seven verses of the Singgalang song. As the singers warm up, they eye the audience. To knit us together, they sing of familiar feelings, places, and activities. Si Ai begins this thread:

Here we are under the *beringin* tree of the market of Munggu
In front of the nagari office
Oh, help to bring the news.
Tonight we want to listen and enjoy
We are gathered together
Seeking to be of one mind.
We come to have a good time
Later we will be taken home.

In this early part of the performance, people come and go shouting out phrases to the singers and to one another: "You've come home." "When did you arrive?" "How are you?" Such remarks heighten the impression that we are all of one family. Gadis Suayan develops the thread of union with verses addressed first to me and then to Serge.

Ibu, oh Ibu of the good heart
The one who is so wise and polite.
We can see you only, Ibu
We can't make a life with you.
For soon you will leave for your country.

Si Ai takes it from there:

> Oh Ibu Peggi, the one who is so beautiful
> Why do you look so sad, lost in thought?
> Do you dream about your sick child?
> We hope that she will be well.
> We hope that you will bring us here again.

Gadis Suayan then shifts to Serge:

> Oh, Pak Sus of the good heart
> He follows us tonight to have a good time.
> Even if we must separate tonight
> We will meet again.

Using the example of the pandanus tree that is uprooted and split, she says about me:

> Even though we will separate
> Like the pandanus,
> We remain as one in heart
> When we remember one another.
> Don't let your heart change, oh Ibu
> Never change, wherever you are.

This line goes on for some time, about fifteen more verses, mostly saying the same thing but using different rhyming couplets.[3]

Song threads about Serge and me and other members of the audience are interwoven throughout the evening and as the night wears on the verses become more intimate. These are always sung by the women, never by Nijon. Often the songs have a sexual connotation and are delivered with much advice. With respect to Serge and me, the women comment on our relationship, suggesting that because we sit lost in thought we may be dreaming about other lovers. We are told that if the other is not satisfactory, we may take another lover but we are reminded also that the old lover is always the best. Repeatedly the women suggest we come up and sit with them. Not understanding a word, Serge doesn't move and sits lost in thought through the night. Not wanting to interrupt his chain of thought, I don't tell him that his musing is constantly the subject of the verses. The singers want us to look happy by laughing and having fun. Serge is far away in France, where he grew up as a young man. I get up to join the women, who treat me like a dear friend who has come home.

The song plot thickens as the audience shouts out requests and the singers continue to make up verses about selected audience members as well as singing standard lagu pusako of their own choosing. In interviews with the singers they use many descriptors to characterize their songs: "happy" (*gimbira*), "sad" (*sedih*), or "funny" (*lucu*). They tell me that the songs are about feelings (*perasaan*), suffering and misfortune (*perasaian*), and love (*cinta*). Or, the songs are filled with advice on character and morals (*budi perkti*). Fate (*nasib*) is another important topic. The most affecting songs are the laments (*ratok*). Finally, many of the songs sing about particular places or villages—how life is in those places and what day the local market is held.

Love Songs

One might say that saluang songs are mainly about love because so many express longing for connection. The most heartrending songs tell of the loss of a mother or child. For example, there is the famous "Ratok Koto Gadang," a lament from the village of Koto Gadang in Agam. I chose this song as a book epigraph because it is such a beautiful poetic expression of feelings engendered by one's mother and village of origin. The song is about the fate of a person who comes back to his village after a long stay in the rantau. He goes to his mother's house and calls out for his mother. No one answers and there is no ladder leading up to the door of the house. All the windows are closed. It is sung in verses of four lines each.

> If there is no winnow for the rice
> How can it be cleaned?
> If my mother is no more
> On whom can I lean?

> I have come home to Canduang
> To her rumah gadang.
> The stairs are broken and the door is closed.
> Oh, tell me my people where has she gone?

> If my dear mother is at home
> My worries are over.
> When I am sad, she soothes my heart.
> When I need her, she gives advice.

Without her I am nothing.
With whom will I talk?
I feel so lost, I can only cry.
It is late, I must hurry home . . . Oh, Mother.

Si Ai comments, "This is a sad song. The rhythm conveys the pain."
She continues:

It's about Mande, our mother. The song is about the desperation we feel if we lose our mother. Our mother is always there for us. If she has no money for us, she gives us rice. If there is no mother, we have no rice. If we want our child to marry, we discuss a candidate for marriage with Mande. Her home is the place where we have the wedding. If we have our Mande, we always have someone to talk to. If we don't have our Mande, then we have to handle life on our own. Our rice is filled with our tears when our Mande has gone. This is the meaning of "Ratok Mande Kanduang."

Many love songs describe feelings like this: what it is like to lose connection to a loved one. Often the words combined with the melody induce tears. One of Pak Edi's favorite songs is like this. Normally reticent, speaking rarely to us, Pak Edi was positively effusive on the subject of saluang. He accompanied us to all performances choosing always to sit near us rather than to join the card players or his buddies in the village. Many times he and Serge shared the same bench in the hours after I left because I wasn't able to stay awake. I often had the feeling of being close to Pak Edi because it seemed to me we shared common emotions, even though we spoke so little to each other over the years.

The following song, "Pinang Sabatang," Pak Edi told me, takes him to the heart of the problems and emotions of his life.

This is the song of the areca palm
The tree that stands alone
With no children, and no other trees.
How painful it is to see you so lonely, dear friend.
Yes, I am alone in the world.
My rice is mixed with tears
My mother is gone, Oh, Mande.
I am alone in the world
My food swims in my tears.
This is my fate, Oh, Mande.
Fate is like trees that fall
It can go any way.
My fate has fallen
When I get sick, I have only my tears for medicine
What can I do, Mande?

The song concludes with the mother's answer:

> I sing this sad song
> For the cassette.
> The child I wait for is so far
> He has gone rantau, he doesn't return
> Oh, its getting late.

I was never able to ascertain from Pak Edi whether this song had anything to do with the fact that his own mother and father were living a fair distance away. I thought of asking, but I felt such a question would be inappropriate. One is like a tree that falls in a certain direction; fate is to be accepted not questioned. I felt that this was how Pak Edi experienced life.

Laments often give advice as to how to heal a breach and go on with life. One of my favorites is "Lament of Suayan," named after the village where Gadis Suayan got her start. In the following verse a wife thinks of her husband who has gone, but the song could apply also to unmarried lovers. The woman doesn't want to tie her husband down, but she misses him terribly. She knows that he may be going to another wife or to the rantau, situations faced by many women. The wife reminds her husband that they are bound by good deeds, not by a rope. This allusion to the importance of persuasion rather than force is common in personal relations.

> Suayan, Sungai Balintiak,
> The third is Koto Malintang.
> If you leave, come back quickly, Oh, Tuan.
> It's hard for me to enjoy life without you.
> Where are you, Oh, Tuan.
> We are bound by good deeds. Oh, Tuan.
> If we are bound by a rope,
> Its easy to untie the knot and run, Oh Tuan.
> I hesitate to use a rope
> I don't want to tie you, Oh Tuan.

Another song in the Suayan series laments the mother who is separated from her children by death. The title of the song is "Maik Ka Turun" (The corpse that is laid out just before burial).

> Her breath is gone
> Her body lies on the floor in the middle of the house.
> Oh, Amak (Grandmother).
> The family sits around her
> She cries in her grave, oi Amak.
> She remembers her children left behind,
> Children left behind, oi Amak.

She lies on the floor in the middle of the house.
Wrapped in layers of cloth, Oh, Amak, oi.
She tells those she has left behind
Be happy and prosperous, don't cry, oi Amak.
Be good so that people will be happy with you
So that your Mande can depart in peace.

Generally it is the women who sing the emotion-laden songs during the evening. Nijon also sings about emotion, but the emotion is less expressive and the tone is more playful. About the feelings children have for the father who has gone from the house, he sings:

The ship leaves in the middle of the night
Taking the people to the market in Kambang
The child cries in the night
He sees that his father has not come home
In the morning his pillow and mattress are still cold.

Nijon's composition can be compared to another song about the father sung by Si Ai.

Abak, oi Abak (Father) . . . please come home
The children are crying
Crying at the door, waiting for their father.
They wait but he doesn't come home
They call out for their father.
The mattress is thick, cold in his absence.
The children call others bapak
Abak, oi Abak, come home soon.

Songs about Sexual Performance

At some point during every performance, usually late at night, there is a great deal of laughter as some males in the audience cry out, "Sawah liek! Sawah liek!" looking at me. I feel a little uncomfortable because I wonder if the request for this song makes oblique reference to Serge, whose white hair puts him in the "sawah liek" generation. It would take me some time to realize that the song is a huge joke addressed to all men, old and young. The song is about female sexual desire; both about what happens when women don't have sex and why they may go for a long time without it. Whenever the song is sung it is accompanied by much joking and ribbing about men in the audience.

Literally translated, *sawah liek* means a hardened rice field, one that is unwatered and uncultivated. The song is a lagu pusako because it takes place in a village near Bukik Tinggi. Unlike other songs, this one is never found on a commercial cassette and can only be heard in performance. I have heard many versions over the years. The song begins in the usual way, by reference to its place of origin. Si Ai begins:

> The crossroads on the road to Jambu Air
> The area of the people of Birugo village.
> It has been hot for one long year
> The seedlings are dry
> Where will the sawah get water?

Later Si Ai told me that "hot" here refers to a woman who wants sex regardless of with whom, for she has been long without it. From whom will she get sex (water)? Si Ai asks. She explains that the seedlings refer to pubic hair that is dry and matted from lack of use.

Gadis Suayan takes up the next verse, improvising a bit:

> Hai, come here and sit by me
> Our time for fun and song is not long
> Don't worry about the hardened rice field
> Slowly, the mouse eats the seedlings.

Gadis Suayan, whose husband has left her, tells me that here she is saying that it doesn't matter if the sawah is hard. She wants the gathered men to know that she is not looking for a boyfriend because boyfriends are too slow. Rather, she is looking for a husband who is adept at satisfying his wife's desire because he knows what she wants. Lovers are too slow, she says, because they are caught up in the courtship.

Si Ai takes up the thread, improvising about Pak Pera, who has been sitting near her throughout the evening.

> Pak Pera's dream has finally come true
> Why does he sit with a faraway look?
> Why is the sawah still hard?
> Because his hoe has been stored away.

When I asked her about this song, Si Ai explained that Pak Pera's dream has been fulfilled because Gadis Suayan has admitted to being sawah liek. Why does he still dream? she asks. Because the sawah is still hard, she answers. Pak Pera is unable to satisfy his woman because his hoe no longer works.

Si Ai continues still improvising:

> Don't sit far away from me
> Let's be one and have a good time tonight.
> If my husband doesn't hoe the sawah
> At least he can pick the rice seedlings by hand.

Which means that even if her husband's hoe is put away, he can use his hands to clean her rice field, i.e., satisfy her desire.

Gadis Suayan responds in kind:

> From the market of the people of Matur
> Couples go home together,
> A sign that they want to cultivate the land
> But, the border is broken by the hoe.

Couples meet at the market and go home, walking together, a sign that they are lovers. The young man is too active with his hoe, too hurried, and he hurts the wall of the vagina. His desire is too strong because of his age.

Another popular song about sex is called "Kutang Barendo." Interestingly, Wik and many women say that this is their favorite song. They like it because it is a funny song—it's *lucu*, people say, it makes us laugh. It is also a song that older men appreciate. The rhythm is bouncy and people laugh throughout. *Kutang* means "bra" and *rendo* means "lace." The song is about a young woman who wears a lacy bra which can be seen through her outer garment. Si Ai sings,

> When they see the lacy bra on the young woman
> The old men lick their lips.
> O la la, kutang barendo
> Barendo, please buy it.

The last line advises women to buy the lacy bra for their husbands.

> Buy transparent clothes so that kutang barendo can be seen.
> O la la, kutang barendo.

The verses continue:

> If you meet the person of your dreams
> Only then will your heart rejoice
> Separation breaks the heart.
> When remote control was invented
> Lacy bras were no longer needed.
> O la la, kutang barendo, barendo.

Remote control in this verse refers to the ability to disrobe a woman by pressing a button, like one would turn on the TV. Another verse of the song refers to the young woman whose breasts are like a "blooming flower," "round like coconut shells." But the old man who looks and imagines can only dream.

According to Si Ai this is a song about the dreams of older men who are past their sexual prime but still have a young spirit. They still want sex but can't get it. When old men see young women in transparent clothes, they see their kutang barendo and they feel desire. Old and young like this song because it is funny. Basically, the implication is that sex is fun and exciting for men and women, old and young.

Nijon's Compositions

As the evening wears on and the female singers tire, they give more time to Nijon's songs, many of which are about love. Nijon doesn't sing the lagu pusako, preferring instead his own compositions, which take place somewhere in the villages of the Four Koto. He sings about his home village Sungai Talang, the center of the Four Koto.

> The center of the Four Koto is Sungai Talang
> Monday is market day in Payakumbuh
> Go home at night
> Remember your garden
> Before the coconut falls
> Don't throw out the monkey.

Nijon is saying that one must always go home to one's wife and children. As long as they are working together to raise a family, the husband should not put his wife and children aside for someone else. They need one another to make a living, to keep the garden going.

Another song is about Balubuih (the traditional name for Belubus).

> We are performing in Balubuih having a good time
> It's raining
> If you want to join with us (referring to himself)
> I'll give you anything you want
> Sawah, sex, food, or song.

The hour is late, almost quitting time. Nijon gets carried away, bowing his rabab in imitation of male sexual performance—thrusting the bow along the strings and then stopping for a moment, repeating the thrust, then moving it very fast, back and forth, faster and faster, all the while singing about the joys of life. He speaks of eating, of the hoe sinking into and out of the earth, of the delight and the screams of pleasure. Everyone is with him, smiling, laughing, or talking loudly egging him on. There is no sign of disapproval, but by now it's 4 A.M., we are only a few.

Going Home

After Nijon's performance, Gadis Suayan sings of the upcoming separation:

> The night is late, we can see
> The sincerity is high, we can see
> We are panning for gold
> We have struck gold in Bangko.
> He asks for another song
> Wherever the song goes
> I am there.
> It's time to go
> I am sad, I don't know where I will go.

The song that officially closes the performance is "Jalu Jalu," which is the name of a large-leafed plant found in gardens. As with the opening song, permission is now asked to leave with the hope that good feeling is left behind. Once again the performers are likened to traders who come to the village to sell their goods. The three singers alternate with different verses of this song.

> Jalu jalu in the garden, oi in the garden
> It's the food for the children of the forest, of the forest
> How about it, mamak? Do you agree?
> Take the red brick for building the wall, for the wall
> So that the bathroom is completed, the place for the bath.
> Give us your blessing for our journey
> So that all will be well, like people who buy and sell.

Turning to me, they begin to sing discretely about the money I will give them for the performance. Si Ai starts:

> Give us the ship from Surantiah, the ship from Surantiah.
> The ship of Si Esuik from Java, from Java.
> Give us your blessing [money]
> With a sincere heart, Ibu Peggy.
> Ibuku Peggy, oh Ibu, give.
> We help with our voice, with our voice.

The good-bye and request for money becomes more direct. Si Ai sings:

> En take the car, take the car.
> Take us home with Ibu Peggy
> Please, Ibu Peggy, take us home.
> If we live long, have a healthy life
> Please come back.

Gadis Suayan adds,

> It's four o'clock, we must stop.
> My own dear friend, Ibu Kanduang, are you sad?
> People are sleeping or falling asleep
> Soon the morning light will come.
> What about me, what about me?
> The song has been good, we can stop now.
> If our life is long we will repeat, we will come back.
> When will we meet again, I don't know.

Nijon adds his thoughts:

> We cut the string of the kite
> We cut near the tail that balances the kite, oi Amak.
> I'm happy here
> No one will cry, we are all happy
> Our time together has been good.

Si Ai takes it up:

> We keep what is good and throw away the bad
> We give out of love
> We will long for one another
> The longing we have for one another is unbearable.
> Those of us who have passed this evening together
> We long to be together once again.

Gadis Suayan ends:

> We must separate, but that's okay
> What is important is that we have been one in the sawah.
> Separation is okay
> We will keep the memory in our hearts
> We will meet again.

Later, after Wik serves coffee and cakes, I pay the performers and En takes them home.

Thoughts about the Saluang Performance

The songs I selected for presentation come from a list I made of the favorite songs of men and women in the village. I was intrigued by their choices. Both sexes chose songs about female sexuality. Everyone showed a high regard for the funny songs. Songs of love, lamentation, and loss were the most deeply felt. I was especially moved by Pak Edi's favorite song, which likens fate to a tree that might fall in any direction during a storm—such is the uncertainty of life that males must feel. The song also laments separation from the mother, demonstrating that men as well as women are emotionally attached to the maternal place.

Nijon's songs, all composed by him, are mostly about his home nagari. He sings about the everydayness of life—tilling the fields, harvesting rice, going to market. Some of his songs express longing for the father. "The child cries in the night," he sings, when the child feels the cold spot on the bed usually warmed by his father's sleeping body and realizes that his father has not come home. The theme of longing for the father is reflected in several of Nijon's songs, but the longing is never quite as intense as the longing for the mother in the lamentations the women sing. I was very saddened to hear of Nijon's death soon after this performance. He died from smoking too much, I was told.

Listening to the saluang performance with its emphasis on women and decidedly female ethos, I thought often about what we miss in the West when we equate female-centeredness with female political rule. This narrow focus obscures the character of the emotions and the relations between the sexes in a female-oriented society like the Minangkabau. I was struck by the ease and restrained familiarity between the sexes. The ease is reflected in the melodic interaction between female singer and saluang flute. The saluang player follows the woman's song wherever she wants to go, or he changes the melody, beckoning her into a new song, and she follows. The two are inseparable as they jointly bring emotion alive by weaving women's words and male melody. Males listen in rapt attention, perhaps finding release from the social constraints of maleness which has separated them from their own maternal household.

Sexual tension and disappointment are handled as a joke. The songs about unrequited love are hilarious, especially "Sawah Liek." Men roar appreciatively, women in the audience smile. No one, not even Pak Pera himself, minds when he becomes the butt of the joke in this song about the arid rice field that he is unable to cultivate or water. I often thought of this as a Viagra song, a way for women to tell the men in their lives that sex matters. The implications of this song and those about male sexuality—impotence in older men and aggressive sexuality in younger ones—communicate a female sensibility to the male listeners. The song about the lacy bra that Wik found so funny demonstrates that women like to be looked at and appreciated. As the songs continue into the night, the sexual innuendoes get more passionate, as Nijon mimes male sexual performance using the thrusts of his bow. One wonders how many fields will be cultivated and watered later when the men arrive home.

I was struck by the honesty with which women bear their souls to create a shared emotional space in a context where the goal is to have a good time. Psychologically, the songs seemingly are about the existential void and fulfillment created over a lifetime by separation from and reunion with maternal love. Maternal love is given not just by mothers but by fathers, lovers, spouses, and children. We all long for reunion with that which nurtured us as children. The existential wound at separation from the maternal is perhaps more traumatic for Minangkabau men than it is for women because they are the wanderers, the ones who are dislodged from the maternal breast, whereas women stay in the home of their birth, on the ancestral land, and conceive, bear children, and take them to their maternal breast. The heartfelt outpouring of the emotions of union, love, loss, and sexual desire resembles a stream-of-consciousness psychoanalytic session in which the wound of existential loss is temporarily relieved with a soothing balm. One ends the night feeling less a stranger to oneself. The confusion and bewilderment of life's emotional burdens turn to wonder and clarity as the darkness of night gives way to the light of morning.

This is my reaction to the night of the saluang. I can't speak for anyone else, but I watched closely the faces of my saluang comrades as we gathered close during the long night. I felt at one with the people of Belubus during these nights. I was deeply impressed by the way women, singing of love and meaning, occupied center stage. The performance enhanced and confirmed my sense that this society is more than just woman friendly; it instills female sensibilities in men. It is a society in which there is little or no domestic violence or rape, where women express a joy of living as they celebrate together their children's life cycles and sing their hearts out on the ceremonial stage. These revelations changed the way I saw and related to the world.

I wonder if the sense of release and joy I felt was not a human reaction to the discrepancy between the ethos of misogyny and the nurture of maternal bonding. Misogyny, based on the desire to diminish the feminine in the self, limits the human spirit and separates the soul from maternal nurture; the mantle of female nurture, based on love, gives one a sense of belonging, brings joy and laughter, provides peace and protection.

I wonder also whether the maternal nurture I witnessed and experienced in West Sumatra doesn't also mute the ugly power of the fear of death by preparing the living to cross more easily to the world of the dead.[4] I was deeply touched by the Minangkabau reaction to death. Ibu Idar's regular visits with her father, and reports of others who spoke of direct contact with their departed parents and ancestors, made death less frightening. The lamentations sung during the saluang performance flooded me with memories of those who had nurtured me. As I watched Pak Edi and other men responding to these lamentations, I felt that the performance gave them the space to remember and mourn as well.

The performance ends in the typical Minangkabau way; on a note of goodwill, appreciation, thanks, and apologies. I got used to the polite reminders about the fee that had been promised. The Minangkabau are at heart traders, always aware of the importance of payment for services rendered. Reciprocity suffuses Minangkabau interactions, whether at home, in the marketplace, or during a ceremony.

Serge's reaction to the saluang performance was instructive. In all the many performances he attended, he sat entranced in a faraway world of his own. When I looked at him during the night, I could see that he was moved. How, I was not sure, but I understood that he was in the distant land of his past. After looking at him, my eyes would wander to Pak Edi, who often came to sit by Serge. I was struck by the similarity of their reaction. Both remained silent through the night, lost in thought, clearly engrossed. I appreciated the silence cloaking them in the cool night and never asked questions.

After the first performance, Serge shared some thoughts. "It's a celebration of the emotions and feelings of the generations," he said. "It's like the blues in the States, the fado in Portugal, an expression of the simplicity of deep human feeling. Nostalgia and sorrow grounded in the activities of daily life." He concluded, "It brings together everything you know about village life."

I'm not sure exactly what he meant, but I don't disagree. When the performance is over we go home with Pak Edi by the light of the stars. Serge and I are exhausted but content. We fall asleep in our little room at five o'clock in the morning, feeling soothed by the emotions and comradery of the night.

IV

HOW MEN UPHOLD
MATRILINEAL ADAT

CHAPTER ELEVEN

Being and Becoming a Penghulu

In the traditional Minangkabau nagari, the penghulu was the richest, most knowledgeable, most powerful, both politically and judicially, and most prestigious person.

Tsuyoshi Kato, *Matriliny and Migration*

If we are not rich, it is very difficult to be a penghulu, Dt. Penghulu Besar told En. We must be ready to help others settle disputes whenever they arise. At these times we cannot work in our sawah or ladang. We can go bankrupt or stay poor because we don't have the time to *cari uang* (look for money) like other men in the village. Whether the dispute be about land, harta pusaka, or a family affair, we are called upon. We must be very careful to stay neutral.

Field notes, 1997

The archetypal role of the penghulu places other men and children in a special relationship to him as expressed in the following proverb:

The kemenakan (nieces and nephews) are subject to the mamak,
The mamak (mother's brother) is subject to the penghulu,
The penghulu is subject to mupakat (consensus),
Mupakat is subject to the power of reasoning,
The power of reasoning is subject to what is appropriate and possible,
What is appropriate and possible is subject to truth,
Truth is our king.[1]

This proverb reflects the judicial role played by the penghulu in administering adat law *(adat limbago)*. When they meet in the village council house to settle disputes, the titled male leaders refer to the body of law codified by the original adat lawgivers. This body of law establishes a procedure for the resolution of disputes according to *mupakat*, consensus decision making in search of the truth. Mutual agreement is the ultimate sovereign in Minangkabau life, taking precedence over the power of men or women as a group. Anyone who stands in the way of truth by acting discourteously or resorting to the use of force is exiled from the community or shunned.

The primary function of the penghulu in Belubus is to resolve disputes, negotiate marriage, confer titles on new candidates, and engage males from other lineages in an official exchange of speeches at adat ceremonies. In addition to his role along with senior women in negotiating marriage, theoretically it is the responsibility of the penghulu to look after the young people of his clan by helping them find spouses. In practice, this is a job that usually falls to the mothers involved. It is also up to the penghulu, meeting as a group, to incorporate outsiders who want to live in Belubus under the umbrella of adat through a special adat ceremony in which the individual is "adopted" by a particular clan.

In dispute settlement, the penghulu resolve the competing land claims that lead to harsh words and outright conflict in the village. The process is very careful and deliberate, for the proceedings must follow consensus decision making in search of the truth according to the saying "Loosen that which is tight, so that the sound is like a tinkle rather than a crash."

The man who inherits the penghulu title oversees the management and use of ancestral land in conjunction with his sisters. Because this puts him in a position where he could abuse clan interests for his own profit, he must display more than the correct genealogical link. He must be deemed honest, truthful, straightforward, and strong enough to uphold the rules of adat.

A man who breaks these rules by selling land without the appropriate agreement from his female relatives suffers the consequences of the curse of the ancestors. The symbolism of the curse seems to have been devised with the penghulu in mind. The curse likens the penghulu to a tree; if he breaks the oath of the ancestors, he will be like the tree that decays and dies after bees have bored into its heartwood.

Tree Symbolism and the Penghulu

According to Minangkabau gender meanings the male is believed to be rooted in nature, from which he grows into culture by being educated in

adat or by taking on an adat title. Becoming a penghulu involves the verbal and ceremonial forging of the cultural man out of the natural. This
interpretation is suggested by the name for the ceremony, *batagak
penghulu* or *mendirikan penghulu*, both of which mean "raising a
penghulu." The concept of raising refers to the penghulu as a pillar or
tree. For example, in the booklet of adat rules published locally to guide
and educate the penghulu of the Four Koto, the penghulu is likened to

> a big tree in the field whose roots are very deep, whose trunk is big, with strong
> branches brimming with leaves and fruit. The roots are for sitting, the trunk is for
> resting one's back, the branches are for hanging one's clothes, the fruits are for eat-
> ing, the leaves give shade from the sunlight and shelter from the rain. The penghulu
> shelters his nephews and nieces, guides them in the rules of adat, teaches them the
> rules for measurements. He is the umbrella that shelters all. (Elok 1995:2)[2]

The metaphors of planting or raising, suggestive of growth from the
natural to the cultural, are found in another proverb.

> A title descends through the generations
> Within the measure of adat
> Under the one umbrella, in the maternal line of those
> Who are the occupants of virginal territory
> Who have their own grave and cemetery.
> When the title falls [when the penghulu dies]
> There a mushroom grows [a new one grows]
> From the red earth of the newly dug grave.[3]

In line with the tree metaphor, numerous references to "raising a pillar" appear in other ceremonial contexts where males play the focal role.
For example, the ceremony of building a traditional house is called *batagak rumah adat* (raising the pillars of the longhouse), a task that is performed by all the penghulu of a village aided by village men. Building a
regular house is called *batagak kudo-kudo* (raising the roof rafters), a task
performed in the same way.

The concept of raising is also associated with the menhirs in Belubus,
which are sometimes referred to as *batu tagak* (raised stones). Some people say that these stones were planted long ago by the original settlers to
mark clan land, including the cemetery of the original clan.[4] A common
feature of the menhir sites in Belubus is the occurrence of two separate
but connected groups of stones. An archeological excavation at one of
the sites revealed that the stones in one group marked burials. Near these
burials is a pair of stones, one very large and the other quite small. People say that the large stone commemorates the first penghulu title erected

in the area, while the small stone signifies the *kemenakan* (nephews and nieces) under the umbrella of this title.

Oath of the Ancestors

The tree metaphor is at the symbolic center of the legendary oath administered to the adat lawgivers of the tambo when they received their penghulu titles. In Belubus and much of central Sumatra, the oath is called *sumpah biso kewi*, which literally means "oath of the ancestors." The oath is also referred to as "the curse of the ancestors" to indicate the penalty that befalls those who break the oath. Although I never saw this oath administered as such, many people talked about the curse of the ancestors in Belubus. I have also read eyewitness accounts of the administration of the oath in several sources.

Early in the twentieth century the oath was witnessed by the high-ranking Dutch colonial official, L. C. Westenenk. In his long article on the Minangkabau nagari, Westenenk writes that he observed titled male leaders swearing the oath to claim rights to land under the umbrella of their title. According to Westenenk, the oath was always taken at a sacred place in the presence of all the penghulu of the village. New leaves of the sugar palm were laid upon the ground in a circle, and at the center a stick was planted, to which were fastened the very hard fruits of the *anau* tree. A cooking pot from the hearth of the traditional house was filled with *jarak* leaves and attached to the stick. Westenenk observed a penghulu who took the oath entering the circle with the one woman and man closest to him by blood, descendants from one *kanduang*—that is, from one womb or from the common ancestress Bundo Kanduang. The circle also included one of the most distant relatives so as to represent the center and periphery of the family tree claiming rights to the land. Within the circle the penghulu swore that he was not lying, that the property belonged to the whole family, and that if he was lying the whole family would be ruined.[5]

According to Westenenk the entire family tree is subject to withering like a tree that neither sprouts leaves nor develop roots. The family becomes like the stick planted in the ground that cannot grow, its core bored out by bees. The oath is so heavy, he says, that "a native and especially his entire family dreads taking such an oath without being sure about the matter being sworn" (Westenenk 1918:95–96). The words of the oath are the same as those mentioned in the penghulu inaugural ceremony observed by Frederick Errington some seventy-five years later.

Errington observed the oath being administered in a penghulu inaugural ceremony he recorded in the village of Bayur on the shores of Lake Mannijau in the early 1980s. According to Errington the penghulu candidate was told the following:

> If you are not true in carrying out [adat] you will be struck by the oath and the poison of the kris, the emblem of the greatness of Minangkabau panghulu, possessed by Datuak Perpatih nan Sabatang and Datuak Ketemanggungang. If you are not true to adaik, [you will be as a tree and] on the top, buds will not sprout; on the bottom, sap will not circulate; in the middle, bumblebees will bore holes. Thus will strike the poison descended from Datuak Perpatih nan Sabatang and Datuak Ketemanggungang. I hope that you accept all of my advice, that a drop becomes an ocean, a handful of sand becomes a mountain. (Errington 1984:134)

The allusions in this speech to the dying tree, the sons of Indo Jelito, and to the famous proverb about growth in nature expressed in a village far from Belubus (about four to five hours drive) on the periphery of alam Minangkabau demonstrate the wide circulation of adat traditions. The case of Pak Indra, which I observed, provides dramatic evidence of the continued belief in the power of the curse at the end of the twentieth century.

The Case of Pak Indra

In 1996 while I was in Belubus, Pak Indra was installed with the title of penghulu in one of the villages of Nagari Sungai Talang.[6] En and I heard about the upcoming inauguration of Pak Indra to the title Dt. Raja Kecil from one of the top adat specialists, Dt. Pucuk. It was obvious from the way that Dt. Pucuk spoke that there were problems with Pak Indra's candidacy. With typical Minangkabau circumlocution and sense of propriety, no one actually spoke directly about the problem. The details filtered out slowly; we didn't learn the whole story until some two years later, when Pak Indra's replacement received a formal reprimand from the village adat council. What started in 1996 with great fanfare and hope for a prosperous future ended in 1999 with a family facing shame and depleted resources due to their disregard of adat law and, some said, punishment by the curse of the ancestors.

Conferring a title, especially one that has fallen into disuse (as was the case of Pak Indra), requires separate meetings of the family, clan, village, and nagari in which the qualifications of the candidate are discussed. The qualifications include an examination of the man's character, his knowledge of and commitment to adat, his morality, his leadership abilities, his religiosity, and his character as a proper citizen of the Indonesian nation. In addition, the candidate's family tree is carefully examined to determine his relationship to the penghulu whose title his maternal relatives want him to adopt.

The central importance of the family tree in conferring a title highlights the different valuation placed on blood relationships as opposed to adoptive ones. Relationships by blood are referred to as "the line of Bundo Kanduang" or as *warih nasab* (lineal heir). This is the first and most desired class of heirs. Such individuals are said to be *sapayung sapatogak*, that is, under one umbrella and in one maternal line. The high social value placed on this kind of relationship in the transmission of titles and property is indicated by the number of times I heard people using these phrases in the case of Pak Indra.

The second general class of heirs is labeled *warih batali sabab*, which applies to people who have been adopted or who are linked by adoptive-like relationships rather than by blood ties. Such a tie, at best, was what Pak Indra had with the family of the deceased penghulu whose title he wanted to assume. To support this claim, however, he produced a family tree that showed a blood relationship.[7]

The title in question had fallen into disuse for nearly forty years which meant reviving a sunken title *(mambangkik batang tarandam)*. No one was sure of the exact relationship between Pak Indra and the dead penghulu, only that Pak Indra was probably not warih nasab—not a direct lineal heir. Nevertheless the living male and female relatives who were warih nasab of this penghulu agreed to Pak Indra's candidacy by giving their stamp of approval and signing the family tree Pak Indra had prepared. No doubt they did so because they felt that Pak Indra was a man who could work for the family and draw them together under the umbrella of the resurrected title. At the time of the initial phases of the inaugural ceremony there was no open disagreement, just a lot of muttering.

Putting on the Headcloth

Once the family tree was signed by the appropriate family members, it was then signed by the governmentally appointed head of local adat affairs (the KAN). The next step was the ceremony of *pasang deta* (putting on the headcloth). The night before the ceremony we visited Pak Indra in the house of his older sister, where the ceremony would be held. The scene was festive; piles of bananas filled the kitchen area, and many women were cooking and preparing silomak. I understood from this scene that the main acts of the ceremony would involve the usual adat feasting and food exchanges.

Pak Indra explained that the first order of business would be to receive his ceremonial clothes from his bako relatives. I was surprised to learn that the bako were supplying the appropriate clothes *(kain sapotagak)* including the kris. My confusion had to do with the fact that *kain sapotagak* refers to the dress of one ancestral line, which meant that the pusako (heirlooms such as the kris) should have come from the mother's line. I could understand the bako providing the clothes but not the kris. After all, the kris is the only object that is explicitly associated with the inheritance of titles. In answer to my questioning, I was assured that it was common for bako to supply the clothes to the new penghulu, but the maternal relatives always supplied the ancestral kris. In this case, the bako supplied the kris because there was no kris from the maternal side. This may have been due to the fact that the title had been buried for many years or because the kris had been sold to an antique dealer, a common fate of many family heirlooms throughout West Sumatra. The most likely possibility, however, was that in the absence of a title in his direct lineal line, there was in fact no kris for Pak Indra to inherit, just as there was no title.

Pak Indra told us that he would be given the complete title of the deceased penghulu—Dt. Raja Kecil—most unusual in cases where the candidate was not warih nasab. As the ceremony progressed, however, we observed that this was not the title that was actually conferred. In fact, Pak Indra seemed to have many aspects of the ceremony wrong. For example, he also said that his patrilateral relatives *(bako)* would crown him with the penghulu headcloth, an unusual procedure given that placing the headcloth was symbolic of passing a matrilineal title to a supposedly matrilineal heir. Just the day before, Dt. Pucuk had told us that the local KAN would put the headcloth on the candidate's head, which turned out to be correct in this case.

We arrived early the next morning to witness the handing over of the clothes by the bako relatives. After quite a bit of waiting they arrived, one man and several women. Among them was an older, official-looking woman, beautifully dressed in ceremonial clothes. I was told that she was the younger sister of Pak Indra's father, which made her bako kontan. She carried the penghulu outfit in a neatly wrapped bundle with the kris pushed underneath the cord that tied it together. After arriving and eating, this woman gave the bundle to Pak Indra. The procedure was somewhat formal, perhaps for my benefit. Ibu Suria knelt down in the middle of the room, sitting the way women do with her feet under her. Pak

Indra moved to the center of the room and placed himself in front of her, sitting with his feet crossed. Ibu Suria leaned slightly toward Pak Indra, setting the bundle of clothes on the floor in front of him while saying a few words I couldn't catch. He received the clothes silently with bowed head. After a moment or two, during which time I took pictures, the two got up and the brief bow to ritual was over.

As this was taking place, men dressed in the black garb of the penghulu began gathering outside the house where they stood chatting among themselves and village men. Once all had arrived in the yard, they mounted the stairs of the house and joined us in the great room of the traditional longhouse. One important penghulu was not with them, nor was he expected to attend, I was told. This was the first visible evidence of controversy regarding Pak Indra's candidacy. Later I learned that everyone knew that there was disagreement regarding Pak Indra's right to the title; but since the disagreement was not publicly aired in the adat council house, the ceremony proceeded. The job of the penghulu was to formalize the public agreement that had been reached among the family members.

As the men came into the house they took their places on the mat, sitting in a rectangle around the room. It was the first time I had seen so much male energy ceremonially focused in a village household rather than in the more usual state-sponsored cultural celebrations.[8] The gathered throng of men dressed in black sat stiffly in the great room of the adat house. The women, dressed in the usual ceremonial outfits, crammed in a much smaller space between this room and the cooking room, some standing and some sitting—a jumble of color and excitement watching with obvious delight.

After all were seated, Dt. Rajo, the man referred to as the KAN, made his appearance, breezing in, shaking hands as he went, a handsome young man who had an air of distinguished formality about him—obviously a proper leader by the dictates of adat, religion, and government. He took his seat on the mat in a conspicuous position and all attention turned to him.[9]

The head of Pak Indra's clan spoke first, followed by Pak Indra's assistant, Dt. Aji, who made the obligatory opening speech. He began by saying, "In accordance with our customs, we have climbed up the steps and gone down them. It is time now to go to the council house."

The concept of "climbing up the steps and going down" would be repeated many times throughout the proceedings—it was a way of saying that all of the proper people had been consulted at all of the appropriate levels and that the case was ready for the next step, namely, to take it up to the nagari level.

In a long speech Dt. Rajo agreed, saying that all the right bases had been touched, all the appropriate steps had been taken—going up and down. Flowery verses flowed from his tongue, most of which I didn't understand. He referred frequently to the fact that all present shared the same custom (*adat and limbago*), the same measure for rice (*cupak* and *gantang*), and that the *balai adat* (adat council house) in the Four Koto were all under the same umbrella of custom and measurements. The comment about adat and limbago, cupak and gantang, was a reference to the standards codified in the tambo.

Another man spoke up, throwing a public seed of doubt into the proceedings by pointing out that not everyone who should be attending was present. Over the next hour this matter was discussed at great length, but very little of consequence was actually said. The upshot was that all had been done according to the adat way. "Why are we still in doubt?" Dt. Rajo asked. "Last Thursday, we met according to the rules and we agreed on what we are now practicing."

"This is our way," he continued. "Do we want to depart from the straight path?" he asked. "If we want to make something new, it should not be just here in Dt. Indra's home village, but it must also be applied to all of the villages of the Four Koto, including in Sungai Talang, the center of the nagari."

He continued, summarizing most of the material in the local booklet on the adat of Nagari Sungai Talang he had written. He pointed out that Pak Indra was taking on a title that was being revived after having sunk into disuse, and that this was in accordance with the rules agreed on in the meeting conducted last Thursday. He asked if there was anyone present who wanted to speak. His request included the women, who had listened attentively hanging on to every word. When no one spoke up, Dt. Rajo proceeded to the first ritual event.

The high point of the ceremony was the formal placing of the headcloth on Pak Indra's head by Dt. Rajo. Dt. Rajo first asked Pak Indra to don the ceremonial clothes according to adat. He led up to this with a long speech regarding the title. During this speech he named the title, which was not the one Pak Indra had mentioned the night before. As he spoke Dt. Rajo addressed the women as well as the men.

Now we ask that the title of Datuak Indra Gadang be put on. This is the first title. It is the title that we agreed upon. The women in the kitchen have asked for it many times. We hope there is no further comment. The beginning has been accomplished by our mother [who asked for the title to be put on]. So now we come to the second job. What is the second job? It is to fulfill the adat requirements, which now means to put on the clothes. After that we follow and fill the requirement of customs and traditions. Which tradition do we now follow? Which institution do we now fill? We place the headcloth, which will require five liters of rice. We wear the shirt also. It is the requirement. Please put on the clothes. Please place the shoulder sash from the right to the left side. Please place the kris in the outer belt sash.

Pak Indra and his assistant, Dt. Aji, who had made the opening speech, went into the adjoining room to don the black outfit of the penghulu and the red dress of the assistant to the penghulu, the *dubalang*. As they did so there was much conferring between these two men and the men in the adjacent great room regarding the proper way to tie the sash that holds the kris and how to arrange the sash across the chest. When they came out Dt. Rajo sent them back to rearrange several clothing details they had gotten wrong. For example, the sash around the waist was not properly tied, and the kris was inserted in the sash on the wrong side. Everything must be done according to adat, Dt. Rajo said. Once the clothing was satisfactorily completed, Pak Indra came out and sat in front of Dt. Rajo, who resumed the formal speechmaking.

> Our duty, our burden today is to put on the title that has been sinking for a long time. The title will be Dt. Indra Gadang. We know that since he [Pak Indra] was a child he had a name. But as an adult he is given a title. His name is now Mamak Indra Gadang. By agreement we now give him the title Dt. Indra Gadang. If you meet him near the river at the bathing place, in a crowded area where many men sit together, or after having a meal, please address him by this title.
>
> We ask him to be straight in his walk, sincere in his behavior, and to speak the truth. Without the truth his tongue has no power. He must set straight that which is tangled, clean that which is dirty, catch that which drifts, plant that which is sinking. In the village he may speak only for the sake of the prosperity of the villagers. This is a new title, one that will not sink in the future if the ways of the customs and institutions are followed. If this title falls by death, within twenty-one days we will raise a new one, say new words, fold a new headcloth. Walk straight and in the right time. If we do not walk in the right way, nature in our village will be twisted and complicated. There is no clear way if our leader [penghulu] is not good, if he wears a wrinkled headcloth. For then we cannot count its width, we cannot calculate what he means. To villagers, our children, our nephews and nieces, he must be helpful in overcoming problems. This is the conduct of a penghulu. It is based on our agreement. We follow the big trays [the rules, referring to the trays borne by women in adat ceremonies], we fill the ways and institutions [follow adat].

After the hat was placed and the speeches made, there was a round of money giving. Dt. Aji went around the room on his knees bending before each of the penghulu to give them the agreed upon sum on behalf of Dt. Indra Gadang. Everyone seemed pleased—the women served the food, after which everyone went outside for a round of picture taking. Then, they all proceeded in a procession to the road, making sure that an umbrella shielded the head of the newly raised penghulu. A small truck awaited them at the road, which had been rented to carry everyone to the second half of the ceremony held in the adat council hall in Sungai Talang, the mother village.

The Balai Adat in Nagari Sungai Talang

The ceremony started two hours later in the adat council hall. Most of the penghulu from the first ceremony were there along with a large group of penghulu from Sungai Talang. Altogether some fifty men were in attendance, most dressed in the black garb of the penghulu with four red-clad dubalang also present. The leaders of the four suku sat on the raised platforms at either end of the council hall. The speeches were long, and almost everyone present had their say.

The ceremony started with the usual Islamic greeting: *Assalamulaikum warahmatullahi wabarakatuh*. Then there was a litany of salutations addressed to the political, religious, and adat nobles of the Four Koto, who theoretically were in attendance.

"Hai, to the respected leader of Sungai Talang Barat, we salute you," referring to the elected leader of the administrative entity, which had been turned by government fiat into a desa and which included two of the villages of the former adat entity known as the Four Koto, the four villages of Nagari Sungai Talang.

"Hai, to the respected leader of Sungai Talang Timur, we salute you," referring to the elected leader of the other desa included in the Four Koto.

Then came the greeting to the adat leaders, the penghulu pucuk of each of the Four Koto, followed by a greeting listing all the religious leaders. The salutation ended with a statement bringing everyone together in one social group sharing a common social charter. "We are all part of a common *prao* (boat). We are led by Allah to stand on earth under the sky and to follow the same institutions anchored by the same roots and covered by the same round top, to be guided by the same customs. Through these customs and traditions we give special respect to Allah and to Bundo Kanduang."

The head of Dt. Indra Gadang's suku then initiated the discussion regarding the matter for which they were assembled.

> *Assalamulaikum.* Today we have the decision that we the people of our suku have come to. Like chickens clucking or metal tools clinking, we are all of one voice.

Penghulu inaugural ceremony in the Sungai Talang adat council house, 1996

We decided that Indra should become a datuak, a leader who has been given the title Datuak Indra Gadang. He promised the Chief of Adat of our village that he would follow the right way and step in the common road in order to guide our children, nephews, and nieces. We have brought him to you from our village. He stands in front of you in order to listen and to learn the regulations on how to guide them. He will follow the regulations just as day flows into night. He will use them as pillows in the morning and afternoon and as lights in the evening. Only in this way can he keep our children, nephews, and nieces safe.

Dt. Rajo then announced that the title being conferred involved awakening the "sinking stalk," that is, a title that had been dormant for many years. A great deal of discussion ensued regarding the requisite requirements. Dt. Rajo spoke once again about the necessity of "climbing up and down the steps," in reference to following all the appropriate procedures, visiting all who were involved, getting agreement from everyone.[10] Most of the four-hour discussion involved a summary of the procedures, a discussion of the proper payments, and giving these payments one by one to all those assembled.

During the discussion one of the penghulu asked about the title that would awake the sinking stalk: "Is it the old or new one from now on?" he asked.

The answer was: "We use the old to be mixed with the new one," which referred to the inclusion of one part of the name from the old title in the new title. In answer to the same question, Dt. Rajo added that another "great" ceremony was necessary to finalize the new title. "To awaken the sinking stalk we need roasted chicken [referring to singgang ayam] as we agreed in our meeting. To make it awaken we must fill the customs, follow the regulations, and use the institutions as they were meant for us to use. After that in three months we will have a party. This was our agreement last month."

The requirements for awakening the sinking stalk were repeated, with special emphasis placed on having a party for the entire village, killing a buffalo to be eaten in a common meal, and mounting the head of the buffalo in full view of all in accordance with the proverb:

> The custom must be followed
> The institution must be filled.
> A sacrifice is presented
> Signified by the horns of the buffalo
> Whose meat is eaten.
> A tent is erected
> A big umbrella is carried
> The yellow umbrella is unfolded [penghulu insignia].
> The big drum is sounded [from the mosque]
> Along with the drums of the people.

The speeches continued. One penghulu spoke eloquently of the personality requirements for all penghulu and other notables. He started out by saying that there were fourteen requirements but ended up listing forty, many of which touched on proper behavior with respect not just to adat but to Islam as well.

> Please remember to finish every job and shoulder every burden. Be diligent; follow religion and what our religious scholars teach us; pity the handicapped and the poor; talk politely and honestly; guide the people; be modest, but show your talent in getting what you want; be patient and never angry; be sparing in your words; show respect to your elders, love to your equals, and pity for the young. Understand and follow the four customs and traditions; understand the four rules; understand the four villages; understand our measures [referring to the twenty-two rules of Dt. Perpatih and Dt. Katumunggungan]. Protect the people; sleep little; study Islam; care for the mosque; father orphans; find husbands for widows and wives for unmarried men; always keep liters and measurements so that you will be fair; encourage the people to work better; be good; abandon the sinful ways of the past—do not engage in ritual displays of invulnerability, do not play games and gamble; keep the roads and bathing places clean and safe; teach the people; always be fair in judging conflicts between two parties; be just in your punishment.

Penghulu eating in groups of four from a tray mounted on four feet, 1996

The proceedings ended with an air of festivity as the subject turned to the upcoming party. A date was set for Sunday of the following week. Pak Indra was advised once again that he would have to slaughter a buffalo to feed the entire village and mount its head in a conspicuous spot as a sign of the grand occasion. All would eat together. The penghulu spoke with detailed knowledge about the required dishes for the occasion. There should be twelve traditional cakes (*kalamai*) for the top penghulu of the nagari, nine for the common penghulu, and six for their assistants. Betel should be taken by the dubalang to all the top penghulu of the Four Koto as a sign that they were invited. They also mentioned that some invitations should include bringing singgang ayam.

At the party itself, they said, separate houses should be prepared to feed the various dignitaries. One house was to be reserved solely for the penghulu, one house for the Islamic officials, and one house for the rest of the villagers. The penghulu were to eat according to the "old way," from trays mounted on four feet. On each tray rendang, the Minangkabau curried beef, should be placed in the middle along with fried fish and pieces of singgang ayam surrounded by rice.

During the speeches the women watched through the open windows. They were mostly woman from Dt. Indra Gadang's maternal family along with his wife and daughters. Their pride was abundantly evident with much smiling, nudging, and laughter. I was the only woman inside. At one point, I noticed one of the women gesturing at me laughing and smiling. I went outside to speak to her and she gave me her bright red scarf. I gratefully accepted it because I felt uncomfortable being bareheaded with all the male notables dressed in their finery. Her gesture was one of friendliness, not disrespect or ill will. . . . Four days later I realized that she was Dt. Indra Gadang's wife: I saw her sitting on the mat beside her husband's lifeless body. The last time I saw the datuak alive, he was climbing onto the truck in his penghulu finery along with the others, ready to go home and continue preparations for the grand finale.

CHAPTER TWELVE

Death of a Penghulu, Reprimand of Another

"If we try to profit from our position, we are struck by the curse of the ancestors—what we call *kena biso kewi*," Dt. Penghulu Besar told me. "The curse afflicts everyone who breaks the law of adat," he said. "I know people who have died because they were struck by biso kewi. Adat is strong for many reasons. People are afraid of kena biso kewi. But it's not just fear that makes adat strong. Adat works side by side with *agama* (religion) and *permerintah* (government). If the tie between these three strands of our life breaks, our heritage would be lost," he concluded.

Field notes, 1997

"Harus beradat" (we must follow adat), Ibu Wel often said. "As long as we respect adat we are safe," she explained, "safe from *kena biso kewi*."

Field notes, 1997

If you don't want to observe adat you should leave Minangkabau. A man who doesn't follow the decision of the ninik mamak is better off living in the jungle.

Penghulu announcing the decision to the adat
council in the case of Dt. Indra Gadang, 1997

Eggi was the first to hear the tragic news. Four days after the ceremony in Sungai Talang, she came running home from school completely out of breath. Always with her senses attuned to the pulse of the village, she brought the breaking news.

"Pak Indra was riding on the back of Dt. Kayo's motorcycle," she said. "They were going real fast. There was an accident with another motor-cycle," she explained.

"They were taken to the hospital in Payakumbuh," she told us. As far as we could gather, Dt. Kayo had a broken leg. Eggi didn't know much about Dt. Indra's condition, only that blood was coming out of his ear and he was unconscious.

A woman visiting us jumped immediately to a conclusion. "This prob-ably happened because the title given him last Sunday was not accord-ing to warih nasab. If something is not according to warih nasab, bad things happen," she said.

En made no comment. It would be wrong to jump to a premature con-clusion, wrong especially to utter it aloud. The thought crossed his mind that maybe Dt. Indra had been struck by the curse of the ancestors, *kena biso kewi*. There was no evidence of this, just what the woman said and what En thought.

That afternoon En talked with Jon, the young man who was driving the other motorcycle. There had been no collision, he told En. His mo-torcycle had stalled suddenly because of a failing piston and thrown him off. But he wasn't hurt.

According to Jon, Dt. Kayo was coming behind him, about five me-ters away, driving very fast as he always does. When Dt. Kayo tried to avoid colliding with Jon, his cycle spun out of control. Dt. Indra fell off and hit his head and shoulder on the pavement. Dt. Kayo's leg was bro-ken when his motorcycle fell on top of him.

We heard more about the injuries from a member of Dt. Indra's fam-ily. He had a bruise on the side of his forehead and the back of his head was soft where his head hit the ground. Blood was flowing from both ears and his nose.

The two had been traveling from village to village to acquire the req-uisite signatures on the official government document granting approval for the final ceremony. Much later we learned that the penghulu title mentioned in this document was not the title that had been conferred on Dt. Indra but the full title of the long-dead penghulu. Had this docu-ment been signed, it would have given Dt. Indra official title to the land held by the former penghulu.

The next morning, Eggi told us that Dt. Indra died during the night and his body had been brought back to the village early in the morning. He died in the ambulance on the way to the hospital in Bukik Tinggi, she said. Just outside Payakumbuh, the nurse attending him found that his heart had stopped. One of his children was riding in the front seat and one of his kemenakan, a niece or nephew, was in a car just behind. They brought the body home in the ambulance.

On hearing the news En said, in the Muslim way, "What is given by God comes back to God." All thoughts of kena biso kewi flew from his mind. He told me later that it was sinful to think about the curse, rather than to assume that the death was due to God's will. It would be a long time before the ancestral curse would be mentioned again.

I decided immediately to go to the house to view the body and *ikut sedih* (follow in sadness). I knew that the body would lie in the house for only a short time before it was washed and wrapped for burial. En agreed with my decision telling me the proverb:

> If the news is good we bring it to others
> If the news is of death, we go quickly before being called

I put on a long skirt and a black T-shirt, tied a scarf over my head, and added a black shawl *(selandang)*. While I was dressing Wik prepared the burial offering, a bowl of uncooked rice with three eggs. She made two bowls, one for the family of Pak Indra's daughter, where the body had been taken for viewing, the other for his older sister's house, where the body would surely be taken for washing. The two bowls reminded me of the tension between daughters and their bako kontan in the case of a father's death. The daughter desperately wants to prepare her father for the grave, even bury him on her own land. If the father's maternal family has the same desire, however, they may insist on washing and burying the deceased.

Men in Between, in Life and in Death

Pak Indra's daughter lived in a large, well-built house off the main road. Inside, his body lay on a mat placed in the middle of the room. A much larger mat covered most of the floor where mourners were sitting. As I came in, the woman who had given me the red scarf at the inaugural ceremony stood up to greet me. I realized then that she was Dt. Indra's wife. She gave me her hand and I brought it to my face expressing the greeting of sorrow.

We sat down by her husband's body and she showed me the ugly bruises on the side of his forehead, his shoulder, eye, and his left side, moaning as she pointed. I shook my head in pure disbelief. I couldn't believe my eyes. Just a few days before I had seen this man at the pinnacle of his life about to graduate to a respected social status. Only about fifty, he had years to live surrounded by a large family who depended on him. The shock of seeing his body, its life so abruptly halted, threw me off balance, bringing me face to face with emotions from which my natural inclination is to flee. Having experienced loss from the moment of my birth into the vulnerable years of my childhood, I couldn't stand the sight in front of me.

I cried quietly, grieving not just for this man, whom I barely knew, but for all those who had died during my years in Minangkabau: my mother, my father, and members of my Minangkabau family: Umi, Onchu, Ibu Idar, and Dt. Paduko Sati. I was riveted to the spot, unable to move. It was one of those moments which I often face as an anthropologist when the personal obliterates the professional. At these moments it seems to me that anthropology cannot capture the grandeur or the tragedy of people's lives. In the face of death, life takes on a meaning that words cannot represent, at least my words. It is the desire to hold on to these moments, to comprehend them through the social dramas framing the irony, the paradox, the despair, and the exhilaration of living that motivates my writing and research.

As I sat there I understood that the younger woman sitting with her mother was Pak Indra's older daughter, Ibu Ina, whom I had met just four days before as she joyously mingled with the other women at the ceremony. She was very distraught—moaning loudly as she ran her hands along her father's body, soothing his wounds, looking under the batik cloth that covered his body and under the veil that shielded the wounds on his head and forehead. Her eyes glazed and wild, she was overcome with grief.

My reverie was broken by the entry of men carrying a bier on which to transport Dt. Indra's body to his sister's house for the washing ceremony. As they tried to lift the body, Ibu Ina threw herself on her father, letting out a piercing shriek when the men gently but firmly tried to disengage her.

One of the men, a nephew of Dt. Indra whom I had also seen at Sunday's ceremony cried hard, loudly imploring Ibu Ina to let them take the body. Two other men tried to drag her away. But she persisted, flailing at them with her arms. This went on for sometime, a scene of unfettered emotion expressed on both sides, the likes of which I have never witnessed in Minangkabau.

The men relented only when Ibu Ina jumped up on the bier and lay there like a corpse. Then she ripped off her shirt and yelled, "If he can't be washed here, wash me first. I'll kill myself with a knife if you take his body," she screamed.

This presented quite a dilemma. The families had met after the body was brought to the village in the early morning. They had agreed that the body would be taken to the daughter's house for viewing and afterward to the house of his older sister for washing. The meeting included three of Pak Indra's five children, two daughters and one son.

As a rule, I was told, children prepare the body of a parent for burial by washing and wrapping it in the appropriate cloth. If the deceased is male, they then take it to the house of his maternal relatives, where it lies briefly before final burial. In other villages I have seen the reverse. The body of a deceased male lies briefly in the house of his children before being taken for washing and burial at the house of his maternal relatives.

Negotiation over washing and burial of a male is a time when the interstitial nature of Minangkabau men is prominently on display. Anthropologists have written a great deal about "women in between" and men in charge, but very little about the situation I observed in Minangkabau. I have seen men cry out of sheer frustration due to the divided loyalties that pull them simultaneously in two directions. The sense of being in between begins early in a boy's life when he leaves his mother's house so that his sisters feel their rights to the matrilineal property are secure.

As adults, males are caught between their wives and children and their mothers and sisters. Marriage places them in an ambiguous position. As the proverb puts it, a husband is here today, gone tomorrow—like ashes on a burned-out tree stump *(abu diatas tunggul)* easily blown away by the wind. A man is a guest in his wife's home, treated like a king if he is a good provider, discarded like a pair of old shoes if he is not.

While males may feel ambivalent about their position, some say that they wouldn't have it any other way. They are emphatic that it would be unjust to put women out of the house at divorce. A society is only as good as it is to its women, they claim.

All these thoughts were crossing my mind while the drama of the washing continued. The men gave up on removing the body and remained to help. Before lifting the body onto the washing bier, they first had to disengage Ibu Ina, who clung to her father as if to life itself. She calmed down somewhat by taking charge of the washing in another room, where she was helped by several women and the men who had wanted to take the body to the maternal relatives.

Once the washing was completed the body was carried back into the living room, covered by the batik cloth supplied by bako relatives. In accord with Islamic custom, the body was then wrapped and tied in white cloth, taking care so as not to expose it to the roomful of women who had crowded around the body. Family members would be embarrassed for other people to see the unclothed body.

There were many men present, but they stood outside the house. Only a few came to view the body. With the exception of En, who always showed exquisite tact on such occasions and a refined ability to relate to others, the men who viewed the body were close relatives.

Once wrapped in white and then again in a new batik cloth, the body was ready for transporting to the grave site. As in all funerals, the body was taken out a window, not through the door. But before this, a maternal relative of Pak Indra, one of the men who had tried to take his body to his sister's house, spoke to those standing outside: "If there are any mistakes, any debts, please forgive them. If you cannot forgive the debts, please contact our family. Please pay all debts that you owe to Pak Indra. Do you all agree to forgive and forget?" After the obligatory "yes," the body was brought out through the window. As it was carried down the road, shielded from the sun by an umbrella, people fell in behind.

The body was taken first to the house of Pak Indra's older sister. The old woman was beside herself with grief because she had not been able to wash the body. I heard people telling her gently but firmly to calm down, not to cry. According to Islam, it is no good to lament and mourn loudly because that makes it doubly hard for the spirit to leave the body. Pak Indra's nephew held her as she sobbed, comforting her in a quiet, gentle voice.

The body remained inside her house for less than an hour. After it was brought out through the window, the procession made its way to the local mosque for prayer. Because so many people were present, more than forty, it was said that the spirit would not hang around on earth for the usual forty days but fly straight to heaven.

At the Graveyard

After the ceremony at the mosque the body was taken to the adjacent graveyard, where the grave diggers had not yet finished their work. As everyone sat around waiting, one of Pak Indra's daughters spoke about the events of the previous day. She remembered that in times past her father often felt sick when riding with Dt. Kayo because of the bumpiness and excessive speed. But her father had to get the requisite government permissions for the ceremony that Sunday, he had said, and no one else could take him. The daughter spoke of how fast they were going when they came through the village. I too remembered the roar of the motorcycle when the two men drove past our house. The daughter spoke sadly of her last words with her father. She had stopped the two men on the motorcycle to plead with Dt. Kayo to slow down. Seeing that her father was without a helmet she gave him one and insisted that he put it on. But her father carried it in his hand, fearing that it would bounce off his head and be lost when they went over a bump. How often people cut corners when money is tight, I thought.

At the regional office, the daughter recounted, Pak Indra had met Dt. Rajo and was able to obtain his signature on the letter of permission. The man he was looking for had been out of the office, however, so Pak Indra continued on to Payakumbuh. Dt. Kayo drove very fast, eighty kilometers per hour. After Jon, the other motorcyclist, passed them and then suddenly stalled, Dt. Kayo swerved and Pak Indra fell off . . .

As she was talking both En and I noticed that she appeared very angry. But she did not lay blame. Dt. Kayo was of her mother's clan, which meant that he was her mamak. All that she admitted was that Dt. Kayo's intention was not evil. It was fate, she said, sent by God.

After the body was placed in the ground clad only in the white and batik cloths, the gravediggers filled the hole with fresh red earth. Everyone left the graveyard either to go home or to the nearby house of Pak Indra's sister.

En and I remained behind talking to Dt. Aji, Dt. Indra's assistant, and another man who was Pak Indra's brother-in-law. The subject was the title—what to do about it? The family wanted to go ahead with raising the title and having the ceremony. According to adat they had to decide on a replacement within twenty-one days while the earth was still red on the grave as specified by the proverb "When the title falls, there a mushroom grows from the red ground of the newly dug grave."

Dt. Aji and Pak Axton discussed the potential candidates as we sat pensively by the grave. They discounted the various possibilities one by one. One nephew was a wastrel, unable to make decisions or manage money. Another lived too far away to manage the extensive properties that would be inherited under the title. They agreed that they should find a young man, because he would better represent the generations. Finally they decided on the most reasonable candidate, Pak Indra's nephew. Being his sister's son, Pak Herman was the obvious choice, definitely warih nasab, a direct matrilineal heir. Several weeks later the headcloth of the penghulu was placed on his head in a ceremony in the same house.

The Second Ceremony

The second ceremony drew the same number of penghulu and women. This time, however, Dt. Rajo did not attend, nor were the speeches formal or lengthy. When the young Pak Herman came into the room the women greeted him with tears and joy as he went among them shaking their hands. To an onlooker, the atmosphere was one of cordiality and agreement.

Every thing proceeded as if all was a foregone conclusion. The head of the four suku of the village started off by asking, "Does the clan accept Herman as the next Dt. Indra Gadang?"

One woman answered that she agreed only if Pak Herman promised to take care of her family to the same extent that he looked after his own. This was something of a challenge because she was suggesting that he might not. It was a harbinger of what was to come.

The penghulu in charge did not respond in a friendly way. Unlike the penghulu in Belubus, who are careful to address everyone with respect, especially in a ceremonial context, he criticized this woman.

"Let men teach, not women," he said.

To this the woman replied, "But I am older, I can give advice to Pak Herman," indicating that as a senior woman she had this right.

Whereupon the same penghulu responded, "It is not good for women to give advice to datuak."

This exchange threw something of a pall over the meeting as it proceeded and presaged the controversy that would arise later. Pak Herman was told to put on his clothes, which he did. Afterward the hat was put on, as happened previously with Pak Indra, only in this case it was put on by the man who was considered head of adat in the village. In the speech he gave, the head of adat referred to the tree metaphor once again. "To be a leader, a man must be like a big tree. Its roots are for sitting, its stalk is for resting against, its branches are for taking shelter. A leader looks like a banyan tree in the desert. It becomes a pillar against the wind. Everything must be done patiently. The field should not be full of rubbish."

When this phase of the ceremony was completed, the group walked to the local adat council hall, since it was unnecessary to go to Sungai Talang to complete the ceremony. (The requirements and payments for raising the title had already been met by Pak Indra. Pak Herman was simply receiving his uncle's title within the requisite period of twenty-one days after his death.) This did not end the matter, however. Although the title was not contested, the land claimed under it was.

The Aftermath

The following year, in July 1997, Dt. Indra Gadang's claim to the land under the title of Dt. Raja Kecil—the title he had tried to adopt—was debated by the council of penghulu in his village. The debate took place in the adat council house and was conducted by the titled male leaders of the village. These men listened to the evidence presented by all interested parties including women. While the oath and associated curse of the ancestors never came up in the discussion, it was alluded to privately; people said that the bad fortune that fell on the family of Dt. Indra Gadang was the effect of the curse.

Upon my return to the village at this time, I heard the whole story. According to Dt. Kayo, the driver of the motorcycle, Pak Indra and Dt. Aji constructed a family tree that attached Pak Indra's genealogical line directly to Dt. Raja Kecil's line so as to put Pak Indra's family under the umbrella of the land covered by Dt. Raja Kecil's title. In reality only Dt. Aji and another penghulu, Dt. Kurus, had rights to this land. Dt. Aji agreed to the scheme because he was old and needed Pak Indra's help to manage the land. The deal was that once he was confirmed as penghulu, Dt. Indra Gadang would work the land for both of them and the two would split the proceeds fifty-fifty.

The problem with this strategy was that the genealogical line that Dt. Kurus represented as penghulu was left completely out of the reconstructed family tree. It was as if Dt. Kurus's and all those under the umbrella of his penghulu title didn't exist. Dt. Aji had agreed with this strategy, hoping that if Pak Indra helped him work his rice fields he could pass some of the proceeds along to Dt. Kurus.

To make matters worse, Pak Herman tried to grab all the land, freezing out not just Dt. Kurus but Dt. Aji as well. This infuriated them to the degree that they told the story to members of the adat council. First Dt. Kurus claimed that the new Dt. Indra Gadang (Pak Herman) had taken all the land. Then Dt. Aji backed his story saying that the family tree was false. He admitted that the real inheritors were himself and Dt. Kurus.

Dt. Kayo admitted that he had helped Pak Indra construct the bogus family tree. He confessed to having signed the tree knowing it was false. From the start the plan had been to sell or rent the land. According to Dt. Kayo neither the old nor the new Dt. Indra Gadang had any right to the property they claimed under the newly created title. The land belonged only to Dt. Aji and Dt. Kurus.

In private Dt. Kayo told me that Pak Indra's death was due to the curse of the ancestors. The words he used were the same as cited in the last chapter. It's like a rock that doesn't grow roots, Dt. Kayo said.

Echoing Westenenk's 1918 explanation of the curse, Dt. Kayo said that it falls on those who break the oath made by people when they opened new, unclaimed land in the jungles and forests. The one who claims the land utters the oath as a form of land deed entitling all direct descendants to the land. Anyone not entitled to the land is struck by the curse of the original oath taker. According to Dt. Kayo this was the fate to which Pak Indra succumbed.

During the summer of 1997 the case dragged on in the adat council house as the penghulu met to adjudicate the conflicting claims of Dt. Kurus and Pak Herman. The discussions were referred to as a war of words, because Pak Herman continued to fight for all rights to the land despite the decision of the adat council. Pak Herman argued that the rights were his under the family tree prepared by Pak Indra and signed by the very people now contesting these rights, which included Dt. Kayo, Dt. Kurus, and Dt. Aji. The public discussion in the balai adat involving all the penghulu of the village provided an unusual opportunity to observe adat in action outside of the ceremonial context. En attended the discussion and with the agreement of the penghulu taped it. Excerpts are presented below to provide a feel for the flow of speech (no real names are used).

The Dispute: 1997

The debate took place in the balai adat of the village. According to En, eighteen men clad in ordinary clothes attended, sitting as was customary in a circle on a mat with their backs to the wall. They began with the usual exchange of greetings by the chosen speakers, who were either the heads of the four major clans in the village or their representatives. Then the presence of En with my tape recorder prompted a long discussion about the importance of my work for telling the world about adat Minangkabau.

Several of the penghulu in attendance were well-known adat experts, one of whom I interviewed extensively in 1985. Now, twelve years later, he repeated much of what he had said then about the nature of adat and its history, from the ancestors' descent from Mt. Merapi to their settling of Sungai Talang. He also reiterated that even though the government had broken the Four Koto into two administrative districts (*desa*), the adat of East and West Sungai Talang was one. He recited the proverb specifying the unity of adat in the nagari: "Cupak has the same measurement, adat has the same application."

Someone else spoke against the governmental division of Sungai Talang into two desa and talked about the necessity of considering it one entity, because "our balai adat originated from there." Referring to Sungai Talang as "the mother" of the Four Koto, he likened Sungai Talang to "the center of the fishnet."

Discussion in the adat council house, 1997

Turning to the purpose of the meeting, the penghulu pucuk referred to the report made at the last meeting regarding the disputed land. "This report was delivered last week to the mamak in the balai adat, giving our conclusion on the matter," he said. "In delivering our report, we indicated that the muddy water will be made clear."

But the water was still muddy. "Our decision has not been executed," he told the gathered penghulu. "Pak Herman and his family refused to comply because they did not agree with the adat decision." They also claimed that they had not been in attendance at the meeting when the decision was announced, he said. "Our conclusion was not fully heard, agreement was not finally reached," he announced. "As yet we have no final verification that the matter is settled."

In response one of the penghulu explained, "It's like this. Before it becomes bright, it is darkened. There is still conflict, the matter is not yet settled."

In answer, the penghulu pucuk cautioned, "If this matter is not settled, only bad things will grow. We must watch this matter carefully. The conflict is such that if Dt. Indra Gadang continues to go to the rice field he claims is his, he will experience bad things. If disagreement continues, we must take the matter to the next step, that of the nagari."

This man explained that the matter had been taken by Pak Herman and his family to the locally elected official *(kepala desa)* and to the police. This news was taken by the group as a direct assault on the power of adat in village affairs.

Expressing a minority point of view, one man declared, "The eagle has its own food, and so does the sparrow. This is a matter of civil, not criminal law. This is not a police matter but one for the kepala desa or the district head."

This comment caused something of a uproar. By saying that the matter should be taken to government officials, the speaker was wedding state law to local adat law, a matter under great dispute in the villages where adat is strong. A long discussion ensued reaffirming the jurisdiction of adat.

Disagreeing with the speaker emphatically, the chief of adat in the village spoke. "No, this matter should be decided here, in the balai adat, not by the courts or the district head. We must go up the steps and down the steps, as arranged by the original measure"; in other words, all the steps of adat must be followed before the matter goes to the courts or the police.

In agreement one of the senior penghulu gave a long speech summarizing the case, speaking about the way adat is applied when there is a land dispute.

> The Nagari has four suku, we have applied our adat, we have solved the problem, we have looked for a solution from the bottom up to the top and back down. We have climbed the ladder, we have come down the steps. We promised twenty-one days ago to have a decision; up to now there is no result. We must continue to work to find a solution in the way of adat. If they [Dt. Aji and Dt. Indra Gadang] don't agree with our decision it is because they are not observing adat. We feel calm because we are of one voice, we work in one rhythm. Now they, the other side, are not of one voice. They have chosen to go to the police. But, according to our custom, it must first go to the nagari.
>
> We met and we agreed that the property should be divided into two. One portion for Dt. Kurus the other portion for Dt. Indra Gadang, who would share his portion with Dt. Aji. We made this decision long ago but it was not executed. We must ask why not, why wasn't it applied?

At this point Dt. Indra Gadang (Pak Herman) entered. The head of adat turned to him, saying, "Ah, he is here. Let's listen to what he wants to say. Hai, Indo Gadang! All has been heard, all has been discussed, all has been agreed. Why has the decision not been applied? What do you have to say to this? We the many have reached agreement. How come the decision wasn't executed? Is there still disagreement?"

In response Dt. Indra Gadang said, "Can we answer you now? If I am right, the decision was made. As we understood the decision, it was only suggested that we give some land, not divide it into half. We were told to give one fourth. This was the decision, but it wasn't written. We want to see your decision in writing."

This raised a whole new set of issues. It is unheard of to ask for a decision in writing from the adat council where verbal consensus always rules.

The discussion was intense. One of the penghulu jumped in, "We came to a decision. If there are four each gets two; if there are two, one gets one, the other gets one. What letter do you ask for now?"

Dt. Indra Gadang repeated his request that the decision be in writing.

Another penghulu responded with a long speech chastising the young man, giving him a lesson in adat.

> The decision has been given according to the words of adat, the words of pusako. This is our tradition. That's it. You can expect no more. Adat is tightly sealed, the fist is clenched according to tradition. As the promise is breathed, it should not be broken. As they who keep the promise are many, it cannot be broken. I am not the only one who agrees, all of us agree, the whole nagari. When you received the folded cloth of the penghulu hat and paid the requisite gifts to all of us, there was no letter. The ceremony was the only witness. This is our adat now and from long ago, our adat which speaks with one voice and follows one measure.

Then the head of adat in the village repeated what he had said in a meeting at the office of the kepala desa.

> I was called to the office of the village head to give an account in the presence of Dt. Kurus and Dt. Indra Gadang. The regional head was also present. When they asked me for a letter stating our conclusions, I told them that we do not decide in that way. When we discuss a matter, we discuss openly and then apply our conclusion. Adat is not written—the black of the pen on the white of the paper is not our way. We live by the legacy of adat, which was given us by our ancestors of long ago. Even the regional head understood this, although he is not Minangkabau. He said to those at the meeting, "Minang adat is not written."

In support, another penghulu spoke up saying that whatever the penghulu agree on must "be fisted strongly" (followed strictly). This is true of all lands associated with all penghulu titles. There is no letter, no written deed, unless it is land that has been bought during a person's lifetime.

Even the chief justice in Payakumbuh understands this fact, this man noted. All problems associated with *pusaka tinggi* (inherited land) as opposed to *pusaka rendah* (bought land) are solved by the penghulu of the four suku, not by elected officials. Inherited land, matters having to do with the legacy of adat, aren't solved in the office of the desa but in the balai adat of one of the Four Koto according to the steps of adat—going up and going down, he said.

"This is our way," he concluded looking sternly at Dt. Indra Gadang. "We, the penghulu of the four suku, are of one voice; we speak in one rhythm. Those who don't want to observe adat must leave Minangkabau. If we don't follow adat—going up and going down, each step of the way—we are left with the arbitrary law of the state. This law is not our way. It has three elements, all of which rely on rule by force: soldiers, the court, and the law."

> The law of adat is different [he continued]. We seek peaceful settlement by words and agreement according to the proverb: We measure using wood, we decide using words, we seek peace. This case has been settled according to adat, not according to the police. This is the way our ancestors have taught us. We have followed that way, so also should you. Accept our decision. If you take the matter to the courts, adat and brotherhood are broken. The costs to pay for the trials will be prohibitive, shrinking all your assets. We know that Dt. Kurus is of the same line as Dt. Rajo Kecil, sharing the same cemetery, the same rice fields. He is warih nasab, part of the line of Dt. Rajo Kecil. We have the proof of this from the words of other relatives. Now, because of you, because you excluded him from the new family tree, he has nothing. He is old and it is pathetic to see him in such condition. That is not the way of adat, to take from the old or to sell land.
>
> If you do not accept our decision, please make an appeal. Take the matter to the adat council of our mother village. We have worked hard on your behalf, we have done our job, we are tired of this matter. We don't want to be burdened with it any longer.

Epilogue to the 1997 Meeting

Later one of the penghulu spoke to En off the record. He described the evidence. Dt. Kurus and Dt. Aji belonged to one house, shared the same cemetery, and their lands were adjacent. It was wrong to deny Dt. Kurus his rights, especially as he was getting old and needed help. People should not be driven by greed, he said. Nor should they sell adat land. People like this are struck down by the curse of the ancestors for violating the oath of the penghulu, he concluded.

He went on to talk about the character of a penghulu. He must be truthful, trustworthy, intelligent, and informative. His job is to protect the assets entrusted to him. Above all he cannot sell land. Rather he must make the land grow according to the proverb "When less, he adds; when short, he lengthens; when defective, he fixes." A penghulu cannot sell land because he must preserve it for future generations. *Pusako* (land) is for inheriting, not for selling, he said. The same goes for *soko* (titles). Together, the two constitute the soul of Minangkabau. If a family does not have pusako and soko, they are no longer Minangkabau. For every family there must be land, a penghulu title, all sheltered under one umbrella (symbol of the penghulu), all shaded by one tree. This makes the Minangkabau family.

He ended by reiterating that the penghulu of the village had come to an agreement—they were of one voice, one opinion. Those who don't want to follow the decision of the penghulu are better off living in the jungle.

Finale: 1998–99

The case of Pak Indra's right to the land dragged on for two more years, concluding only in 1999 with two decisions, one by the adat council and the other by the courts. As I heard it, the adat council took the ultimate step. Because Pak Indra refused to follow the adat decision, he and his family were symbolically excluded (shunned) from adat by a decision known as *tingalkan* (leaving behind). As one of the participating penghulu told me, the case illustrates both the power and the problems that *adat Minangkabau* was facing on the eve of the twenty-first century.

It seems that sometime in 1998 Dt. Aji finally agreed to the adat decision to split the land. He entered into an agreement with Dt. Kurus, which was put into writing in a jointly signed letter, called a letter of peace. This letter was signed by all the penghulu of the village. At the same time, Dt. Aji agreed to give part of the land to the son of the long dead penghulu. This was legal according to adat law because it was land that had been bought by Dt. Rajo Kecil *(pusako rendah)*.

To seal the final agreement, Dt. Aji invited all of the penghulu and all the women who had any interest in the land to the house of the deceased Pak Indra's sister. Together the women of Pak Indra's matriline cooked for the ceremony, showing their agreement with the final decision.

The new Dt. Indra Gadang, however, did not agree. Egged on and supported by his father, he came to the ceremony prepared to continue the dispute. Upon entering the house, before he sat down to eat, before any greetings were exchanged, he interrupted the proceedings in a loud voice.

"Why are all of you here?" he asked. Whereupon he ordered all of the gathered penghulu to leave.

The men responded by saying to the head of Dt. Indra Gadang's clan: "We were invited here in the adat way. He cannot order us like this." Nevertheless, they all left, filing out one by one as the women looked on in stunned silence. That was not the end of the matter, however.

That night all of the penghulu gathered in the balai adat at the request of the head of Dt. Indra Gadang's clan. There was unanimous agreement that his manner and speech was not that of a penghulu.

The head of his clan suggested that the young man be thrown out of adat *(dibuang oleh adat)*. This is the most serious punishment that can be meted out by adat. It would amount to social death in the village and affect not just Dt. Indra Gadang, who would thereby be divested of his title, but everyone under the umbrella of his title. It would mean that no woman or man falling under the aegis of the title could be invited to or hold an adat ceremony in the village. The shunning would effectively mean that no one related to Pak Herman in the maternal line could be incorporated into alam Minangkabau at birth, nor married in the adat way.

After some debate the penghulu decided not to take such a drastic step, just yet. They chose instead to take the preliminary step of tingalkan, that is, leaving him temporarily outside of adat. Tingalkan is a kind of shunning, but it can be reversed if the offending party pays the appropriate fine. This fine is not nearly as heavy as it would be if the person is thrown outside adat. For example, the fine for reentering adat if one is left behind is only a goat, as opposed to a buffalo if one is thrown outside adat altogether. Upon payment of this fine together with the appropriate speech of reconciliation in the balai adat, the family can reenter adat. The only permanent stain is ultimately carried by Dt. Indra Gadang. No matter what happens in the future, he will never be able to resume the penghulu title, which he disgraced by refusing to follow the adat decision and by behaving so egregiously in the public attempt at reconciliation.

The decision to tingalkan, along with the letter of agreement signed by all of the penghulu of the village, was taken as a sign that in the Four Koto at least adat is strong *(kuat)*. "Adat Minang is still strong," I was told in August 1999 just before I left Belubus. It was a time of ferment in the village due to the rise in expectations brought about by the overthrow of Suharto in 1998, the national parliamentary elections in 1999, and the upcoming presidential election. I ended my stay in Belubus, on the eve of the new century, by investigating how people stood on the question of the viability of adat.

MILLENNIAL MUSINGS

CHAPTER THIRTEEN

Adat in the Twenty-first Century

Adat doesn't rot in the rain
Or crack in the sun.
As long as there are Minangkabau
Adat Minangkabau will survive.

Minangkabau proverb

M illennial endings and beginnings are a time for thinking about past and future, a time for summing up the old century and injecting hopes and dreams into the new. I thought a great deal about endings and beginnings in late August 1999 as I prepared to leave Belubus for what I felt would be the last time before completing this book. Time was running out. I had been traveling to West Sumatra almost every year since 1981. Eighteen years is a long time to devote to one intellectual passion with little concrete to show for it except a wealth of experience and the joy of living my passion.[1] I was not getting any younger, and Serge was suffering more than usual from asthma brought on by the smoke wafting all across central Sumatra from the burning of forests in eastern Sumatra and Borneo in the late 1990s. After sitting up several nights with him while he gasped for breath in our little room shuttered against the night and marauding spirits, I felt that the time for summing-up had come.

I was ready because En and I experienced a breakthrough in translating the saluang verses I had recorded and he had transcribed over the years. For the first time I felt that I understood the totality of the saluang performance, both its poetics and female ethos. It was an understanding that had eluded me for years but that I felt was essential to telling this story, for while the soul of the Minangkabau people is in their adat, their heart is in the saluang performance. I wanted to record both heart and soul in these pages to the best of my writing ability.

As we translated the saluang songs from past years, I told En and Wik that this might be my last trip until the book was published and I came back bringing copies. With their usual equanimity they took the news quietly, but I could tell that they too were feeling moved to pour their intellectual energy into some sort of final statement. For several weeks over breakfast, lunch, and dinner En and I talked about what we had learned since 1985. Wik listened attentively to our discussions, as she always did, before offering her views. Together the three of us waded boldly into the interpretive stream, using adat as our text but restricting our focus to the question of whether adat would survive in the twenty-first century.

The political climate was ripe for such musings. It was the era of *reformasi* (reform), which had brought about Suharto's downfall in May 1998, a time of resurgent nativism in West Sumatra. There was a palpable feeling of wanting to shore up adat Minangkabau, to revive what had been eroded by Dutch colonialism and interference from Jakarta. A cultural revolution was in the air, manifested by widespread discussion about returning to the adat of the past, including the old nagari system that Suharto's desa system had undermined.

En and Wik's passionate feelings about adat and its possible future made me want to hear what other villagers had to say. The conversations that ensued—free flowing and full of critiques, hopes, and dreams—illuminated local attitudes about adat at the turn of the century. As we discussed and debated, I abandoned the role of observer and took an active role in the conversation. Ibu Wel participated at times as did two well-known penghulu in the village, Dt. Patiah and Dt. Gondo Besar (not their real names). These conversations, joined by En and Wik, exemplified *mufacat*—trying to discover truth through discussion and consensus.

The Political Context of the Conversation

The student riots in Jakarta brought President Suharto's thirty-five years of power to a grinding halt in May 1998. I arrived in Padang the following month to find a new air of hope. University students had followed the lead of their colleagues in Jakarta by occupying the provincial parliament building. It was a time for change and redressing old wrongs.

Serge and I with the family just before departing in August 1999. *Left to right:* Ibu Wel, Ibu Ida, Serge, Pak Edi, Ibu Os, Yeni, Peggy, Eggi, Adis, En, Adek. Ibu Wik is in front with Ronald and Agoes.

People talked about *reformasi damai* (peaceful reform) with an unparalleled excitement and outspokenness. It was definitely a heady time.

Just before my arrival in Belubus that July, villagers, mostly women, started seeking redress for past wrongs at the instigation of local organizers, some of whom came from Jakarta. A group of forty from Belubus joined with people from other villages to converge on Payakumbuh to *menuntut hak* (demand their rights) and to call for the end of corruption. Similar demonstrations took place all over West Sumatra. Indeed, I ran into them throughout central Sumatra that summer. The action was peaceful and yielded significant concessions by government officials, who for the first time responded to the voice of the people rather than the power brokers of the Suharto regime.

In Belubus people spoke their minds not just to government officials but to one another as well. I felt the effect of this greater freedom because for the first time I was able to visit Eggi's family without having to present official letters from the museum in Padang to the local government and police officials. The Suharto government's tight control of the local population extended even to outsiders like me. The rationale was always the same: Should I be involved in an automobile accident or disappear for some reason, as sometimes happened to visiting foreigners, the local police wanted to have all the particulars about me to inform the appropriate American officials, or so they said.

During the my stay in Belubus a group of villagers demanded compensation for land that had been seized by the government in the 1980s to construct a small dam. This was just one of several unprecedented public meetings with government officials. Most of the people involved in these meetings were women, because they were the overseers of the land that had been seized. The following year they received compensation.

The change in atmosphere I observed after the parliamentary elections the following year was even more dramatic. Reformasi damai brought about a realignment of party affiliation in the general election. For the first time, the people of Belubus along with people all over West Sumatra abandoned the official party, Golkar, in favor of the party they thought of as the "party of reformasi," PAN, headed by Amein Reis. Golkar came in second throughout Indonesia. The party of Megawati came in third in Belubus on the grounds that she favored democracy.

People lost their apathy and experienced a huge rise in expectations. The change of attitude was evident in the unprecedented straightforwardness of the criticisms and opinions people expressed when I asked them about adat in the twenty-first century. Their targets were not just the Indonesian government but local authorities as well. En started it all by criticizing the adat books for leaving women out of the picture. Wik abandoned her usual deferential attitude and spoke of the strength of women's adat and its role in preserving adat. The two penghulu expressed bitter criticism of local government officials for ignoring adat decisions.

En's and Wik's Views

The summing-up started when En commented at dinner one night about the importance of women's ceremonies for understanding adat Minangkabau. Referring to my observations about adat weddings, En declared out of the blue, "I never knew that the sumandan (in-married wives) played such an important role in wedding ceremonies until I saw them going out to meet the bride and groom here in Belubus. In my village I was never interested in what women were doing. I always thought that the only women who did anything were from the bride's mother's family. But that's not the way it is in Belubus. My village is probably just like this one, only I just didn't notice," he concluded.

En's admission that as a male growing up in a Minangkabau village he had never bothered to understand what went on in women's ceremonies confirmed my impression that women's ways are relatively foreign to many men. Until this conversation, however, I had no idea how strongly En felt about his newfound knowledge.

Finishing his chain of thought with the flair of the anthropologist he had become, En continued: "After seeing women's adat in Belubus, I understand why it has to be the sumandan. Like bako relatives, these women must be honored and respected so that the ties between the clans are tightly interwoven. The sumandan helps her husband's family and later, as bako, the women of her husband's clan reciprocate. It makes perfect sense. It's drawing all the strands of the fishnet together that counts, not the power of the penghulu that the books talk about."

En's comments gave me pause because I realized that he was articulating a lack of knowledge common to Minangkabau males. I wasn't surprised that he used the fishnet metaphor. We had just translated the proverb equating Bundo Kanduang with the center of the net.

Thinking a little more, En came to a startling conclusion. "It's a shame that none of the books on our adat are written by Minangkabau women," he said. "By emphasizing the importance of the male class and overlooking women's adat, the male writers seem to be after power rather than the truth. If we forget to respect our mothers for all they do for us and for adat Minangkabau, the foundation of our matriarchaat and our adat will crumble."

I understood that En was speaking from his heart. We had just translated the saluang lamentations for the mother. Both of us had been moved to comment on how much we missed our departed mothers.

As I was thinking this, I was even more floored when En recited a proverb that he said came to him in the middle of the night as he lay awake thinking about our talks. The proverb likens adat matriarchaat to the architecture of the traditional house:

> Our mamak is like the roof of the rumah gadang,
> Our mande is like the *tonggak tuo* (central pillar).
> Take away the roof and there is still the house,
> Take away the pillars and the house collapses.
> This is the meaning of our matriarchaat.

My surprise had to do with the fact that adat experts are not unanimous on the subject of who constitutes the central pillar of the rumah gadang. Some choose the penghulu, others Bundo Kanduang. The tree symbolism associated with the penghulu, and the idea that the inaugural ceremony means "to raise a penghulu," argue for the mamak as being the central pillar.[2]

En's comment, however, was not out of step with other views. The first observations of the Minangkabau described the senior woman as being at the center of the multifamily rumah gadang.[3] But since I had never heard anyone in Belubus equating the senior woman with the central pillar, I asked En why he had put her in this role. He responded by saying that his proverb represented the truth as he observed it in Belubus and elsewhere in West Sumatra. According to En, truth must be based on reality, not on speculation or a desire to uphold the power of the penghulu.

"After all, doesn't the proverb 'Growth in nature is our teacher' (*alam takambang jadi guru*) mean that we learn from what we see and experience, not just from what we are told?" he asked.

En elaborated on his concern about the male orientation of adat books, how they don't tell the whole story. As he spoke, the sound of his voice alerted me to the seriousness of his thoughts. "Oh, Bu, because most of the books are written by the ninik mamak of certain villages or by the intellectuals in the cities, we don't get the whole picture. This is because the books are concerned with teaching men and boys about adat. They should include *kaum ibu* [the female class] in their discussions," he said. "Without knowledge of women's activities in the villages, our matriarchaat is hidden from us, so that we don't truly understand its meaning," he went on.

"Baarak and baalek—women's processions and ceremonies—are the adat of women, but in the books we never hear about them," he concluded. "Women's adat knots the threads of the net and keeps adat alive."

I was intrigued by his comments. His insistence on keeping to the facts was a tribute both to anthropology and to the Minangkabau desire to learn from experience. His conclusion was consistent with conclusions reached by the anthropologist Johanna van Reenen and by Pak Idrus Hakimy as well.

Van Reenen titles her book on Minangkabau women *Central Pillars of the House* (Reenen 1996:1–3). In several of his books Pak Idrus Hakimy equates the butterfly (*limpapeh*) with the central pillar of the matrilineal household, the one on which the strength of all the other posts is concentrated. Pak Idrus claims that according to adat, limpapeh is like Bundo Kanduang, the mother on whose strength children depend. Pak Idrus also likens the butterfly to the female class (*kaum ibu*) in their role as "pillar of the big house" and pillar of the nagari (Hakimy 1994a:94; 1994b:41, 172).

I told En that I found his view unorthodox, at least in Belubus, but he stuck to it. When Ibu Well arrived, I asked her, "Oh, Bu! Who is more

Senior woman touching center post of her rumah gadang, 1999

like the central pillar of the household: ibu or mamak—mother or mother's brother?"

Without any hesitation, she answered. "Oh, the mamak."

In response, En asked her. "What would adat be like in this village if women thought only of themselves and their families and not of adat?"

"You can't think of one without the other," Ibu Well responded.

At this point Wik jumped in. Without addressing the question—at least at that point in the discussion—of who should be thought of as the tonggak tuo, Wik embarked on a long disquisition about adat ibu, responding not just to En's question to Ibu Wel but to our discussion in the days before.

"It's mainly women who follow adat here," she said. "Women understand the ceremonies, men don't. Husbands follow their wives, because they don't know about adat. If the mother doesn't follow adat, its certain that the father won't. He's got his job in the garden and sawah. Life's hard enough as it is, trying to do the best we can for our children. Even though we have little money, we must marry our children in the adat way and sponsor our children when they are born."

Wik continued by talking about those who don't follow adat. "There is a lot of gossip about those who don't follow adat," she said. "If the children are naughty, people say: 'Oh, when that child was born it wasn't brought to the spring for the first bath.' Or, they say about a man and wife who weren't married in adat: 'Oh, those two have many problems because there is no mamak to help them resolve their problems.'"

As she gathered steam, her voice filled with emotion, Wik delivered a lengthy lecture about the importance of adat. As she talked I thought back to May 1985, fourteen years before, when Ibu Idar expressed very similar thoughts to me as she spoke passionately of women's role in adat. It was as if Ibu Idar had joined us in the conversation.

"We follow adat because it is the way of our parents and their parents before them. We respect their experiences in life and learn from them. We learn from their suffering, from their joys and sorrows, and from the bitter and the sweet they have tasted and we don't forget. This is what we mean by 'Growth in nature is our teacher.' If we don't learn from our parents, if we ignore what they tell us, if we are blind to their experiences, what was the use of their lives?

"We must pass on what we know to our children. If Eggi goes out to a ceremony dressed the wrong way, I teach her the right way. If she follows my advice, she is happy because she sees that she is like everyone else. If she is stubborn and dresses any way she likes, she is ashamed."

When Wik said this about Eggi, I smiled, remembering the time several years before when Eggi had insisted on wearing a miniskirt to her cousin's baby-naming ceremony. On the morning of the ceremony I heard Eggi moaning in her room. Not knowing what inspired her tears, I guessed when I saw Eggi's attire for the ceremony. In a short skirt and tight blouse, she looked like a nine-year-old Asian MTV star. Later at the ceremony Eggi moped around, looking out of place and ill at ease. I finally took her aside and suggested that she go home and put on the clothes her mother had bought for the ceremony. Maybe because it was me and not someone else in the family, Eggi disappeared and came back a little later beautifully attired in the baju kurung her mother had bought for her. I could tell by the light that shone from her eyes and the smile on her face that she felt infinitely better.

As I was thinking all of this, Wik ended with the following statement about the strength of adat in today's world: "Although individuals may chip away at adat, although children may be hard headed, half following adat, half going their own way, as long as the mother teaches her children the right way according to adat and Islam, adat will not falter. If children stop listening to their parents and women stop holding and attending ceremonies, adat will be lost. But that will happen only when the world ends and Doomsday is upon us."

Eggi dressed in a *baju kurung* for an adat ceremony, 1996

Wik's comments turned my thoughts again to Eggi. How would she turn out, I wondered? Would she stay in the village and raise her children in the adat way? Or would she leave and go to work in the city as some of her cousins had done? Was Wik speaking to Eggi through me? For years I had watched Eggi grow up, making the transition from infant to toddler to young girl, and now she was verging on adolescence.

I knew that at age twelve the verdict was still out as to which path Eggi would take. My influence, I strongly suspected, would not keep her from following adat Minangkabau. The major lesson I learned while in West Sumatra was the degree to which adat Minangkabau survives because of the Minangkabau ability to live simultaneously in several worlds. It is an ability that I too had developed. Living part of the year in Philadelphia and part of the year in Minangkabau, I had become bicultural.

Returning to the question of who best embodied the central pillar, I was intrigued to find that Wik agreed with her mother. Indeed both mother and daughter took it as something of a insult to suggest that women, not the mamak, should be seen as the central pillar. After some reflection, I realized that their version of the meaning of the tonggak tuo was their way of preserving adat. They equated the central pillar of the household with the mamak to show respect for the male adat role. Obeisance is not about subordination, it is a way to raise a fallen pillar, in this case the pillar represented by the mamak. Since male and female adat domains are interdependent yet autonomous, women's adat must be devoted in part to helping the male domain survive. The same is true of the male domain; only by showing respect for women's ceremonies can male adat survive. Regardless of the books that describe only male roles, in the village context men know that the status of their families depends on their mothers and sisters staging the proper ceremonies. "Going up and down the ladder" according to adat is not restricted to dispute settlement. It applies also to celebrating the life cycle as well.

Thinking this over, I said to En, "Making good ties and showing respect is at the heart of adat. Isn't this the meaning of women's ceremonies? Women uphold adat in their own way, which may include finding ways to keep men involved. There are so many counterforces affecting the energies of men," I went on. "For example, there is the influence of those who don't respect adat, such as we saw in the case of Pak Indra. Then there is the need to make a living, which means that many men must find work outside the village. Men who take on the title of penghulu have more worries than those who don't because they are called upon to settle disputes and look after their kemenakan. In today's world there are many more pressures on the male adat role than on the female, for no other reason perhaps than the fact that women are not required to leave their ancestral homes and they always have their families on whom to rely."

En wasn't convinced. Once again he invoked the proverb "Growth in nature is our teacher." "We must be guided by what is true in nature, not what gives people the most power," he said. "Isn't this what the proverb means?"

Sitting nearby, Wik nodded her head in agreement.

I thought some more, and so did Wik and En. A few days later we came to a much different conclusion, deciding that it would be wrong to assert our opinion in such a way as to create an imbalance between the roles of men and women. Although, the three of us felt that women played the key role in preserving adat, we concluded that the final success of adat in withstanding the inroads of the twenty-first century depended on paying respect to the penghulu as protector and recognizing adat law as the main support of the house of adat.

We agreed that to assert En's point of view would be to yield to a desire to think in terms of power, just like the authors of the adat books. More important was to recognize that the value of women's adat was not the power it had over people but its ability to draw people together into a net of *tali budi*—friendly and respectful ties. Tali budi is what the Minangkabau matriarchaat is all about, we concluded. This conclusion was shaped by our discussion with Dt. Patiah, who emphasized tali budi as the core pillar of adat.

Dt. Patiah's View

Dt. Patiah was one of the few involved in the affair of Dt. Indra who refused to sign the faked genealogical tree. He knew it was fake and was certain that it would cause trouble down the road. Following the letter of adat law, he did not agree with the other penghulu who felt that since the potential claimants had signed the family tree, it was acceptable to graft one family tree to another.

Dt. Patiah's views expressed during our conversation were colored by the problems he and his colleagues had experienced in debating the case of Dt. Indra. He was particularly incensed by the suggestion that the adat decision be put in writing to show to the local government representatives.

When I asked him what he thought about the current state of adat, he replied immediately, as if the question weighed heavily on his mind: "Today, the force of adat has weakened." He referred to the three laws under which every Minangkabau lives—adat, religion, and the government. "The weakest of these three is adat law," he said, sadly. "The regulations of adat cannot be enforced, because the government, represented by the kepala desa, doesn't follow the decisions of the ninik mamak. So by the time our decisions arrive in the office of the kepala desa, they have no meaning. He and those who work in his office act as if they think adat is already finished," he added. Then he spoke with a tinge of anger. "Because they don't enforce our decisions, the people conclude that adat Minangkabau is finished, so they turn increasingly to the government. For adat to survive it has to be backed by the government. In the past when the nagari system was in force, there was more willingness to follow adat decisions, and adat law had more force."

Dt. Patiah supplied more details about the problems faced in the case of Dt. Indra. When the adat council—in accordance with the adat rule that under certain conditions children can inherit use rights from their father—allowed the son of the man whose land was under dispute to harvest a stand of coconut trees on the land, Dt. Indra Gadang attacked him physically and accused him of stealing. He made his accusation in the office of the kepala desa, who advised him to take the matter to the police. This was a terrible affront to the council decision, for it meant that their decision was not backed by the local government.

Dt. Patiah expressed his hopes in no uncertain terms. "I hope that our provincial government follows adat Minangkabau," he said. "We must follow our own adat, not the adat of Jakarta." Laying blame where he thought it was due, he said, "Because of the new desa system, much of adat Minangkabau has been forgotten."

He said that there were many efforts to reverse this trend in the younger generation of males. For example, he pointed out that young men were being taught how to speak at ceremonies. Echoing the female approach to the meaning of ceremonies, he concluded that it was important for young men to learn how to speak at the ceremonies "so we will become one like a family, like before."

At the end of the interview, I recited the proverb that En had constructed about the senior woman being like the central pillar of the house. His response was immediate: "The mamak is the central pillar of the house."

This elicited a long interchange between En and Dt. Patiah in which En repeated much of what he had said to me and Wik about the importance of women's ceremonies for upholding adat. Dt. Patiah didn't disagree. After some fiddling with the proverb proposed by En we all agreed on the following version.

> The mamak is like the roof of the rumah gadang
> That protects us all.
> Our mande is like the center of the fishnet
> That draws us all together.
> Adat law is like the tonggak tuo
> That guides us.
> The adat of our matriarchaat
> Is our foundation.
> The roof rests on the central pillar,
> The pillar rests on the foundation stones.
> Break the foundation stones and the house is destroyed.
> Break adat and our lives are over.

This rendition was agreeable to Dt. Patiah because it included adat matriarchaat, which had to be considered separately from adat law. He defined "adat matriarchaat" as consisting of women's ceremonies in conjunction with the matrilineal principle which he said constituted the foundation for all else.

After further thought, however, Dt. Patiah was not fully satisfied. Something was missing. According to him, above all else adat Minangkabau required people to be respectful and polite, to look for and create tali budi. This, he said, was the major lesson of adat law. "Harus budi" (you must always be polite). "Kalau tidak berbudi, bukan orang Minangkabau" (if people aren't polite and of good character, they are not Minangkabau).

After thinking for a few moments about the importance Dt. Patiah attached to tali budi, we jointly devised the following lines as an ending to En's proverb. The addition sparked a smile of agreement from Dt. Patiah:

> The house is beautiful because of the foundation stones,
> Break the foundation stones and the house is destroyed.
> Adat is beautiful because of good ties,
> Break good ties and adat is destroyed.

These ideas are not inconsistent with those expressed by Pak Idrus Hakimy. In equating Bundo Kanduang with the central pillar of the rumah gadang, Pak Idrus points out that if this pillar collapses all the others fall with it. He cites a proverb not unlike the one constructed by En and Dt. Patiah:

> The house is strong because it has a foundation,
> Break the foundation and the house is destroyed.
> Society is strong because of good relations,
> Break good relations and society is broken.

(Hakimy 1994a: 128)

Dt. Gondo Besar's View

Dt. Gondo Besar is the head penghulu of one of the four major clans in Belubus. Because his opinion and manner are considered wise and careful, he occupies a very important position in dispute settlement. In Belubus he is one of the most respected of the penghulu. I have interviewed him often over the years, usually about adat. Regarding the future of adat, he had a great deal to say, much of it echoing Dt. Patiah.

The difference between the two penghulu was the degree to which Dt. Gondo Besar emphasized the male role in adat. While Dt. Patiah talked about adat matriarchaat, in which he lumped the adat of ceremonies and the matrilineal system, Dt. Gondo Besar refused to acknowledge a separate female domain. According to his account, women's role was to follow what had been decided by men. He even went so far as to say that the recipes for ceremonial foods were originally devised by a meeting of the penghulu in the adat council hall in Sungai Talang.

Dt. Gondo Besar was very frank. He sighed with resignation before saying, "Adat is weak here because of the local government. The kepala desa doesn't know much about adat and doesn't honor adat decisions. To make matters worse, often the penghulu don't know anything about adat as well. Some even go so far as to violate their sacred oath and sell clan land for their own profit," he said with disdain.

Dt. Gondo Besar attributed the weakness to the Dutch, the Japanese, and Suharto's New Order. The Dutch seized clan land that had formerly been reserved for the use of the penghulu so that penghulu could pay full attention to adat affairs rather than rely for their living on the land of their wives. This was a blow to the male practice of adat because it meant that they had to devote most of their time to making a living. The same practice was followed by the Japanese. It was only during Sukarno's Old Order that the Indonesian government respected local adat.

This changed with Suharto's New Order. In the interest of nationalization Suharto destroyed local unity by instituting the desa system and appointing government officials who knew nothing of local adat. This meant that lawyers and judges conceptualized cases in terms of national law, not adat. Penghulu were robbed of their function and lost authority. The role of the penghulu in today's world is vastly diminished, Dt. Gondo Besar concluded.

Regarding the different role of males and females, he placed much more importance on the role of the penghulu. "It is the mamak who safeguard adat and control the women," he said. But he may have been unsure of himself because he added, "Women are in charge of proposing a marriage, while it is men's duty to protect women's property. Unfortunately, too many men sell clan land without getting the appropriate agreement from the women. Our adat is weakened by these men."

When I asked him about the adat of ceremonies, he referred to the four types of adat discussed in the tambo. En and I were both surprised to hear him state that the fourth type, the adat of ceremonies, could not be attributed to women because it was decided upon by the ninik mamak in the council house. As he saw it, the adat of ceremonies changes from nagari to nagari due to agreements arrived at by men.

"The ninik mamak hold a meeting attended by all the penghulu of the four clans of the Four Koto," he said. "There they decide the rules. For example, they decide that the women must take singgang ayam, curried chicken, to the house of the groom when they go to fetch him to the bride's house."

At this point, I jumped in to say, "But the ninik mamak cannot cook singgang ayam. They don't know the recipes."

Undaunted, Dt. Gondo Besar continued. "All customs are decided in the council house of Sungai Talang and then the people are informed. If the people don't follow the customs, they are admonished."

"But," I went on, repeating myself like a stuck record, "the ninik mamak don't know anything about the foods that women make for the feasts and exchange with one another."

Unwilling to yield, Dt. Gondo Besar said, "The ninik mamak decide and then inform the women."

The discussion then turned to whether the women attended the meeting at which such decisions were made. In line with proverbs stating that "agreement rules" and "all decisions must be round, like water in the pipe" (that is, must be arrived at by consensus), I suggested that perhaps women attended these meetings to present their views.

"No," he said. "We never let women attend meetings because they don't know how to speak to the point. All they do is chatter, speaking two words rather than one. It is very hard to come to any decision when women are present."

I responded by pointing out that his wife knew much more about ceremonial procedures than he and the ninik mamak. I also brought to his attention that just a few days ago it was mainly women who met with government officials in the adat council house to receive compensation for the land seized for construction of a dam on the Belubus River. Dt. Gondo looked a bit confused. Perhaps this was the first time anyone had challenged him on what he treated as dogma. But dissension is in the spirit of mufacat. By identifying differences one prepares the way for consensus. Or as a proverb puts it, "Crossing wood in the hearth makes the fire glow."

In the discussion that followed, Dt. Besar came around to my opinion by pointing out that no one ever *creates* regulations in the balai adat. They only follow ancestral ways. "Our adat is handed down to us from our ancestors. In the balai adat our role is only to agree to what we have been doing for many generations," he said.

Pressing my point, I repeated that in the past the ninik mamak were unlikely to have created the recipes. Didn't they get them from the women? I asked.

"Yes, they got them from the women," he said. "Women know all the recipes. Mentioning adat ibu, he said, "Women run the ceremonies. Without women there would be no adat. This is because in today's world the status of the ninik mamak has fallen while the status of women has risen. It is stronger now than it was before."

Dt. Gondo Besar ended by accepting En's proverb. "Yes, today women are like the central pillar," he said. "It's also true that the mamak is like the roof because their job is to protect ancestral land."

He ended with his hopes for the future. "Reformasi will bring democracy, which means that we can go back to the nagari system. Then the local government will respect the decisions we make in the balai adat. The ninik mamak will honor their sacred oath. They will not leave the village. They will look after their nieces and nephews as they once did," he said. "The role of women is very important also. They help us tie good knots in the village—tali budi. Yes, we think of them as the center of the fishnet."

The Meaning of Adat

The conversations I had with key people just before leaving Belubus highlighted all that I had learned about the practice of adat in the village context. Adat is much more than what is written in books. Adat represents a point of view about proper relations, a way of life that follows this viewpoint, as well as a world view. The men's contribution to adat is practiced in discussion and in the oversight of ancestral land with their sisters. Men study the legalisms of adat law and apply them in dispute settlement. They also recite adat proverbs in public adat meetings and write these proverbs in adat books. Women's oversight of adat social relations is reflected in the life cycle ceremonies they organize and stage. The goal is not just to uphold adat but to enfold children within an accepted way of life and set of social relationships. If women stop teaching their sons and daughters, if women stop holding ceremonies, if they neglect adat law in dispersing access rights to ancestral land to their daughters, adat will be lost and so will the Minangkabau people. Wik's sentiments are in keeping with the passion expressed by Pak Idrus when he writes that Bundo Kanduang and the female class are the pillars of the household and the nagari (Hakimy 1994a:65, 67–70, 94).

There was unanimous agreement about the importance of maintaining tali budi, or good character and good relations. Dt. Patiah was adamant in saying that if tali budi is lost, adat is finished. Dt. Patiah also felt that the soul of adat was in its performance—the way it is practiced in ceremonies as well as its aesthetic style and mood. Women share this view.

Dt. Patiah and Dt. Besar decried Suharto's New Order for the destruction it had wrought on the male contribution to adat. Both expressed the desire to revive adat law so that local problems will be decided according to tradition, not according to the law of the nation-state administered by an elected official with no respect or understanding for adat. Both long for the restoration of the nagari system, which will once again join Belubus and her sister villages to their mother village Sungai Talang.

Evidence that the return to the nagari system was not an idle dream came from En, who wrote me in November 2000: "It is the plan of the governor of West Sumatra to come back to the nagari system beginning April 1, 2001. In the future if Ibu comes back to Belubus the nagari system will already have been reinstated. If there are additional developments En will send word." A year later he told me in a telephone conversation that the nagari system had been reinstated in many parts of West Sumatra and would soon reunite the villages of the Four Koto.

Dt. Besar's ambivalence about women's role was hard to fathom. His approach to adat, like that of other men I talked to over the years, was strictly male centered. Although others did not go quite as far, it was interesting to hear how some of the penghulu in the village defined adat mostly in terms of adat limbago. For example, Dt. Perpatih, who claims that he inherited his title from the line of the legendary Dt. Perpatih, told me that adat is the "system of laws arranged by the *nenek moyang* (ancestors), which Dt. Perpatih nan Sabatang and Dt. Katumanggungan left to us in our *pepatah petitih* (maxims and proverbs)." Another leader claimed that all of adat, including the matrilineal social system, was devised by the adat lawgivers.

In view of these opinions it is interesting to note that scarcely any of the men can recite either the tambo or the twenty-two adat rules verbatim. Only one of my teachers in Belubus, Dt. Paduko Sati, knew the tambo and the twenty-two rules by heart. During his lifetime, he was an important man in the adat hierarchy in his capacity as head of the four clans in Belubus. Just a few months before he died in 1987 he told me, "Adat is all that is arranged, that comes into being by regulation."

Conceived in this way adat is legalistic in its orientation to rules and discursive in being communicated and learned through speech and texts. Even though the rules and proverbs cannot be recited verbatim by all the male adat leaders, knowledge of it is nonetheless available to them through the little book written by the officially appointed head of adat (the KAN).[4] Most of the adat leaders I met with had this booklet in their possession.

Irrespective of whether they know the texts of adat limbago, all the male religious and adat leaders in the village understand adat as guide and compass. In 1989, Angku Mudo Panil, a well-known religious official, testified to the importance of adat by saying that adat is "like the ship that keeps people from sinking." This understanding provides a bridge for accommodating adat and Islam, for both are conceived in the same terms. Emphasizing the joint effect of adat and Islam, he added, "If religion is strong we will not fall, so religion determines and adat applies."[5]

This often repeated saying reminded me of the themes of the tambo and *Kaba Cindur Mata* that associate senior women with basic principles and their sons with those who apply the principles by developing the rules of adat. One could well say: "If women are strong, we will not fall; so woman determines and adat applies."

Dt. Besar's comment that women are excluded from reckoning adat matters in the balai adat because they talk too much and nothing gets decided was the first time I had heard a disparaging remark made by men about women. Yet Dt. Besar also agreed that women uphold adat in today's world, whereas the male adat role is slackening. I concluded that his critique of women was an effort to reopen a space for men after so many decades of its diminishment first by the Dutch, then by the Japanese, and more recently by Suharto. At the end of our conversation he voiced a more measured view granting as much to women as he wanted to give back to men.

I never heard women belittle the male role in quite the same way. Wik's comments about how women have to stage the ceremonies because men don't know them came the closest, but she explicitly explained this fact in terms of the economic realities limiting the male contribution. Ibu Wel voiced the most common attitude of women toward the male role—one of obeisance and respect for the penghulu. Obeisance doesn't necessarily mean subordination; it is at the core of tali budi, maintaining good ties. This was the way women sought to raise the fallen pillar, repair the leaky roof, shore up the foundation, and thereby restore the house of adat.

Obeisance and mutual respect are the way of adat. The flowery speeches that flow from the tongue of the penghulu, giving and receiving respect through words so that the plants will grow and the people will prosper, parallels the aesthetics of ceremonial celebrations staged by women. It is also in keeping with the politesse of the exchanges linking women through food. In the end I concluded that adat ibu and adat limbago—food and words guarding the ramparts of adat—are homologous forms operating from the same basic foundation. This foundation is formed by the system of symbols constituting what Dt. Patiah and En referred to in our conversation as adat matriarchaat, which they claim constitutes the foundation of the house of adat. Break the foundation and the house is destroyed; break good relations and society is broken. Such ideas place maternal meanings and women at the center of the regeneration and stability of adat in today's world.

CHAPTER FOURTEEN

Redefining Matriarchy

Twentieth-century social and cultural anthropology has promised its still largely Western readership enlightenment on two fronts. The one has been the salvaging of distinct cultural forms of life from a process of apparent global Westernization. . . . The other promise of anthropology . . . has been to serve as a form of cultural critique for ourselves. In using portraits of other cultural patterns to reflect self-critically on our own ways, anthropology disrupts common sense and makes us reexamine our taken-for-granted assumptions.

George E. Marcus and Michael M. J. Fischer,
Anthropology as Cultural Critique

The Minangkabau matriarchate, which Dt. Patiah referred to as adat matriarchaat, is a world away from the Western conception of matriarchy. Although there are many ways in which women dominate life in Eggi's village, they do not rule, nor do men. Thinking about the centrality of women's ways, I began to reconsider the Western definition of matriarchy. Women's ways include their ceremonial activities and their devoted commitment to raising children according to adat, thereby ensuring the stability of tradition. The aspects of royalty in village ceremonies link women to Bundo Kanduang, the mythical queen mother who sits at the center of the Minangkabau universe. Then there is the panoply of maternal symbols defining the centers of the Minangkabau social universe from Bundo Kanduang to the common ancestress. Mother and children are tied in space and time to this focal ancestress by virtue of their rights to oversee and use the objects and land that descend through the maternal line. All of this gives senior women agency and authority in the affairs of daily life in ways that cannot be compared with the power men exercise over women in male-dominated societies. The exercise of power in male-dominated societies is neither analogous nor a mirror image of the exercise of power in West Sumatra according to the tenets of adat.

From its first delineation in the nineteenth century, the Western definition of matriarchy has been drawn by analogy with patriarchy or "father right," not by reference to ethnographic studies of female-oriented societies and social forms. Because patriarchy developed as a code word for paternal tribal rule based on biblical sources, matriarchy was defined as rule by the mothers. Thus *Webster's* defines a matriarch as "a woman that originates, rules over, or dominates a social group or an activity or a political entity." In the *OED* a matriarch is defined on "the supposed analogy of patriarch," who is the "chief or head of a family . . . or tribe."[1]

The emphasis on political power and rule in these definitions derives in part from the biblical tradition and in part from the work of J. J. Bachofen in the nineteenth century on "mother right." In his famous book *Das Mutterrecht*, published in 1861, Bachofen defined mother right as matrilineal descent and government of the family, which, he said, "falls not to the father but to the mother, *and by a consequent extension of this last principle, government of the state was also entrusted to the women*" (Bachofen 1967:156, my emphasis).[2]

One of the first articles by an anthropologist to use the term *matriarchy* refers to the Minangkabau, among other societies, to develop a cross-cultural model for the "matriarchal family." In his 1896 article "The Matriarchal Family System," E. B. Tylor begins by defining matriarchy as a cluster of matricentric social features, such as those mentioned by Bachofen, including female rule. Surveying a number of societies around the world, Tylor applies the term *matriarchal* to communities in which women enjoy "greater consideration than in barbaric patriarchal life" (Tylor 1896:90). By "greater consideration," Tylor means matrilineal descent, post-marital residence in the wife's household, and the evidence in some societies that "the wives are masters" (89).

To illustrate what he means by the matriarchal family system, Tylor refers to life in the Minangkabau longhouse *(rumah gadang)* as described by a Dutch colonial administrator in 1871.

Built on posts, adorned with carved and coloured woodwork, and heavily thatched, these houses duplicate themselves into barrack-like rows of dwellings occupied, it may be, by over a hundred people, forming a sa-mandei or motherhood, consisting of the old house-mother and her descendants in the female line, sons and daughters, daughters' children, and so on. If the visitor, mounting the ladder-steps, looks in at one of the doors of the separate dwellings, he may see seated beyond the family hearth the mother and her children eating the midday meal, and very likely the father, who may have been doing a turn of work in his wife's rice-plot. If he is a kindly husband, he is much there as a friendly visitor, though his real home remains in the house where he was born.[3]

After a lively description of a number of these "matriarchal" family systems, Tylor unexpectedly switches track and, without offering any credible evidence, rejects the term *matriarchal* on the grounds that although it was "an improvement on earlier definitions . . . it takes it too much for granted that the women govern the family." In its place he substitutes the term *maternal family* because he concludes that "the actual power" is rather in the hands of brothers and uncles on the mother's side (Tylor 1896:90).

The question of whether matricentric societies were characterized by female rule was the major theme in twentieth-century anthropological treatments of matriarchy. Finding no such society, anthropologists discounted matriarchy as a viable social form. To mention a few of the more notable statements, in 1921 the American anthropologist Robert H. Lowie wrote in *Primitive Society* that "matrilineal descent was at one time interpreted to mean that women govern not merely the family but also the primitive equivalent of the state." According to Lowie, anthropologists are "thoroughly in accord" with "the utter worthlessness" of this conclusion.[4]

Decades later, the topic of matriarchy was revisited by the American anthropologist David Schneider in *Matrilineal Kinship*, published exactly one hundred years after Bachofen's *Das Mutterrecht*. Schneider rejects Bachofen's ideas about mother right:

> Bachofen's contention that matriliny (descent through women) and matriarchy (rule by women) were but two aspects of the same institution was accepted only briefly. For as evidence was sought in terms of which his contention could be evaluated it became clear that the generalized authority of women over men, imagined by Bachofen, was never observed in known matrilineal societies, but only recorded in legends and myths. Thus the whole notion of matriarchy fell rapidly into disuse in anthropological work. (Schneider 1961:viii)

In their widely influential edited volume *Women, Culture, and Society*, one of the founding volumes of feminist anthropology, Michelle Rosaldo and Louise Lamphere came to the same conclusion. According to them, the evolutionary theories of Bachofen and Morgan positing "an earlier stage of human development" wherein "the social world was organized by a principle called matriarchy, in which women had power over men" could be dismissed on both archeological and ethnographic grounds. Going one step further, they made their famous (but later retracted) statement: "It seems fair to say then, that all contemporary societies are to some extent male-dominated, and although the degree and expression of female subordination vary greatly, sexual asymmetry is presently a universal fact of human and social life" (Rosaldo and Lamphere 1974:3).[5]

Outside of anthropology, feminist historian Gerder Lerner defines matriarchy as pertaining "only when women hold power over men, not alongside them." According to Lerner matriarchal power should include "the public domain and foreign relations" and instances "when women make essential decisions not only for their kinfolk but for the community." Such power, she continues, should also "include the power to define the values and explanatory systems of the society and the power to define and control the sexual behavior of men." Admitting that she constructs her definition of matriarchy as "the mirror image of patriarchy," Lerner concludes "that no matriarchal society has ever existed" (Lerner 1986:31).

Rule by Women and the Logic of Male Dominance

When David Schneider announced that "the generalized authority of women over men" is recorded only in legends and myths, he neglected to point out that in these legends female rule is often presented as an argument for male dominance. The logic of this argument is the subject of Joan Bamberger's survey of myths about the "rule of women" in South America, which she concludes operate as "social charters" for male dominance (Bamberger 1974:268). According to Bamberger, the "insistent message of the myth" justifies "male dominance through the evocation of a vision of a catastrophic alternative—a society dominated by women. The myth, in its reiteration that women did not know how to handle power when in possession of it, reaffirms dogmatically the inferiority of their present position" (279).

Bamberger labels the basic structure of these stories "the *myth* of matriarchy" because they rationalize male dominance in terms of women's inability to rule. What intrigues me about the stories that Bamberger relates is the degree to which the archetypal scenario of male dominance is formed by references to women as the building block of society. In the South American stories women are depicted as "owning" the sources of supernatural fecundity in the time of mythical beginnings. When men discover that women's supernatural power is contained only in magical objects and is not part of their sacred being, the men steal the objects for themselves. After that women remain "forever the subjects of male terrorism." To maintain their power over women, men coerce them into

"socially acceptable behavior" on "penalty of death." This behavior includes forcing women to give up their children to men: their sons to ini-
tiation in the male cult and their daughters to residence in the house of
their husbands (Bamberger 1974:271, 274–275, 272, 277–278).

The severance of the mother-child bond on the grounds that the symbols of fertility belong more properly in the hands of men is the most
striking feature of the archetypal scenarios of male dominance that Bamberger describes. This theme gives men the right to continually reassert
their authority for each new generation of males to ensure that they too
will follow the dictates of male dominance (Bamberger 1974:276–277).
Although Bamberger and others call this scenario the "myth of matriarchy," it is more properly labeled the *war against women*, or *the case for
patriarchy*. The message of the myth is that men *must* rule by force to
keep women from taking back the sacred objects. Obviously, this is vastly
different from the gender logic I described for the Minangkabau.

Given the importance of unruly female power *in the case for patriarchy*,
it is interesting to ask whether unruly female power figures in Minangkabau lore. Dt. Gondo Besar's comments, reported in the last chapter,
about women not being allowed to speak in the adat council house because they talk too much is the only instance I encountered that comes
even close.[6] Minangkabau lore is much more likely to reflect on the subversive potential of male power. The most prominent example is found
in story cited in *Kaba Cindur Mata* about the land ruled over by the
thieves.[7] It will be remembered that this is a story about how unruly males
who live at the margins of society are brought under the aegis of the law
of Bundo Kanduang. The moral of the story concerns the dangers of the
male character undisciplined by adat.

Both Bamberger's "myth of matriarchy" and the Minangkabau story
reflect on gender transformations in accordance with the social order.
The story of the thieves can be interpreted as a discursive move to
counter the perceived or real horrors of hegemonic male dominance in
a world without adat. The so-called myth of matriarchy, on the contrary,
is more a counter-hegemonic move by dependent men against the perceived dominance of women.[8]

The two stories differ significantly in the role that force plays. In the
Minangkabau story, a male acting as an extension of the queen mother first
defends himself against the unbridled use of male force and then converts
the offending males to adat. In the myths of matriarchy, one is confronted
instead with an interminable battle waged by men to keep women in their
place. The battle appears to be one of the main factors in the conjugation
of gender relations carried over into the social practices of daily life.

Marija Gimbutas and Riane Eisler on Matriarchy

The stories of former female rule can be contrasted with another body of data that tells quite a different story. The hundreds of images of female figurines from ancient Europe excavated by Marija Gimbutas and displayed in the pages of her books provide powerful evidence of a social ontology of the maternal. Whether or not one agrees with her interpretations of these images as goddesses, her analysis does not efface the existence of the images themselves, which at the least suggest a public focus on the hefty, perhaps pregnant, female body.

In her first book on goddesses Gimbutas depicted widespread female figurines from "Old Europe" (7000–3500 B.C.). Her generalizations about goddesses and a goddess culture in this and subsequent books were as widely disseminated as they were criticized.[9] Whatever might be said in reaction to her mother goddess focus, Gimbutas makes some important points about matriarchy. She strenuously objects to defining matriarchy as female rule. Casting matriarchy as the "mirror image of patriarchy" is motivated by "the indolent assumption" that ancient societies must have resembled our own. She sees this approach as a "serious and continuous obstacle to the study of ancient society," for it distorts the reality of Old Europe.

> Indeed, we do not find in Old Europe, nor in all of the Old world, a system of autocratic rule by women with an equivalent suppression of men. Rather, we find a structure in which the sexes are more or less on equal footing. . . . [a society in which] the sexes are "linked" rather than hierarchically "ranked." I use the term matristic simply to avoid the term matriarchy, with the understanding that it incorporates matriliny. (Gimbutas 1991:324)

When Gimbutas speaks of the sexes as "linked," she refers to Riane Eisler's division between "dominator" and "partnership" models of gender relations. Eisler associates the dominator model with both patriarchy and matriarchy ("two sides of the same coin," she says) because both are defined in terms of "the ranking of one half of humanity over the other." The partnership model, on the other hand, is "primarily based on the principle of *linking* rather than ranking." According to Eisler, in the partnership model gender differences are not "equated with either inferiority or superiority." In the place of the labels *matriarchy* and *patriarchy*, Eisler proposes *gylany* for societies where gender relations follow the partnership model and *androcracy* for male dominance and ranking relations (Eisler 1987:xvii; 105).[10]

It is understandable why Eisler and Gimbutas reject the label *matri-archy*. But what about the Minangkabau? Are we going to replace their self-designation as a matriarchaat with a new label on the grounds that their meanings don't fit the Western definition of matriarchy? I think not. My goal in going to West Sumatra was to explore local meanings, not to apply labels devised at home. I think of anthropology as a way of deconstructing, not confirming, the androcentric stereotypes that pervade Western thought.

The problem is not with the term matriarchy but with its traditional definition. Rule by women should be dropped from matriarchy's semantic referents on the grounds that a more appropriate term exists, found in the ancient Greek sources: *gynecocracy*, after the Greek *gyne* (woman) + *kratos* (rule). The Minangkabau themselves would be the first to say that autocratic rule by women is not what they have in mind when they use the term *matriarchaat*. The time is long overdue for rethinking the Western definition of matriarchy. The place to start is with the nature of power in partnership societies.

Rethinking Power

In many societies power is not conceived as we think of it. Comparing the Western idea of power with that of the Javanese he studied, Benedict Anderson says that "the Javanese have a radically different idea of power from that which obtains in the contemporary West." For Western political thinkers, "power is abstract. . . . a word used commonly to describe a relationship or relationships . . . in which some men appear to obey, willingly or unwillingly, the wishes of others" (Anderson 1972:5–6). For the Javanese power is concrete.

> [It] exists, independent of its possible users. It is not a theoretical postulate but an existential reality. Power is that intangible, mysterious, and divine energy which animates the universe. It is manifested in every aspect of the natural world, in stones, trees, clouds, and fire, but is expressed quintessentially in the central mystery of life, the process of generation and regeneration. In Javanese traditional thinking there is no sharp division between organic and inorganic matter, for everything is sustained by the same invisible power. (Anderson 1972:6–7)

Anderson points out that the Western concept of power—its either/or quality in relationships characterized by acts of dominance and subordination—was associated with the rise of secularization that swept over Europe after the waning of the Middle Ages (Anderson 1972:5). This is an important point, for it suggests that the modern Western idea of power was specifically associated with the expanding public sphere of male debate and politics associated with the drive to colonize. Power lay in conquest, expansion, and acquisition of riches, not in the realms of life associated with women—the family, life cycle rituals, religion, and magical lore. It was the raw power of force in civil society, not the power associated with the regeneration of life.

Annette Weiner's account of the nature of women's power in Trobriand culture provides a stunning example of a case in which the Western idea of power is irrelevant for understanding gender relations. According to Weiner, "Trobriand women have power which is publicly recognized on both sociopolitical and cosmic planes." Critiquing the Western focus on secular power, she says that

> the "discovery" that Trobriand women have power and that women enact roles which are symbolically, structurally, and functionally significant to the ordering of Trobriand society, and to the roles that men play, should give us, as anthropologists cause for concern. . . . We have accepted almost without question the nineteenth-century Western legacy that had effectively segregated women from positions of power. . . . We have allowed "politics by men" to structure our thinking about other societies; we have led ourselves to believe that, if women are not dominant in the political sphere of interaction, their power remains at best peripheral. We unquestioningly accept male statements about women as factual evidence for the way a society is structured. We argue the problem of emic and etic [local versus analytical meanings] but not with reference to women's perception of their roles. From this view, since we compare women to men in the context of politics, we should not be surprised that we arrive at the almost universal notion that women's status is secondary to that of men. (Weiner 1976:227–228)

Anderson's ideas and Weiner's conclusions apply to Minangkabau village culture in general. "Politics by men" is not the whole of life in a village like Belubus, nor is it where life is primarily focused. This fact has significant consequences for the quality of social interaction. For example, as might be expected in a situation where secular politics doesn't rule life, social behavior departs markedly from the zero-sum, either/or approach that the Western idea of power leads us to expect. In Eggi's village, people whose interaction with others follows the command/obey formula are thought of as *kasar*, which means "rough," "coarse," or "ugly." Social interaction should be *halus*: smooth, polite, and polished.[11]

The person who is halus promotes tali budi (good relations according to adat). Such a person is endowed with knowledge *(ilmu)* of adat, religion, and the world of the gaib (the hidden). If male, they speak in proverbs during ceremonies. If female, they acquire the wherewithal to hold ceremonies and are always ready to help others who seek their advice. Together senior women and their brothers oversee ancestral property for future generations. They may also pray regularly and make the obligatory trip to Mecca. Their dedication to adat and religion gives such individuals greater access to the potency that flows through the universe, which they use for healing and advice, not for their own prestige or for subordinating others to their will. By this view, the locus of power is in nature, adat, and religion, not in the individual.

The Javanese, Minangkabau, and Trobriand views should not be treated as unique or exotic expressions of the human social vision. The merging of the sacred and secular in the regeneration of life is a theme that crops up in the earliest recorded literature of the Western tradition. We see it in the advice offered by Hesiod, the eighth-century B.C. poet-farmer. When I first read Hesiod's *Works and Days*, I was in Belubus trying to figure out the meaning of the curse of the ancestors so widely whispered in the case of Pak Indra. Particularly striking to me in this connection was what Hesiod had to say about the consequences of breaking the laws dictated by unwritten tradition. According to Hesiod, those who live in harmony with these laws,

> feast on the fruits of their tended fields,
> And the earth bears them a good living too.
> Mountain oaks yield them acorns at the crown,
> Bees and honey from the trunk. Their sheep
> Are hefty with fleece, and women bear children
> Who look like their parents.
>
> (ll. 268–273)

Those who violate the natural order by living "for violence and vice" are dammed by the curse of the gods:

> often a whole city suffers
> For one bad man, and his damn fool schemes.
> The Son of Kronos sends them disaster from heaven,
> Famine and plague, and the folk wither away,
> Women stop bearing children, whole families
> Die off, by Zeus' Olympian will.
>
> (ll. 278–283)

Where Hesiod refers to the gods, the Javanese, Trobrianders, and the Minangkabau construct different symbolic manifestations of the power that sanctions those who go against the laws of nature and the cosmos. Those Minangkabau who transgress the dictates of adat are struck by the curse of the ancestors. The deadly punishment attacks not only the sinner but the sinner's family as well; shunned and rejected, the family dies like a tree with shriveled roots and no buds, bored in the middle by bees. No one ever explained to me who these avenging ancestors might be other than to speak vaguely of the nenek moyang, the forefathers and mothers of long ago, who opened the land, established the titles, and united alam Minangkabau.

Minangkabau gender meanings and social forms are consistent with their understanding of the laws of nature, society, and the cosmos. Matrilineal adat protects the mother-child bond on the grounds that fertility, growth, and social well-being depend on nurturing the newborn. Masculine gender meanings are symbolized similarly. The male role, for example, is likened to the uncoiling frond of the fern leaf, one curve of which reflects the father's nurturing role, another curve the uncle's educative role. The female role is equated with the butterfly: Bundo Kanduang is the butterfly (central pillar) of the household. In the wedding ceremony, male fertility is likened to the rooster that fertilizes the egg; the bride's contribution is the chicken coop where the egg is laid.

On the wedding stage men weave discursive webs of good feeling between the intermarrying clans with metaphors of growth and allusions to adat rules. In their formal adat speeches the penghulu from the two clans liken customs and traditions to flowers that blossom when regulations are followed. When the penghulu from the groom's clan gives the groom to the bride's family, he likens the wedding union to "the seed that is born at this moment," which will "grow bearing flowers and fruit."

Wedding advice given to the bride and groom also provides information on proper social relations. The wedding speaker says that people find truth by sitting together and "seeking common agreement." Consensus, says a proverb, must be "round like the water that flows in the bamboo tube."

As men speak the words of balance, accommodation, and harmony on the ceremonial stage, women set the stage and weave the ties of tali budi through their regal processions, sumptuous feasts, and ceremonial exchanges. The spectacle celebrates marital links between hostess and guest clans. The women of the guest clans, bako and sumandan, parade to the home of their hosts carrying gifts of food on their heads. After they are fed and nurtured, the parading women leave with the all-important king of the bananas (*pisang batu*), the dominant symbol of the husbands that have been exchanged between their clans.

Such practices demonstrate the importance of balance in this strongly matrilineal society. Neither the maternal nor the paternal is left out. Maternal links are protected by matrilineal adat; paternal links are ceremonially marked with grand displays of food, gifts, and words. The adat of ceremonies cloaks the newborn and the newlywed in a mantle of balanced social relations. "Every young couple," I was told, "lives in a social universe supported by four families—the families of the mother and father of the bride and groom. That way their offspring will not want for anything should their parents divorce or pass away."

A proverb aligns the quadripartite social world with the four directions in the physical universe.

> Adat is divided into eight:
> Four fly to heaven
> Four remain on earth.
> The four that fly to heaven are
> One: the moon, two: the sun,
> Three: the East, four: the South.
> The four that remain on earth are
> The family house, the carved granaries,
> The great rice fields, and the irrigation works.[12]

According to this proverb, adat encompasses the totality of life, from heaven down to the fields, granaries, and houses inherited through the matrilineal line. Humans exist in a quadripartite physical world defined by the four directions and a fourfold social world comprised of the four clans *(suku)*. Villages in turn are grouped in clusters *(nagari)* of four, which were once organized into larger clusters of four. Similarly, the soul is conceived as composed of four elements, and traditional healing makes use of four sanctified leaves with distinct curative properties. The quadripartite ordering scheme extends to the partitioning of adat described in the tambo; adat law comprises twenty-two rules divided into five groups of four rules and one group of two.

Webs of Significance and the Meaning of Matriarchy

This excursion into the nature of power unlocks the meaning of Minangkabau matriarchaat The key idea is that power relations are inscribed in webs of significance, taking growth in nature as a model for the ordering of culture.[13] The web metaphor is particularly appropriate, given how the interlocking components of adat matriarchaat are associated with the structure of the traditional house—an association reminiscent of the way Charlotte, the spider in the children's book *Charlotte's*

Web, builds her house from the webs she spins for herself and her children. Like Charlotte's web, adat matriarchaat is an interconnected web of meanings on which the house of adat rests. The architecture of the web is constituted by the reinforcing activities of the penghulu and the senior women. One acts as a guide in the application of adat limbago, which shores up the pillars supporting the roof of the house of adat. The other draws people together in the ceremonies of adat ibu, which refurbishes the foundation. Both are essential. Break either of these strands in the web of adat matriarchaat, and the house of adat falls.

Such considerations suggest that the definition of matriarchy as the control of political power by women should be abandoned in favor a definition emphasizing the role of maternal symbols in webs of cultural significance. The focus should be on the structure and content of dominant gender symbols, not just the linked relationship between the sexes as Eisler suggests. The partnership relationship is important, but it alone doesn't define matriarchy because there are at least three types of symbolic structures representing gender in partnership societies: egalitarian, diarchic, and matriarchic. Egalitarian structures are those in which gender differences are not symbolically marked, although sex differences may play a role in the division of labor. Diarchic structures are marked by a pervasive system of symbolic gender dualisms. Matriarchic structures, like that of the Minangkabau, are based on a maternal model. In all three, although the content of the symbols differ, male and female function as two equal halves of a larger whole and neither dominates the other.[14]

I reserve the term *matriarchy* for structures highlighting maternal symbols and meanings such as I have described for the Minangkabau. I have argued that the dominance of maternal meanings in the Minangkabau case is due to the derivation of social meaning from the perceived sources of life and death in the whole of nature according to the proverb "Growth in nature is our teacher."[15] The new life in the rice fields, the gardens, and the chicken coop must be nurtured and protected from magical influences so that it will grow and bear fruit, like the clump of earth that grows into a mountain and the drop of water that becomes the sea. Because growth is key, nurture, not power, is the dominant model for human relations—*tali budi* in Mingangkabau terms. As En, Wik, and Dt. Patiah agreed in constructing their joint proverb, all the talk about adat in terms of house, roof, pillars, and foundation is meaningless without reference to budi. As Dt. Patiah emphasized, "If people are not polite, if they aren't of good character, they are not Minangkabau."

Just as a clump of earth does not grow into a mountain overnight and a drop of water does not quickly become a sea, social life also has a beginning and builds. In the case of the Minangkabau the beginning is marked by the apical ancestress and the oath by which people lay claim to land for the maternal generations to come. The common ancestress is reminiscent of the images displayed in Gimbutas's books. Seen through a Minangkabau lens, the pendulous breasts, expansive buttocks, and rounded hips and stomach of these images suggest that they are icons of fertility and growth. The apical, postreproductive common ancestress is the repository of vital life-force, the centripetal force around which social connections and access rights to land are formed for each generation. These figures represent more than a primordial obsession with the womb, which some have suggested. Rather they represent a philosophy of life and death with everyday consequences for human social connections and ceremonial forms.[16] As such, the figures signify not just the source, origin, and growth of life but the completed life cycle, the union of all that is necessary for the regeneration of life.

Such considerations lead me to propose that matriarchy be redefined in terms of *cultural symbols and practices associating the maternal with the origin and center of the growth processes necessary for social and individual life.* There are etymological grounds for shifting the definition of matriarchy in this direction. The root *matri*, from the Latin *mater*, means "mother, nurse; origin, source." The *-archy* suffix, which can be traced to the Greek word *arxi* or *arche* (ἀρχή), also refers to origin or source. Liddell's *Greek-English Lexicon* (1961:252) lists *two* definitions for *arche*, one focusing on origins and the other on political power. According to the first definition, *arche* is defined as *"beginning, origin; lay a foundation; source of action; from the beginning, from the first, from of old; the original argument; first principle, element; practical principle of conduct; principles of knowledge."* The second meaning defines *arche* as "first place of power, sovereignty; empire, realm; magistracy, office." The first meaning applies to adat Minangkabau, while the second with its implied emphasis on hierarchy, rule, and control does not.

The Centrality of Maternal Symbols in Adat

Maternal symbols related to origin and center ramify through the Minangkabau social universe from Bundo Kanduang (Our Own Mother), who sits at the center of the Minangkabau world, to the common ancestress who is at the apex of the family tree *(ranji)* that legitimizes rights to ancestral property. The common ancestress is succeeded by new generations of women who oversee access rights to this land. In their role as mothers, women are the beloved *mande* (mother), the one who is at the emotional center of her children's lives.

Maternal symbols define the nagari social universe to which Dt. Patiah and Dt. Gondo Besar long to return. In the Belubus area this universe is composed of four villages, the oldest of which is the "mother" village. Traditionally this nagari was encompassed within a set of four, the oldest of which was, again, the "mother" nagari. This nagari republic, known as Empat Batua (Four Stones), traced its origin to the kingdom of Pagarruyung, at the foot of Mt. Merapi, to which the adat houses in Belubus look.

The cultural focus on origin and center is carried over into the naming of saluang songs. Songs are named for their village of origin. The first saluang song in any saluang performance pays homage to the village where the saluang originated. The laments sung during the performance demonstrate that the mother is the center of the emotions; listeners, moved by the songs, connect not just to their biological mothers but also to one another.

The senior woman of the rumah gadang is equated with the central pillar of the house. Because it is the first to be erected, this pillar is defined as the origin, center, and navel of the house, which makes it the ritual center. In the wedding ceremony when the groom enters the bride's household, he circles the post seven times. He comes bringing seedlings and shoots for planting and a rooster for the chicken coop, which symbolically convey his inseminating role. People say that circling the post ensures the well-being and fertility of the marital union.[17]

Adat ceremonies are at the crux of village social life. Women are more involved than men for a number of reasons. Traditionally, unmarried young men were expected to leave their homes and villages in order to prove their worth in the rantau, while their sisters and mothers remained securely in charge of the matrilineal property. Ibu Idar explained, "Women cannot leave their home to go somewhere like men do. A woman stays in the place where she was born and upholds Minangkabau tradition. The way a woman behaves is part of custom; she keeps adat going through her behavior." The same sentiment was expressed by Dt. Ampek when he told me that in their role as Bundo Kanduang women "fulfill" adat.

In their roles as husbands, men sometimes complain that theirs is a poor lot, because if divorced or widowed they must leave the home of their wives and abide either with their matrilineal relatives or in a local prayerhouse. Yet, men are proud of their roles as brother, uncles, and adat leaders and decry societies that force women out of their husbands' homes if a marriage ends through death or divorce. Generally speaking,

Minangkabau men feel morally superior because of the protective nature of adat, which they uphold as a matter of masculine pride.

In their adat roles senior men and women act as partners in authenticating and regenerating the adat social order, through practices and beliefs that elevate it to sacred status and reproduce its meanings. They also conjointly weave the newborn and newlywed into a mantle of social ties and stamp a social identity onto individual consciousness. This identity includes accepted ways of feeling, acting, and being Minangkabau. As the emotions, dispositions, sensory predilections, and cognitive schemata of the ceremonies are embossed on the psyche of the newborn or the newlywed, they are reinscribed in the collective psyche.[18] Thus, like the discourse of male adat and the texts of the tambo and kaba, women's ceremonies reproduce from one generation to the next the adat way of being in the world.

The Role of Islam and Other Codes

In this discussion of matriarchy in West Sumatra it is important to recognize that Islam stands as one of the three dominant sacred elements within Minangkabau symbology, along with nature and the maternal. The centrality of Islam did not happen easily or overnight but was worked out historically as Islamic fundamentalists and adat leaders resolved the tensions and conflicts dividing them.

Today the matrilineal principle and Islam are firmly ensconced in the most sacred of adat categories, the "adat that is truly adat." The continued stability of the tie connecting adat and Islam puts a modern stamp on the sacred nature of maternal symbols. The support of Islam ensures that respect and harmony will not be dislodged as prime social values. The enforcement of such values in everyday village life explains the near absence of rape and wife abuse. Having come to West Sumatra wondering what the ethos of male-female relationships would be like, I learned that roughness (*kasar*) in male behavior is not tolerated. In the years I lived in Belubus I heard of only one case of wife abuse. The problem was resolved by sending the husband back to his mother's house. People defined rape as non-consensual sex and spoke of it as the epitome of evil. I did not hear of any cases of it occurring while living in the village. Since gossip about sexual affairs circulates widely, I have no doubt that I would have heard about instances of sexual violence or abuse.[19]

Generally speaking, the accommodation of Islam and adat applies to the other codes of village life. Together these codes support alam Minangkabau as the world where adat matriarchaat lives. It is fair to say that without women's ceremonies backed by adat limbago, without the support of Islam and the imagined oversight of the ancestors, the hegemony of the matrilineal principle and adat matriarchaat would have been dissipated by the growing consumerism, entrepreneurship, and self-interest that changed the face of Indonesia during the Suharto era.

Today women's ceremonies are more part of the daily rhythm of life than male adat practices because of the whittling away of male adat by the desa system of regional governance. But the erosion of the male domain does not mean that it is lost or that males alone will be responsible for its resurrection. Women's respect for the male contribution to adat will contribute to its revival when the desa system is changed back to the old nagari system. If, however, the social passion the Minangkabau people show for their adat is supplanted by a resurgent Islamic fundamentalism, an expanded market mentality, or a nationalism insensitive to local adat, the doomsday of which Wik spoke, a time when adat ends, will surely loom closer.

I don't see this as happening anytime soon. The most sacred principles of adat Minangkabau can be found throughout alam Minangkabau creating a lifelong attachment to family, place, and community.[20] The focus on growth, fertility, and the maternal creates a sense of well-being and purpose that competes with the ennui, alienation, and despair so common in the world today. So does the importance attached to maintaining balance through accommodation. Had the Minangkabau chosen to fight rather than to accommodate the numerous influences that impinged on their world over the centuries, had they chosen to assert cultural purity, no doubt their adat would have long ago succumbed. The moral of the Minangkabau story is that accommodating differences can preserve a world, in this case alam Minangkabau with its sacred adat customs. Although quiet and unobtrusive, gentle in its humility and politesse, the cultural order Minangkabau women uphold with the help of their brothers has had a remarkable staying power. Its emphasis on nurturing the weak so that society will be strong offers a model for living in a world that has lost sight of the healing powers of the maternal.

Notes

Introduction

1. *Adat* is the term used all over Indonesia to refer to local customs. *Adat Minangkabau* refers specifically to the unique system of customs the Minangkabau call their own. *Alam Minangkabau* (the Minangkabau world) refers to the traditional heartland of Minangkabau culture (called *darat*), in which all villages are united under a common adat.

2. In Indonesia it is common to address adult males with the title *Pak* (father) and adult females as *Ibu* (mother). I was called Ibu Peggy. It is also common to shorten names, so that Pak Boestami was Pak Boes to those who knew him well. Those I knew very well, such as Endri and Wik, I addressed by their nicknames without the more formal title of Pak and Ibu.

3. This approach to anthropology, established by Franz Boas in the early twentieth century, has produced some classic anthropological studies of the role of women in society, as relevant today as when they were first published. A long list of anthropologists comes to mind ranging from Margaret Mead to Marjorie Shostak, Annette Weiner, Maria Lepowsky, and Lila Abu-Lughod. In the case of the Minangkabau there is the work of Nancy Tanner and Lynn Thomas, the first American anthropologists to spend a long term in residence in West Sumatra, and more recently the work of Joanne Prindiville, Cecelia Ng, Johanna van Reenen, and Evelyn Blackwood.

4. Like all family trees in Belubus and anywhere in West Sumatra, this one was kept as a semi-legal document giving the names and relationships of family members who had access rights to the ancestral land claimed by the first ancestress who came to Belubus.

Chapter 1 Adat Matriarchaat as a World View

1. Each of Indonesia's many ethnic groups proudly proclaims its own adat, which developed before Dutch colonial rule and world religions made their impact on the Indonesian archipelago. Today, even after a half-century of independence and the development of a national culture and economy, most of Indonesia's ethnic groups pride themselves on living according to their unique adat. This is true of the Minangkabau.

2. Normally, Minangkabau men (indeed all Indonesians) have only one name. In West Sumatra the men who inherit the penghulu or datuk titles in the matrilineal line get a fancy

title tacked on to their name. Such men are usually addressed by the title "Datuk." In the case of Pak Idrus (as he was also called) his title means "the Datuk who is the king of the Penghulu." Pak Idrus was appointed penghulu in his home village of Batusangkar, the largest town in the oldest of the three traditional districts in the Minangkabau heartland. All the years that I knew him, however, he lived in Padang. When we first met he was a member of the provincial parliament of the Minangkabau state government and chairman of the Adat Council of West Sumatra, a body appointed by the governor to build a bridge between adat and government activities.

3. Throughout my stay, Suharto was the ruling president. Suharto fell in 1998, the year before my last trip to West Sumatra. The third president, Abdurrahman Wahid, was elected just after I left in the fall of 1999.

4. See Abdullah 1966, 1972, and 1985 for the context of these proverbs in Minangkabau history. See also Kato 1982:101.

5. See discussion in Abdullah 1966:1, 3, 7; 1972:194, 244–245.

6. Over the years Bahrizal translated many old Minangkabau texts for me, a language which I did not speak. In time I learned Indonesian, which I spoke in Belubus and with En. While I came to understand a little Minangkabau, I never spoke it. The Minangkabau language is very close to Indonesian, so close that children who have not yet learned Indonesian in school get along quite well in it.

7. See Abu-Lughod 1993:45 for commentary on this tradition in the patrilineal Islamic society where she worked in Egypt.

8. Abdullah (1966:9) says that "those who brought Islam to Minangkabau, like any other sufi-oriented 'missionaries,' were more concerned with the purity of an individual's heart than with the religious correctness of his actions."

9. The elaborate ceremonial food exchanges among women mark the key social relationships of Minangkabau social organization. Cecilia Ng (1987; 1993), who studied women's ceremonies in the city of Payakumbuh near Belubus, also remarks on the social centrality of ceremonies. My account confirms Ng's analysis of the relevance of ceremonies in marking and celebrating adat social relations. See also Blackwood 2000.

10. A number of readers of the early drafts of this book have noted that Minangkabau philosophy "essentializes" the female contribution to the ordering of culture by reference to maternal functions. This is true, but it can also be said that the Enlightenment and Darwinian views essentialize the male contribution by reference to male physical strength. Both can be labeled as essentialist, biologizing views. The difference is that one view gives women agency and authority and the other subordinates women to the power of male strength.

11. For his argument see Nasroen 1957:33–37.

12. A Minangkabau proverb, quoted to me in many villages. It is also cited in Nasroen 1957:37.

13. This is my interpretation of the proverb based on discussions with many adat experts.

14. Quoted in Abdullah 1972:231.

15. J. J. Bachofen and Lewis Henry Morgan presented strong arguments for sovereign female authority in the mid-nineteenth century. Bachofen introduced the notion of "maternal law," which he defined as "government of the family" and of the "state" in his 1861 book *Das Mutterrecht* (Bachofen 1967). Morgan described "mother right" among the matrilineal Iroquois and, like Bachofen, spoke of "gynecocracy" in early human society. Although this might seem to credit Bachofen and Morgan with the definition of matriarchy as female rule, neither actually used this term.

According to the classicist Stella Georgoudi (1992:450–451), although "matriarchy" is considered to have been Bachofen's "great discovery," which French feminists in the early twentieth century compared to "Columbus' discovery of America," the term does not appear in his work. Rather, Georgoudi points out, matriarchy was forged later in the nineteenth century by analogy with patriarchy. As far as I can surmise, E. B. Tylor (1896) is the first to use this term in the context of anthropological analysis (see chapter 14 for more on Tylor's contribution).

Although Bachofen and Morgan didn't actually use the term *matriarchy*, they can be credited with the association of matriarchy with female rule because of the degree to which both conflated gynecocracy and mother right. As Georgoudi notes, Bachofen used these terms "side by side," as if to say these were "inextricable characteristics." Thus, where he found matrilineal kinship, Bachofen assumed gynecocracy.

Lewis Henry Morgan can be credited with the most extensive and earliest examination of the social meaning of matrilineal descent. His famous *League of the Iroquois* was first published in 1851, ten years before Bachofen published *Das Mutterrecht.* In his later work Morgan seems to have been influenced by Bachofen, as Bachofen was undoubtedly influenced by Morgan. Morgan spoke of Iroquoian "mother-power" and claimed that "mother-right and gynecocracy among the Iroquois . . . is not overdrawn" (1965:66). See also Morgan 1870, 1964.

Schott (1979:354) points out that Morgan used the term *mother-power* in his 1881 book on houses of the "American aborigines." See also the discussion in Leacock 1981:151.

According to Morgan, mother-power represented "an ancient phase of human life which has had a wide presence in the tribes of mankind" (Leacock 1981:151). Bachofen also thought of mother right as representing an earlier stage in human cultural evolution.

The notion that mother-power represents "an ancient phase of human life" illustrates the second most important attribute that came to be associated with matriarchy: its evolutionary priority to patriarchy. For example, Bachofen associated mother right with "the pre-Hellenic peoples," and "patriarchal forms" with the more advanced Greek culture (1967:71). His preference for one over the other is seen in his conclusion regarding "the triumph of paternity," which he said liberates the spirit from nature and sublimates human existence over the laws of material life (109).

Bachofen and Morgan were not the only commentators to accord women high status at a low level of evolutionary development. In *Primitive Marriage*, another well-known book of the times, John McLennan (1970 [1865]) claimed that matrilineal societies were more primitive than patrilineal societies because at an early stage of cultural evolution there was no knowledge of paternity, which meant that social ties to the father were not relevant. In the absence of knowledge of paternity, the mother-child bond furnished the only relation on which kinship could be established and the family held together. Tylor notes that McLennan's conclusion followed Bachofen's earlier treatise on mother right (Tylor 1896:81).

16. See my discussion of the historical and cultural meaning of Sonan Sari in chapters 3 and 6.

17. This proverb is also cited in Nasroen 1957:63.

18. See chapter 12 for an account of this case.

19. Okin 1979:198–200, quoting Hobbes and Locke.

Chapter 2 The Divine Queens

1. A substantial number of Minangkabau have also made their home in other parts of Indonesia and in Malaysia, where the state of Negri Sembilan was formed from groups tracing their origin to the heartland. These areas are also called the rantau.

2. There is no agreement on the exact identity of Rum. Some say it is Rome; others, "the old Eastern Rome," by which they mean Constantinople, or Turkey (Abdullah 1970:4). Yet others suggest Macedonia, the home of Alexander the Great.

3. According to Mahmoed and Manan 1987, the formalization of matrilineal succession happened in 250 B.C., which fits with Nasroen's (1957:32) idea that the matrilineal principle came before the influx of Hinduism and Buddhism into the area. The problem with this idea, however, is that most genealogical charts I have seen place Indo Jelito closer to Bundo Kanduang.

4. In *Kaba Rantjak Dilabueh*, a famous legendary story translated in Johns 1958, the twenty-two rules are taught by a mother to her son as follows. She lists the four types of adat in the third group of four rules.

As for the four types of adat:
First is adat that is truly adat,
second, adat that has been made so;
third is adat which has become so,
and fourth is the adat of ceremonies.

5. Summarizing what little we know of Minangkabau history, the name *Minanga* appears in a seventh-century inscription. Although found in the coastal city of Palembang in southern Sumatra, this name is applied to a population far away. According to the inscription, in 686 A.D. soldiers from a population called "Minanga" were conscripted for service to a king in southern Sumatra. Some scholars suggest that the people referred to as Minanga came from the eastern Sumatran coast near the mouth of the Kampar River, which historically connected the highland area of West Sumatra with the eastern coast.

The title Sri Maharajo Dirajo is first found in an inscription of Kota Kapur in the seventh century. "Sultan" is an Islamic title that appears in eastern Sumatran coastal states much later in the thirteenth century, the time when Islam started spreading in Sumatra. Thus, the use of "Sultan" as a prefix to Sri Maharajo Dirajo dates the imagined world of the tambo to the thirteenth century at the earliest. However, the early fourteenth century is the most likely origin of the tambo events because it is at this time that the title Maharaja Diraja (king of kings) appears in one of the first inscriptions in the Minangkabau area (Casparis 1992). These inscriptions are imputed to a royal personage from the famous kingdom of Majapahit, which flourished in Java in the fourteenth century. Another inscription is associated with a group of Tamils who may have migrated into the area from South India.

J. G. de Casparis, the well-known translator of early Javanese and Minangkabau inscriptions, says that the northern part of Sumatra was Muslim for half a century before the first inscription mentioning the name *Maharaja Diraja* was found in the Minangkabau area bearing the date of A.D. 1316 (Casparis 1992). The inscription is attributed to Akaraendrawarman, uncle to the famous Minangkabau ruler Adityawarman. This was the ruler who used the illustrious title Maharaja Diraja, according to Casparis. Akaraendrawarman was the successor of another king, who was ruling in 1286, the year when the famous statue of Amoghapasa was sent from Java by King Kertanegara to the gate of the Minangkabau area, at that time located downriver from Pagarruyung on the Batang Hari River. In all likelihood this king originally hailed from Java. Akarendra later moved his kingdom into the area now associated with the center of the Minangkabau universe. Casparis (1992) says that "from all this data we can draw a conclusion about the existence of a dynasty in the state of Melayu," which included these three kings.

Other evidence supports this conclusion. The famous Javanese fourteenth-century narrative poem, "Nagara-Kertagama," mentions the Minangkabau as a tributary of Majapahit. This evidence—taken with the evidence of the inscriptions, all of which are associated with the king known as Adityawarman, who himself hailed from Majapahit—suggests a Javanese connection. The resemblance between the government of Pagarruyung and the royal kingdom of Majapahit according to some Minangkabau thinkers confirms the influence of Majapahit in the kingdoms that developed at the center of alam Minangkabau (Yakub 1987:34).

The possibility of a direct Indian connection is suggested by the name of Indo Jelito's second husband, Ceti Bilang Pandai. Trading castes of Tamil Nadu known as Chettis may have had contact with people of the Minangkabau area as early as the ninth century. Archeological evidence on Sumatra suggests that South Indian mercantile groups established ties with the local economies of central Sumatra. A number of inscriptions in South Indian scripts and languages have been found along the coast of Sumatra and within the central highlands, including specimens engraved by trading corporations. These records refer to the period between the ninth and fourteenth centuries when South Indian political and economic expansion was at its height (Nilakantha Sastri 1932; Suleiman 1977:5, 10).

6. Dt. Madjoindo was born in 1896 in Supayang, Solok, and educated in the Raja's School in Bukik Tinggi. He notes in the introduction that he stayed as close as possible to the original text of *Cindur Mata*, adding what he was able to learn from experts of Minangkabau adat. He says, however, that his rendering of the story is a considerably shortened version of the original and that he has rearranged its composition. The version by Dt. Madjoindo (1982) was translated for me by Peter Just. The version by Dt. Sanggono Dirajo was translated by Bahrizal, son-in-law to Pak Idrus Hakimy.

7. My experience confirms Madjoindo's comments. In one village I saw the kaba performed before the whole village as part of a marriage ceremony. This performance was all male. I was told that the reason had to do with the fact that women are not allowed to travel at night to other villages for performances. This, however, suggested to me only that the kaba is connected with Islam, since there is another even more famous performative genre (discussed in chapter 10) in which well-known women singers travel all over West Sumatra to perform at village ceremonies. These groups (composed of two women and one male flutist) perform through the night. In my experience of such groups in Belubus, no one ever complained about women traveling about at night.

8. For the 1683 account by Tomas Dias see Reid 1995:152–160.

9. Johor is one of the many place-names mentioned in the older adaptation of *Kaba Cindur Mata* by Dt. Dirajo.

10. See Andaya 1975 for an account of the queens of Minangkabau who wrote to the Dutch.

11. Abdullah (1970:4, 11–12) says that the references to Islam in the many versions of *Kaba Cindur Mata* place the events after the coming of Islam. He points out that the aphorism "Adat is based on Islamic law, Islamic law is based on adat" appears in the story, which dates it to the early alignment of adat with Islam.

Yet, one could also argue that the published versions of the kaba have incorporated the appropriate references to Islam. That Islam is not entirely incorporated in the story is suggested by the presence of well-known pre-Islamic practices such as gambling and cockfighting, which were discarded from adat as a result of the nineteenth-century Padri War.

12. The theme of the mother educating her son found in *Kaba Cindur Mata* is prominently on display in *Rantjak Dilabueh*, another kaba (see note 4). The protagonist in this kaba is a mother who in her role as senior woman teaches her son adat law. Comparing the similarities between the two kabas, Johns has this to say: "Neither of the husbands of Bundo Kandueng or Siti Djuhari (the female protagonist of *Rantjak Dilabueh*) play any part in the story; in both the woman is the centre and source of wisdom in the house and the state; both use the framework of the story to present the social ideals of Islam and *adat* as forming a perfect harmony" (1958:xii). Similar themes appear in the tambo when Indo Jelito acts to prevent civil war between the two half-brothers over the division of the territory as they move about bringing groups under the aegis of the Queen's adat.

13. This model of matriarchy is a classic example of what Marija Gimbutas (1991:324) referred to as a "matristic" society in Old Europe in which the sexes are "linked" rather than hierarchi-

cally "ranked." Gimbutas uses the term *matristic* "to avoid the term matriarchy, with the understanding that it incorporates matriliny." For more on Gimbutas and the notion of "partnership" societies proposed by Riane Eisler, in which the sexes are "linked," see chapter 14.

Chapter 3 Looking toward Mt. Merapi

1. See Sanday 1990a and 1996.
2. Westenenk (1918:6–7).
3. Sungai Talang is about one hour's walk from Belubus. There is considerable evidence in Sungai Talang attesting to its greater antiquity. It is more densely populated and there are many more upright stones at the center of the village and on the hills overlooking the village. There are also many flat rocks gouged with holes, which some people say were used for sacred purposes. The greater age of Sungai Talang is also suggested by the broken chips of Chinese porcelain people extract from their newly plowed rice fields, which resemble shards dated as early as the fourteenth century, possibly the time period of the events related to the tambo.
4. See discussion in Watson 1987 and Blackwood 2000:33.
5. The whittling away of the effectiveness of adat by the desa system of government will become evident in chapter 12.
6. For more on the political events associated with this news, see chapter 13.
7. Sudibyo, Boestami, and Sanday 1984.
8. According to the tambo summarized in the last chapter, Pariangan was part of the first kingdom established by the immigrant king, Sri Maharajo Dirajo. Later, Pariangan was incorporated as part of the kingdom of Dusun Tuo, established by Indo Jelito and her sons.
9. See chapter 11 on inaugurating the penghulu and chapter 12 on dispute settlement for more on the oath and associated curse in Belubus today.
10. Sudibyo, Boestami, and Sanday 1984.
11. Additional evidence in support of this hypothesis comes from isolated groups thought to have split off long ago from the population now known as the Minangkabau. Many of these groups are characterized by matrilineal descent and matrilocal residence such as found in the Minangkabau population. One of these groups, the Talang Mamak, live in isolated forest areas in eastern Sumatra. According to their lore they split from the Minangkabau when Islam entered the area. The Talang Mamak accept matrilineal descent as a given in the absence of a specific code of laws such as the twenty-two adat laws described in the tambo.

Chapter 4 Diversity in Daily Life

1. According to the 1996–97 census count, 87 percent of the inhabitants of Belubus and its two neighbor villages are farmers. All families own or have access to rice fields. Some families turn their fields over to a tenant farmer who farms it in exchange for some portion of its yield; or the land may be pawned (i.e., rented for a certain fee). No matter whether a family farms or not, its basic needs are first and foremost dependent on the ability to acquire rice, be it directly from its own land or through some other means.
2. This should not be taken to mean that the names of the four clans in Belubus are the same as those established in Dusun Tuo. However, the clan names in Belubus can be found in many other villages, including those located in Tanah Datar, the region where the original villages were established.

3. Kinship rank based on original *(orang asal)* and later settlers *(orang datang)* and those who are adopted into a lineage is recognized in Belubus, but not to the degree it is in other villages, such as Taram studied by Evelyn Blackwood. Blackwood (2000:38–39) distinguishes between three types of kin statuses: elite, client, and servant. Following Bachtiar, who studied Taram before her, Blackwood says that the elite are members of the original clans, descendants of individuals from the royal court at Pagarruyung. This group has the right to titles, the traditional rumah gadang, land, and certain types of ceremonial dress that set them apart from the other ranks. Blackwood calls those who came later and were adopted into one of the original seven clans "client kin." Such kin are "expected to fulfill certain duties and obligations toward their elite kin, while elite kin provide guidance to their subordinate kin in matters concerning adat." Finally, there is the category called "servant kin," who were slaves before the Dutch outlawed slavery in 1860.

Ng (1987, 1993) also describes how kinship rank is distinguished by dress, by seating arrangements at ceremonies, and by whether a ceremony is held in a traditional house as opposed to a modern one.

As will become evident in the chapters to follow, in Belubus such distinctions are muted, barely recognizable in today's world. There is no folklore about the original four suku coming from Pagarruyung. It is believed that all but one of them originated in the mother village, Sungai Talang, which in turn owes its origin to Pagarruyung. Each of the four suku have menhirs, which different greatly in size and number. The suku with the greatest number of menhirs, land, and wealth is reputed to have originated from a town on the road to Bukik Tinggi, not from Pagarruyung. In the past it is likely that more distinctions existed, for it is quite common for members of two of the more wealthy clans of Belubus to intermarry and to look down on marriages with members of other clans. Ceremonial dress does not code these distinctions. All women wear the same general outfit according to the latest style.

Chapter 5 Discovering Adat Ibu

1. Although I never heard this proverb recited in full in Belubus, men quoted parts of it in speeches. I cite it here because the ideas and images fit my observations of the importance of women in their ceremonial roles and daily life. The meaning of this proverb is reflected in the lamentations about the loss of the mother that female bards sing on the ceremonial stage (see book epigraph and chapter 10).

2. My translation, which I worked out with Endri, is based on the proverb presented by Gerard Moussay (1995:722) in his Minangkabau-French dictionary. For a slightly different version of this proverb and a different translation see Reenen 1996:1–3. See chapter 13 for more on this proverb.

3. These classes of relatives include affinal kin (relatives by marriage) and consanguineal (blood) relatives of mother and father. I will have much more to say about these classes of relatives and their function in ceremonies in the following chapters.

Chapter 6 Eggi Becomes Minangkabau

1. Sonan Sari is manifested in the group of seven rice stalks, one of which includes a stalk with four rice leaves, known as Raja Padi (Queen or Mother of the Rice). People say that the seven stalks grow facing toward the village. The seven are tied and taken to the rice house in a ceremony honoring the soul of the rice before the harvest. Like the seven grains of rice mashed for the baby to eat, the symbol of the seven rice stalks assuage the hunger of the people.

In the first-fruit ceremony of the past, abandoned when the Indonesian government introduced new strains of rice in the early 1980s, a special prayer was said to the seven stalks before they were collected (cited in chapter 3). The rice that comes from the mother of the rice is referred to as *buah kuldi*, because one plate of Sonan Sari makes people full, just as Adam's apple filled Adam's throat, according to one of the lines of the prayer. This allusion to the fruit that Adam ate is another example of the melding of adat and Islam.

Reciting this prayer guarantees a bountiful harvest by paying proper respect to the mother of the rice. When the seven stalks are placed in the rice house, they attract the rice in the field, which then fills the house. Thus Sonan Sari constitutes another archetype of the center defined in maternal terms (see chapters 1 and 3).

Chapter 7 *Exchanging Husbands and Bananas*

1. I adopt Ng's (1993:118) terminology here. Ng notes that the categories of husband givers and husband takers "constitute one of the most significant ways of ordering social relationships in Minangkabau society." The material presented in this and the other chapters on the birth and wedding ceremonies (chapters 6–9) confirm this observation in the case of Belubus.

2. See Ng 1993 on feeding husband givers in house-raising ceremonies. The relationship between husband givers (*bako*) and husband takers (the matrilineal clan) can be diagrammed as follows.

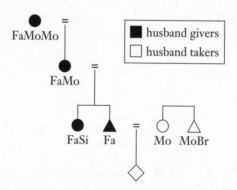

3. Although my description of Eggi's birth ceremony corresponds more or less to what happened, in this chapter I draw from several such ceremonies, which is why I use fictitious names. The compilation is designed to provide a general picture. Not every ceremony follows exactly the particulars I report here. For example, it is not always the paternal grandmother who carries the dulang tuo on her head. If she is a much older woman, the same objects may be carried by a surrogate bako relative, who is always a close female relative of the father of the child.

4. See chapter 10 for a description of a typical saluang performance.

Chapter 8 *Negotiating Marriage*

1. Chewing betel in the adat way means wrapping the areca nut in betel leaf and including lime and gambir.

Chapter 10 Songs and the Performance of Desire

1. The saluang, a bamboo flute, can have anywhere from three to ten holes. In the Minangkabau heartland, however, the traditional *saluang daret* has four holes. The instrument originated from the village of Singgalang on the slopes of Mt. Singgalang. Some say that the instrument originated from the bamboo flutes played by boys herding their flocks and that the songs evolved from the lullabies mothers sing to their children.

2. This impression was confirmed in 1999 when a new saluang group performed in Belubus for the first time. This group was formed by a popular male radio announcer and featured a famous saluang singer from Bukik Tinggi. The performance opened with an Islamic prayer and there was no gambling. Although no one said so, I assumed that the melding of adat and Islam in this performance explained why nearly the whole village attended and women stayed through the night. The gambling that takes place during the more traditional ceremonies, even though discrete, is not welcomed by women, especially the wives of the gamblers. Although performances usually attract fewer than a hundred spectators, many men and women consider themselves to be experts on saluang songs, telling me their favorite songs and naming their favorite singers.

3. For an example of how the rhythm and rhyming works in one of the extemporaneous verses addressed to Serge and me, witness the following, in which the first and third lines rhyme, as do the second and fourth.

> Uda urang Cing–ka–riang
> Pak Sus pang–i–riang–nyo
> Ma–nan–gih sang–kak di–jin–jiang
> Bu–ru–ang ba–tin–dak lah ta–bang sa–jo.

4. This thought is inspired by Foley's discussion of reactions to the Eleusian mysteries (1994:133).

Chapter 11 Being and Becoming a Penghulu

1. Cited in Madjoindo 1982:10. See also K. von Benda-Beckman 1984:1.

2. This booklet of local adat rules was published in 1995 by Dt. Marajo Nan Elok, the man known as the KAN, the head of the adat assembly of Nagari of Sungai Talang. These positions were established in 1983 for the whole of West Sumatra. In addition to the adat assembly representing West Sumatra in Padang, the local penghulu also comprise an assembly. It is the responsibility of the local KAN to encourage men to learn adat lore and rules as well as to oversee the ascension to adat titles in the villages. The goal of the local and Padang adat assemblies is to keep adat alive in the modern world in parallel with the activities of the Indonesian government. The local KAN encourages "the unity of custom" that once united members of the nagari.

3. Elok 1995:3. This proverb mentions one of the most important conditions under which a penghulu title is conferred, namely at the grave of the deceased. There are seven conditions under which a man may be raised to "greatness" (the word often used to refer to a penghulu title).

> 1. The greatness can be conferred by words through which all agree that a new title can be established.
> 2. The greatness can be created by splitting an existing title into two due to increasing population.

3. The greatness can be revived if a title has fallen into disuse, literally "sunk into the water."

4. The greatness can pass from a disabled, but still living, older man to a younger man.

5. The greatness may be conferred by appointing a successor either at the grave of the newly dead penghulu or while the earth of his grave is still red.

6. The greatness may be conferred by appointing a successor later but still during the mourning period.

7. The greatness may be conferred by reviving a title that has been put aside (folded) at the request of Bundo Kanduang (the senior women), because no appropriate relative exists to take it.

4. This hypothesis fits the meaning of stones reflected in the tambo.

5. For Westenenk's account see Westenenk 1918:95–96.

6. In this account I have changed all names including the name of the village in order to protect the identities of those involved. I begin with the inauguration of Pak Indra, which took place in a village near Belubus. The pictures of the penghulu inaugural ceremony presented here are from another village.

7. As a rule adopted heirs cannot inherit a title but are allowed to inherit wealth and property. There are exceptions to this rule, as in some cases (Pak Indra, for example) adopted relatives may receive a title. There are three categories in the group of adopted relationships, all defined in terms of the nature of the social relationship. The three types of adoptive relations, described by Elok (1995:27–30), are based on the nature of the tie.

Warih sabab batali adat. The relationship is established among individuals who are tied by a common adat through adoption. Members of the original group incorporate such individuals because they have become tied by mutual interaction through sharing customs, so that they feel that they have a common adat.

Warih batali buek. This situation is similar to the previous one. In this case, however, a group inherits from another not just because of having forged a common tie but because the original group does not have a female heir. For example, a penghulu may have under his title a great deal of land but no female heir to use it. He passes the land to members of another group who need property and with whom he has a good relationship.

Warih batali budi. People inherit wealth and properties from a penghulu because he has no descendants and they have worked for him during his lifetime.

8. The state sometimes sponsors desa-wide inauguration ceremonies as a way of encouraging adat leadership in the villages. During the years I traveled to Belubus, to my knowledge no such ceremony was ever held for the men of Nagari Sungai Talang.

9. For Dt. Rajo's full title see note 2.

10. F. von Benda-Beckmann (1979:91) explains the decision-making procedure of "climbing up and down the steps" in some detail for the area in which he worked in Agam. Whether the decision refers to lowly issues or involves the whole village, it must follow a step-by-step procedure. "'One has to go up the stairs—one has to go down the ladder.' No step may be left out. If people approach a higher forum immediately, this is 'wrong' according to adat; the parties will be reprimanded and the issue not entertained."

Chapter 13 Adat in the Twenty-first Century

1. I published three articles on the Minangkabau during this time. Two of these were illustrated articles appearing in the journal *Expedition* (Sanday and Kartiwa 1984; Sanday 1997). The third article was Sanday 1990b.

2. Defining *soko* (ancestral title), the author of the local adat booklet who installed the first Dt. Indra with his title equates penghulu titles with the "pillar of the Rumah Gadang" (Elok 1995:3). See the discussion in chapter 11.

3. For example, in his 1896 article on "The Matriarchal Family System," E. B. Tylor features the 1871 observations of Verkerk-Pistorius, a Dutch colonial administrator, who wrote about the position of the senior woman in the traditional household. See the next chapter.

4. See chapter 11, where I present some of the material of this booklet written by Dt. Marajo Nan Elok (1995).

5. This is the spirit of the message communicated by Pak Idrus Hakimy and found also in the work of Taufik Abdullah on the accommodation of adat and Islam, cited in chapter 1. In interviews and his published books, Pak Idrus goes further in the direction of the idea that Bundo Kanduang, as pillar of the household and nagari, determines the core principles and that men in their roles as mamak apply these principles.

Chapter 14 Redefining Matriarchy

1. *Webster's New International Dictionary*, 3d ed.; *Oxford English Dictionary*, 2d ed., s.vv. "matriarch," "patriarch."

2. To give Bachofen his due, the Minangkabau philosophy merging adat and the maternal in nature and culture is reminiscent of his doctrine of "naturalism," Bachofen's term for the underlying philosophy of matriarchal social systems. In a comment strikingly reminiscent of the Minangkabau nature philosophy, Bachofen says that "matriarchal people feel the unity of all life, the harmony of the universe" (79). He describes the existential components of life in mother-right societies as "regulated naturalism" in which the basis of human society is maternal love.

Like the Minangkabau, Bachofen sees women as "the repository of all culture, of all benevolence, of all devotion, of all concern for the living and grief for the dead." This idea is consistent with the comment made by Pak Idrus (reported in chapter 1) that the importance of the mother in adat is "in accordance with the flora and fauna of nature in which it can be seen that it is the mother who bears the next generation and it is the mother who suckles the young and raises the child."

3. Tylor 1896:86, citing Verkerk-Pistorius.

4. Quoted in Schott 1979:354.

5. But see Rosaldo 1980, Lamphere 1995, and articles in Sanday and Goodenough 1990 for other views.

6. His comments are mild compared to the stories Bamberger reports and at most demonstrate a male tendency to define an adat sphere that is separate from women's way.

7. See chapter 1 for Minangkabau ideas of male and female nature and chapter 2 for the story of the thieves in *Kaba Cindur Mata*.

8. I use the term *hegemony* much as Ortner does in her application of Raymond Williams's definition to a discussion of "gender hegemonies." According to Williams, the hegemonic denotes "a lived social process . . . practically organized by specific and dominant meanings and values" (Ortner 1996:146). Defined in this way, the hegemonic does not rule the whole of life because other patterns are always discernible—perhaps not occupying the same importance in daily living but present nonetheless.

Applying this concept to gender meanings and practices, Ortner says that when one examines the "multiplicity of logics operating, of discourses being spoken, of practices of prestige and power in play," some gender practices will be "dominant—'hegemonic.'"

Others will be "explicitly counter-hegemonic—subversive, challenging." Others will be "simply 'there,' 'other,' 'different,' present because they are products of imagination that did not seem to threaten any particular set of arrangements" (146–147).

Ortner's discussion is reminiscent of the notion of multiple logics and conflicting gender discourses proposed by anthropologists at a conference honoring Simone de Beauvoir in 1984. At one of the symposia, a number of anthropologists talked about the contradiction and paradox in gender relations. In the edited volume based on the papers presented (Sanday and Goodenough 1990), Anna Meigs (1990) discusses the female-centered practices of the seemingly male-dominated Hua of New Guinea she studied. Alice Schlegel (1990) distinguishes between general and specific gender meanings among the Hopi. Maria Lepowsky (1990) provides powerful evidence of female-controlled social practices among the egalitarian Vanatinai (see also Lepowsky 1993). Other authors note that in the event that males dominate the political order, one must ask whether that order works in the service of both sexes or only one—and, where women are excluded (as in the more segregated social orders of New Guinea), one must ask to what degree the male order has public sway over females. As Lila Abu-Lughod (1990) and Rena Lederman (1990) point out in their contributions, even where the public order of male politics subordinates, excludes, or hides women, women are still heard from.

9. Gimbutas 1974. The criticism came largely from archeology. Unfortunately, some archeologists seem more bent on discounting the tendency of Gimbutas to see mother goddesses in these figures than on developing a model to explain them. For one of the most thoroughgoing critiques see Tringham and Conkey 1998.

10. The term *gylany* refers to the linkage (*l*) between female (*gy*) and male (*an*). She says that the letter *l* "stands for the resolution of our problems through the freeing of both halves of humanity from the stultifying and distorting rigidity of roles imposed by the domination hierarchies inherent in androcratic systems" (Eisler 1987:105).

11. See Anderson 1972:38–43 for an analysis of *kasar* versus *halus* in Java.

12. See F. von Benda-Beckmann 1979:404 for a discussion of this proverb.

13. Here I am guided by Clifford Geertz's well-known definition of culture. Geertz espouses a semiotic approach to culture as being constituted by the "webs of significance" people transmit in patterns of meanings embodied in symbols such as can be found in the life cycle ceremonies of Eggi's village and in the coercive power of the curse of the ancestors. It is by such means that humans "communicate, perpetuate, and develop their knowledge about and attitudes toward life" (Geertz 1973:5, 89).

14. Janet Hoskins defines diarchy as "an ideology of balanced powers" in which the members of the male/female pair are "linked in a fundamental relationship of interdependence." The linkage is essential to the symbolic meaning of the pair. As Hoskins points out, "mythological justifications of diarchy stress the unity of the whole, whose two halves must function as counterparts, neither one effective without the other to complete the union" (1988; 50, 36). See also Fox 1982 for a discussion of diarchy.

Such symbolic male-female pairs are not found in the symbology of egalitarian or matriarchic systems. In the former, differences are muted, while in the latter dominant gender symbols are structured on a maternal model. Although different in symbolic structure, the three systems are similar in establishing a linked relationship between the sexes.

15. For more on this proverb see chapter 1.

16. For example, explaining why the depiction of the human form is female rather than male, Eisler suggests that when people "began to ask the eternal questions . . . it would have been natural for them to image the universe as an all-giving Mother from whose womb all life emerges and to which, like the cycles of vegetation, it returns after death to be again reborn" (1987:xvi). My argument expands this viewpoint by suggesting that humans predicate

the sources of life and death on the human form by observing all that grows and all that dies in nature.

17. The equation of the central post with the fertility of the house is reported by Cecilia Ng, who conducted research in the nearby city of Payakumbuh. She notes that the central post is symbolic of the potential of clan fertility and continuity represented by unmarried girls. For example, in the houses she studied young girls sleep near the central post. In house-building ceremonies these girls symbolically pull the central post erect. She also notes the practice of burying the placenta and the umbilical cord of the newly born at the foot of the post, which confirms her hypothesis regarding the post as symbol of lineage continuity (Ng 1993:127).

18. I see the ceremonies as developing the *habitus* of local identity and emotional form. I use this term as it is defined by Pierre Bourdieu (1977:159–197) and discussed by Dirks, Eley, and Ortner (1994:13).

19. The one case of rape that a few people mentioned to me happened in the 1940s and involved men from another village who ganged up on a mentally retarded woman from Belubus as she walked through that village on her way home. The outcome of that case shows how swift justice can be, at least according to this story. The rape was stopped by men who found it in progress, the leader committed suicide out of fear for his life at the hands of male relatives of the young woman, and the other men were jailed. I could never substantiate the details of this perhaps apocryphal story and only heard it from two people who played central roles as close relatives of the young woman. To this day, however, the people of Belubus avoid the road through this village. I have been told many times not to go there on my daily late-afternoon walks with Eggi and Serge. I take this to mean that there is a culture of protecting women against possible abuse by men. The story itself says something about the social response to rape.

20. The spirit of what I found in Belubus is reflected in the work of ethnographers such as Tanner 1974; Tanner and Thomas 1985; F. von Benda-Beckmann 1979; K. von Benda-Beckmann 1984; Prindiville 1985; Reenen 1996; Ng 1987, 1993; and Blackwood 2000. Frederick Errington's report (1984) of the village where he worked includes reminiscent themes, but it appears that he did not have access to women's culture in the same way that he did to men's, with the result that he highlights the chaotic potential of male subversiveness without balancing it with an analysis of the role of women's culture in the cycle of adat ceremonies. Errington provides a vivid account (1984:134) of the penghulu inaugural ceremony that conforms with the ceremony I describe in chapter 11.

Glossary of Minangkabau Terms
and Selected Names

Spellings are often based on local pronunciation in Belubus. Some words can be found in Moussay 1995, others in Echols and Shadily 1997.

adat: custom and tradition (a word with multiple uses and meanings)

adat awak: our *adat*

adat ibu: women's life cycle ceremonies or women's *adat*

adat istiadat: the *adat* of local ceremonial customs

adat Jahiliah: pagan *adat* predating the advent of Islam

adat limbago or *adat dan limbago*: customary law, norms, and rules that have been formalized, applied by adat male leaders in dispute settlement

adat nan sabana adat: the true *adat* (which includes matrilineal descent and Islam)

Adityawarman: Javanese-Minangkabau king, associated with royalty and patrilineal succession

Agam: one of the three traditional areas in the Minangkabau heartland

alam: world, nature

alam Minangkabau: the spiritual and physical world where *adat* lives in the Minangkabau heartland

ayam jantan: rooster

baalek: *adat* ceremony

baalua: *adat* speeches given by men during *adat* ceremonies

baarak: procession of women bearing offerings of *adat* food

baju kurung: piece of cloth, usually batik, wrapped around the waist as a skirt, held in place with a corset and topped with a long-sleeved jacket or blouse

bako: father's close matrilineal relatives

bako kontan: father's immediate maternal relatives, i.e., his grandmother, mother, female siblings, and female cousins

balai adat: council house where male *adat* leaders meet

Balubuih: the traditional name for Belubus

banang pincono: a necklace of many colors for wearing amulets

bapak: father

baringin: variety of tree

baso-basi: Minangkabau etiquette in speech

batagak kudo-kudo: ceremony for building an ordinary house

batagak penghulu: raising a man to penghulu status

batagak rumah adat: literally, raising the pillars for the traditional house; the ceremony associated with the building of a traditional house

Batu Manda: a large sacred stone, called the leaning stone, located on Bukik Parasi

batu mejan: gravestones

Batu Mengigil: a stone that shakes when people are sick, when rice is diseased, or
when someone dies unexpectedly

Batu Sangkar: the largest town in the oldest of the three traditional districts in the
Minangkabau heartland

Belubus: the village in which Eggi and her family live; also known as Balubuih

beras: hulled rice

bergurau: to have a good time

berkembang: to grow and expand

bernazar: the practice of going to sacred places, such as to the graves of famous
Islamic leaders, to pray for a special intention

Bimbingan Adat: adat guide containing a detailed account of the rules for the transmission of ancestral land, wealth, objects, and titles

binih mamak: wives of maternal uncles

bokor: vessel used to carry ingredients for chewing sirih (betel leaf, areca nut, gambier, and lime) for *adat* occasions; called a *cerano* in other parts of West Sumatra

budi: propriety in human interaction; politesse

Bukik Apik: daughter village of the *nagari* of which Belubus is a part

Bukik Parasi: hill that rises over Belubus

Bundo Kanduang or Bundo Kandung: queen mother of Minangkabau legend; queen
who allegedly ruled over the kingdom of Pagarruyung, which united all Minangkabau under one *adat*

cabe: red pepper ground with onion, garlic and a little lemon

cerano: see *bokor*

cinta: to love someone (romantically)

cocok: fit, good union of two ideas

cupak: a standard rice measure

darat (*darek*): Minangkabau heartland; consisting of three traditional areas, Agam,
Fifty Koto, and Tanah Datar

datuk or *datuak* (Dt.): honorary title given to a penghulu

Datuk Prapatieh nan Sabatang and Datuk Katumanggungan: sons of the first queen,
Indo Jelito

Datuk Soyieh: a local spirit

desa: villages under the oversight of the regional government

dubalang: assistant to the penghulu, wears distinctive red outfit

dukun: magical healer and practitioner of ilmu gaib

dulang tuo: ceremonial antique brass tray inherited and passed on from mother to
daughter, used to carry special ingredients to ceremonies

Dusun Tuo: Old Settlement

Empat Batua: literally, four stones; name of the *nagari* republic of which Nagari
Sungai Talang was once a part

empat suku: four clans

gadis: young girl or maiden

gantang: a standard of rice measure

gindo: a title that can apply to an assistant of a *datuk*

gotong royang: working together, cooperation

Guguk Nunang: village adjacent to Belubus, part of Nagari Sungai Talang

gurindam: rhapsodic type of free verse

halus: smooth, polite and polished, sensitive

hantu: ghost

Hari Raya: an important religious holiday at end of the Islamic fasting month

harta pusaka: ancestral objects or ancestral land

hukum adat: *adat* law

iblis: devil, Satan

ibu: woman, mother; form of address for adult women

ibu or mande kanduang: own mother, biological mother; can also mean common ancestress

ilmu: knowledge; often refers to special knowledge

ilmu gaib: knowledge of the hidden or magical

Indo Jelito: first queen of the Minangkabau

induo bako: see *bako kontan*

jas: jacket worn on special occasions by men

jin: spirits

kaba: narrative, performed as a sung narrative drama

Kaba Cindur Mata: famous Minangkabau legend, performed as a sung narrative drama

kamar mandi: washroom

kambing gulai: goat curry

KAN: Kerapatan Adat Nagari, a government-sponsored adat organization; head often referred to as KAN

kandang ayam: chicken coop

kasar: rough, coarse, ugly, crude

kata mupakat or *mufakat*: mediation, discussion, and consensus

katidiang jombak: ceremonial basket usually filled with uncooked rice and cakes during a ceremony

kaum bapak: the male class

kaum ibu: the female class

kebesaran: greatness, meaning the land under one *suku* or *penghulu* title

kemenakan: nephews and nieces

kena biso kewi: widely known Minangkabau proverb promising that those who go against the law of matrilineal inheritance will be struck by the curse of the ancestors (see also *Sumpah biso kawi*)

kepala desa: local mayor in the *desa* system

keras: tough and hard

koto: city, town; sometimes applied to villages

Kotyanir: clan of Eggi's maternal relatives

kris (keris): curved Malay dagger

kuasa: power; acting out of power and self interest

ladang: garden

lado: red pepper

lagu pusako: ancestral *saluang* songs

lembaga (limbago): institutions associated with *adat*

Lima Puluh Koto: Fifty Koto, district in which Belubus is located
limbago: rule or custom; *adat* law, norms, regulations (see also *lembaga*)
limpapeh: butterfly; central pillar of the matrilineal household
luhak: traditional division of districts; can also refer to bathing place
Magrib (Arabic): evening prayer time
mak or *amak:* mother; address for senior women
mamak: uncle (mother's brother); sometimes also refers to the *penghulu*
matriarchaat: Dutch term for matriarchy used by the Minangkabau self-referentially
memberi makan: giving first food
memberi minum: giving first drink
memberi nama: giving name
mendirikan penghulu: literally, raise the *penghulu* to a title (see also *batagak penghulu*)
menjelang: literally to call on or to pay one's respects; the invitation stage of the
    wedding ceremony
menjemput junjuangan: literally, fetch the groom; part of marriage ceremony
Merapi: mountain from which the Minangkabau are said to have descended and
    where *adat* was instituted according to the *tambo*
mufakat, mufacat, mupakat, mupakaik: consensus decision making
musyawarah: discussion
Nabi Ulah: prophet of Belubus also known as Syekh Muda
nafsu: passion
nagari: traditional confederation of Minangkabau villages
nasi lomak: sticky rice (sweetened rice for dessert)
nasib: fate, destiny
Negri Sembilan: Minangkabau territory in Malaysia
nenek moyang: ancestors
ninik mamak: *penghulu* or senior males in the maternal family
orang agama Islam: a person of the Islamic religion
orang asal: original settlers of a village
orang datang: settlers who came later to a village
Padang: capital of west Sumatra
Padri War: fought between Islamic fundamentalists seeking to purify *adat* of "pagan
    practices" and *adat* leaders wanting to accommodate Islam yet retain traditional
    practices
Pagarruyung: former center of royalty where Bundo Kanduang is believed to have
    ruled
pak or *bapak*: father, man, title used in addressing adult male
palasik: bloodsucking vampires
PAN: political party headed by Amein Reis in opposition to Golkar in 1999 election
pancasila: five basic principles of the Republic of Indonesia
pantun: rhymed proverb
papatah: maxims and proverbs
Pariangan: village on Mt. Merapi where male *adat* leaders claim that *adat* and *alam
    Minangkabau* originated
paruik: literally, one womb; extended family of matrilineally related kin
Payakumbuh: largest city in the region near Belubus
payung: members of several *paruik* who are under one *penghulu pucuk*
pegawai negeri: government employees
penghulu (pangulu): male holder of the hereditary matrilineal title

penghulu pucuk: *penghulu* who is head of the clan (which can include a number of
   extended families or lineages with separate *penghulu* titles)
pesta adat: ritualized celebrations associated with birth, marriage, house building, and
   ascension by males to ancestral titles
pisang batu: literally, banana of the stone; banana considered of higher value than
   other types, also known as "king of the bananas"
pisang gadang: big banana
pisang manis: sweet banana
pondok: cottage, hut, cabin, usually not a permanent residence
pucuak rabuang: bamboo shoot
pusaka or *pusako*: land, ancestral home, and inherited items
rajo usali: original king
Randai Saedar Jenela: the sung narrative drama composed in Belubus about a young
   man who goes *rantau*
Ranjani: local female spirit said to ride with Dt. Soyieh
ranji: genealogical chart tracing descent through the matrilineal line
rantau: migration area
ratok: lamentations (song)
Reformasi: populist reform movement that brought about Suharto's downfall in 1998
Reformasi damai: peaceful reform; name of 1998 reform movement in Payakumbuh
rendang: Minangkabau curried beef
rindu: longing
rumah gadang: literally, big house; matrilineal longhouse
Sago: mountain; Sanskrit word for paradise (*sarugo*)
sakato: agreement
saluang: form of bamboo flute; performance with female singers and male flute
   player
saluang darat: original saluang, with four holes
saparuik: same womb (common ancestress)
sapayaung sapatogak: one uncle, one common ancestress, one traditional house; to be
   under the same genealogical umbrella, sharing the same maternal ancestors
Sarandib: ancient toponym for Ceylon
sawah: wet rice field
sedih: sad
selendang: shawl worn for ceremonies
silomak: sticky rice
Singgalang: village on the slopes of Mt. Singglang where the saluang performance is
   said to have originated
singgang ayam: curried chicken
sirih: betel nut
sirih langkok: ingredients for chewing betel nut, areca nut, gambier, and lime (see
   bokor)
soko: literally, pillar; the penghulu title
Sonan Sari Padi: Mother of the Rice, title given to a sheaf of seven rice seedlings;
   traditional rice ritual
Sri Bungo: flower, addressed with Indic title
Sri Maharajo Dirajo: immigrant king, who according to legend was the son of
   Alexander the Great and came to Mt. Merapi from Turkey by way of India
suku: clan

suku berempat: the institution of the system of four clans in Belubus
sumandan: wives of male lineage members, usually male siblings and cousins
sumando: in-marrying husbands
Sumpah biso kewi (kawi): the oath to uphold *adat*
Sungai Talang: mother city of Belubus; *nagari* of which Belubus is a part
surau: prayerhouse
syekh: a title for a leader of an Islamic group
talempong: musical instrument (percussion)
tali budi: friendly and respectful ties
tambo: historical account of the origin of Minangkabau *adat* and royalty
Tanah Datar: one of three heartland areas, the area of the early monarchy and first
    settlement
tangka: talisman, amulet, charm, preventive
tepak: ceremonial betel box
tonggak tuo: central pillar of the household
turun mandi: first bath
ulama: Muslim religious teacher or leader
warih nasab: direct matrilineal heir
warung: food stall

Bibliography

Abdullah, Taufik. 1966. "Adat and Islam: An Examination of Conflict in Minangkabau." *Indonesia* 2:1–24.

——. 1970. "Some Notes on Kaba Tjindua Mato: An Example of Minangkabau Traditional Literature." *Indonesia* 9:1–22.

——. 1972. "Modernization in the Minangkabau World: West Sumatra in the Early Decades of the Twentieth Century." In *Culture and Politics in Indonesia*, ed. Claire Holt, Benedict Anderson, and James Siegel, 179–249. Ithaca, N.Y.: Cornell University Press.

——. 1985. "Islam, History, and Social Change in Minangkabau." In *Change and Continuity in Minangkabau: Local, Regional, and Historical Perspectives on West Sumatra*, ed. Lynn Thomas and Franz von Benda-Beckmann, 141–156. Athens: Ohio University Press.

Abu-Lughod, Lila. 1990. "The Romance of Resistance: Tracing Transformations of Power through Bedouin Women." In *Beyond the Second Sex*, ed. Peggy Reeves Sanday and Ruth Gallagher Goodenough, 311–338. Philadelphia: University of Pennsylvania Press.

——. 1993. *Writing Women's Worlds*. Berkeley: University of California Press.

Alisyabbana, Sutan Takdir. 1983. "Sistem matrilineal Minangkabau dan revolusi kedudukan perempuan di zaman kita." In *Dialektika Minangkabau Dalam Kemelut Sosial dan Politik*, ed. A. A. Navis. Padang, Indonesia: Genta Singgalang Press.

Andaya, Leonard. 1975. *The Kingdom of Johor, 1641–1728*. Kuala Lumpur: Oxford University Press.

Anderson, Benedict. 1972. "The Idea of Power in Javanese Culture." In *Culture and Politics in Indonesia*, ed. Clare Holt, Benedict Anderson, and James Siegel, 1–69. Ithaca, N.Y.: Cornell University Press.

Bachofen, J. J. 1967. *Myth, Religion, and Mother Right: Selected Writings of J. J. Bachofen*. Princeton: Princeton University Press.

Bamberger, Joan. 1974. "The Myth of Matriarchy: Why Men Rule in Primitive Society." In *Women, Culture, and Society*, ed. Michelle Z. Rosaldo and Louise Lamphere, 263–280. Stanford, Calif.: Stanford University Press.

Benda-Beckmann, Franz von. 1979. *Continuity and Change in the Maintenance of Property Relations through Time in Minangkabau, West Sumatra.* The Hague: Martinus Nijhoff.

Benda-Beckmann, Keebet von. 1984. *The Broken Stairways to Consensus: Village Justice and State Courts in Minangkabau.* Cinnaminson, N.J.: Foris Publications.

Blackwood, Evelyn. 2000. *Webs of Power: Women, Kin, and Community in a Sumatran Village.* New York: Roman and Littlefield.

Bourdieu, Pierre. 1977. *Outline of a Theory of Practice.* Cambridge: Cambridge University Press.

Casparis. J. G. de. 1992. Kerajaan Malayu dan Adityawarman. Paper presented at Sejarah Malayu Kuno, 7–8 December 1992, Jambi, Sumatra.

Coedès, G. 1968. *The Indianized States of Southeast Asia.* Honolulu: East-West Center Press.

Dirks, Nicholas B., Geoff Eley, and Sherry B. Ortner, eds. 1994. *Culture/Power/History: A Reader in Contemporary Social Theory.* Princeton: Princeton University Press.

Echols, John M., and Hassan Shadily. 1997. *Kamus Indonesia-Inggris* (Indonesian-English dictionary). 3d ed., revised and edited by John U. Wolff and James T. Collins in cooperation with Hassan Shadily. Jakarta: Gramedia.

Eisler, Riane. 1987. *The Chalice and the Blade.* San Francisco: HarperCollins.

Elok, M. Dt. Marajo Nan. 1995. *Bimbingan Adat: Soko-Pusako Dan Sangsoko.* Sumatera Barat: Kerapatan Adat Nagari (KAN) Sungai Talang.

Errington, Frederick K. 1984. *Manners and Meaning in West Sumatra: The Social Context of Consciousness.* New Haven: Yale University Press.

Foley, Helene P., ed. 1994. *The Homeric Hymn to Demeter.* Princeton: Princeton University Press.

Fox, James J. 1982. "The Great Lord Rests at the Center: The Paradox of Powerlessness in European-Timorese Relations." *Canberra Anthropology* 5:22–33.

Geertz, Clifford. 1968. *Islam Observed.* Chicago: University of Chicago Press.

——. 1973. *The Interpretation of Cultures.* New York: Basic Books.

Georgoudi, Stella. 1992. "Creating a Myth of Matriarchy." In *A History of Women,* vol. 1, *From Ancient Goddesses to Christian Saints,* ed. Pauline Schmitt Pantel, 449–463. Cambridge: Harvard University Press.

Gimbutas, Marija. 1974. *The Gods and Goddesses of Old Europe: 7000–3500 B.C.* London: Thames and Hudson.

——. 1991. *The Civilization of the Goddess: The World of Old Europe.* San Francisco: Harper San Franciso.

Hakimy, Idrus Dt. Rajo Penghulu. 1994a. *Pegangan Penghulu, Bundo Kanduang, dan Pidato Alua Pasambahan Adat di Minangkabau.* 4th ed. Bandung, Indonesia: Remaja Rosdakarya.

——. 1994b. *Rangkaian Mustika Adat Basandi Syarak di Minangkabau.* Bandung, Indonesia: Remaja Rosdakarya.

Hesiod. 1993. *Works and Days and Theogony.* Translated by Stanley Lombardo. Indianapolis: Hackett.

Hoskins, Janet. 1988. "Matriarchy and Diarchy: Indonesian Variations on the Domestication of the Savage Woman." In *Myths of Matriarchy Reconsidered,* ed. Deborah Gewertz, 34–56. Oceania Monograph 33. Sydney: University of Sydney.

Johns, Anthony H., ed. and trans. 1958. *Rantjak Dilabueh: A Minangkabau Kaba,* Southeast Asia Program, paper no. 32, Ithaca, N.Y.: Department of Far Eastern Studies, Cornell University.

Kato, Tsuyoshi. 1982. *Matriliny and Migration: Evolving Minangkabau Traditions in Indonesia*. Ithaca, N.Y.: Cornell University Press.

Lamphere, Louise. 1995. "Feminist Anthropology: The Legacy of Elsie Clews Parsons." In *Women Writing Culture*, ed. Ruth Behar and Deborah A. Gordon, 85–103. Berkeley: University of California Press.

Leacock, Eleanor Burke. 1981. *Myths of Male Dominance*. New York: Monthly Review Press.

Lederman, Rena. 1990. "Contested Order: Gender and Society in the Southern New Guinea Highlands." In *Beyond the Second Sex*, ed. Peggy Reeves Sanday and Ruth Gallagher Goodenough, 43–74. Philadelphia: University of Pennsylvania Press.

Lepowsky, Maria. 1990. "Gender in an Egalitarian Society: A Case Study from the Coral Sea." In *Beyond the Second Sex*, ed. Peggy Reeves Sanday and Ruth Gallagher Goodenough, 169–224. Philadelphia: University of Pennsylvania Press.

——. 1993. *Fruit of the Motherland: Gender in an Egalitarian Society*. New York: Columbia University Press.

Lerner, Gerder. 1986. *The Creation of Patriarchy*. New York: Oxford University Press.

Liddell, Henry George. 1961. *A Greek-English Lexicon*. Compiled by Henry George Liddell and Robert Scott. Oxford: Clarendon Press.

Mahmoed, St., and A. Manan Rajo Penghulu. 1987 [1978]. *Himpunan Tambo Minangkabau dan Bukti Sejarah*. Medan: Pustaka, Indonesia.

Madjoindo, A. Dt. 1982. *Cindur Mata*. Jakarta: Balai Pustaka.

Marcus, George E., and Michael M. J. Fischer. 1986. *Anthropology as Cultural Critique*. Chicago: University of Chicago Press.

McLennan, John Ferguson. 1970 [1865]. *Primitive Marriage, an Inquiry into the Origin of the Form of Capture in Marriage Ceremonies*. Edited by Peter Rivière. Chicago: University of Chicago Press.

Meigs, Anna. 1990. "Multiple Gender Ideologies and Statuses." In *Beyond the Second Sex*, ed. Peggy Reeves Sanday and Ruth Gallagher Goodenough, 99–112. Philadelphia: University of Pennsylvania Press.

Morgan, Lewis Henry. 1851. *League of the Ho-dé-no-sau-nee, or Iroquois*. Rochester: Sage and Brother.

——. 1870. *Systems of Consanguinity and Affinity of the Human Family*. Smithsonian Contributions to Knowledge 17. Washington: Smithsonian Institution.

——. 1964 [1877]. *Ancient Society*. Edited with an introduction by L. A. White. Cambridge: Harvard University Press.

——. 1965. *Houses and House Life of the American Aborigines*. 1881. Reprint, Chicago: University of Chicago Press.

Moussay, Gérard. 1995. *Dictionnaire Minangkabau: Indonesien-Français*. Paris: Éditions L'Harmattan.

Nasroen, M. 1957. *Dasar Falsafah Adat Minangkabau*. Djakarta: Bulan Bintang.

Ng, Cecilia S. H. 1987. "The Weaving of Prestige: Village Women's Representations of the Social Categories of Minangkabau Society." Ph.D. diss., Australian National University.

——. 1993. "Raising the House Post and Feeding the Husband-Givers: The Spatial Categories of Social Reproduction among the Minangkabau." In *Inside Austronesian Houses: Perspectives on Domestic Design for Living*, ed. James J. Fox, 117–139. Canberra: Australian National University.

Nilakantha Sastri, K. A. 1932. "A Tamil Merchant Guild in Sumatra." *Tijdschrift voor Indische Taal-, Land-, en Volkenkunde* 72:314–327.

Okin, Susan Moller. 1979. *Women in Western Political Thought*. Princeton, N.J.: Princeton University Press.

Ortner, Sherry. 1996. "Gender Hegemonies." In *Making Gender: The Politics and Erotics of Culture*, 139–172. Boston: Beacon.

Pateman, Carole. 1988. *The Sexual Contract*. Stanford, Calif.: Stanford University Press.

Prindiville, Joanne. 1985. "Mother, Mother's Brother, and Modernization: The Problems and Prospects of Minangkabau Matriliny in a Changing World." In *Change and Continuity in Minangkabau: Local, Regional, and Historical Perspectives on West Sumatra*, ed. Lynn Thomas and Franz von Benda-Beckmann, 29–43. Athens: Ohio University Press.

Reenen, Johanna van. 1996. *Central Pillars of the House: Sisters, Wives, and Mothers in a Rural Community in Minangkabau, West Sumatra*. Leiden: Research School CNWS.

Reid, Anthony, ed. 1995. *Witnesses to Sumatra*. Kuala Lumpur: Oxford University Press.

Rosaldo, Michelle Zimbalist. 1980. "The Use and Abuse of Anthropology: Reflections on Feminism and Cross-Cultural Understanding." *Signs* 5(3):389–417.

Rosaldo, Michelle Zimbalist, and Louise Lamphere. 1974. Introduction to *Women, Culture, and Society*, ed. Rosaldo and Lamphere, 3–15. Stanford, Calif.: Stanford University Press.

Sacks, Karen. 1974. "Engels Revisited: Women, the Organization of Production, and Private Property." In *Women, Culture, and Society*, ed. Michelle Z. Rosaldo and Louise Lamphere, 207–222. Stanford, Calif.: Stanford University Press.

Sahlins, Marshall. 1985. *Islands of History*. Chicago: University of Chicago Press.

Sanday, Peggy Reeves. 1990a. *Fraternity Gang Rape: Sex, Brotherhood, and Privilege on Campus*. New York: New York University Press.

——. 1990b. "Androcentric and Matrifocal Gender Representations in Minangkabau Ideology. In *Beyond the Second Sex*, ed. Peggy Reeves Sanday and Ruth Gallagher Goodenough, 139–168. Philadelphia: University of Pennsylvania Press.

——. 1996. *A Woman Scorned: Acquaintance Rape on Trial*. Berkeley: University of California Press.

——. 1997. "Eggi's Village: Reconsidering the Meaning of Matriarchy." *Expedition* 39(3):27–36.

Sanday, Peggy Reeves, and Ruth G. Goodenough, eds. 1990. *Beyond the Second Sex*. Philadelphia: University of Pennsylvania Press.

Sanday, Peggy Reeves, and Suwati Kartiwa. 1984. "Cloth and Custom in West Sumatra: The Codification of Minangkabau Worldview." *Expedition* 26(4):13–29.

Schlegel, Alice. 1990. "Gender Meanings: General and Specific." In *Beyond the Second Sex*, ed. Peggy Reeves Sanday and Ruth Gallagher Goodenough, 21–42. Philadelphia: University of Pennsylvania Press.

Schneider, David M. 1961. "Introduction: The Distinctive Features of Matrilineal Descent Groups." In *Matrilineal Kinship*, ed. David Schneider and Kathleen Gough, 1–29. Berkeley: University of California Press.

Schnitger, F. M. 1937. *The Archaeology of Hindu Sumatra*. Leiden: E. J. Brill.

——. 1964. *Forgotten Kingdoms in Sumatra*. Leiden: E. J. Brill.

Schott, Rudiger. 1979. Comment on "A Marxist Reappraisal of the Matriarchate," by Carolyn Fluehr-Lobban. *Current Anthropology* 20 (2):354.

Sophocles. 1973. *Antigone*. Translated by Richard Emil Braun. New York: Oxford University Press.

Sudibyo, Yuwono; Boestami; and Peggy R. Sanday. 1984. *The Megalithic Tradition of West Sumatra*. Report. Padang, Indonesia: Museum Negeri Adityawarman.

Suleiman, Satyawati. 1977. "The Archaeology and History of West Sumatra." *Bulletin of the Research Centre of Archaeology of Indonesia*, no. 12:1–25.

Tanner, Nancy. 1974. "Matrifocality in Indonesia and Africa and among Black Americans." In *Women, Culture, and Society*, ed. Michelle Z. Rosaldo and Louise Lamphere, 129–156. Stanford, Calif.: Stanford University Press.

Tanner, Nancy, and Lynn L. Thomas. 1985. "Rethinking Matriliny: Decision-Making and Sex Roles in Minangkabau." In *Change and Continuity in Minangkabau: Local, Regional, and Historical Perspectives on West Sumatra*, ed. Lynn Thomas and Franz von Benda-Beckmann, 45–71. Athens: Ohio University Press.

Tringham, Ruth, and Margaret Conkey. 1998. "Rethinking Figurines: A Critical View from Archaeology of Gimbutas, the 'Goddess' and Popular Culture." In *Ancient Goddesses*, ed. Lucy Goodison and Christine Morris, 22–45. Madison: University of Wisconsin Press.

Tylor, Edward Burnett. 1896. "The Matriarchal Family System." *Nineteenth Century* 40:81–96.

Watson, C. W. 1987. *State and Society in Indonesia: Three Papers*. Occasional Paper, no. 8. Canterbury, England: Centre of South-East Asian Studies, University of Kent.

Weiner, Annette B. 1976. *Women of Value, Men of Renown: New Perspectives in Trobriand Exchange*. Austin: University of Texas Press.

Westenenk, L. C. 1918. *De Minangkabausche Nagari*. 3d ed. Weltevreden: Visser.

Yakub, Nurdin Dt. B. 1987. *Minangkabau Tanah Pusaka: Sejarah Minangkabau*. Bukittinggi: Pustaka Indonesia.

Index